beyond identity politics

beyond identity politics

feminism, power & politics

moya lloyd

SAGE Publications
London • Thousand Oaks • New Delhi

© Moya Lloyd 2005

First published 2005

SAGE Publications Ltd
1 Oliver's Yard
55 City Road
London EC1Y 1SP

SAGE Publications Inc
2455 Teller Road
Thousand Oaks, California 91320

SAGE Publications India Pvt Ltd
B-42 Panchsheel Enclave
Post Box 4109
New Delhi – 110 017

British Library Cataloguing in Publication data

A catalogue record for this book is available from the British Library

ISBN 0 8039 7884 7
ISBN 0 8039 7885 5

Library of Congress Control Number Available

Printed and bound in Great Britain by Athenaeum Press, Gateshead

Contents

In memory of my parents, Bert and Sylvia Lloyd

acknowledgements

This book has taken far longer to finish than I hoped. In part, this was because life intervened all too often during its composition. In part, it was because of the detours, restarts and hesitations that marked its progress. It would not, however, have been completed without the support of several people along the way; not least my editor at Sage, Karen Phillips, whose patience alone deserves immense thanks. I would also like to thank Bob Eccleshall, my former head of school at Queen's, both for his unstinting encouragement and for providing such a conducive environment in which to work. Whilst at Queen's I benefited enormously from the presence of a group of excellent theorists (Alan Finlayson, James Martin and Iain Mackenzie) whose own work on poststructuralism (in its many guises) and whose zest for debate compelled me repeatedly to think again about what I'd written. Thanks are also due to those who read various parts of the book in draft form, in particular, to Iain Mackenzie, Margaret Whitford, Anna Cutler, Terrell Carver, and Véronique Mottier. I owe a special debt of gratitude to Kimberly Hutchings and to Andrew Thacker, both of whom read the entire manuscript in draft form. All my readers offered insightful comments and sound advice, not all of which I heeded. Any errors contained herein are entirely my own.

I owe not only intellectual debts but also personal ones. I would thus like to thank those friends and family whom I haven't already mentioned, for providing distraction and support when I needed it most, especially Anne Strach, Debbie Lisle, Deborah Sugg Ryan, James Ryan (and Mark and Gwendaline, of course), as well as Caroline, Dale and Andrew Lloyd. I also owe a significant debt of gratitude to my late parents. My mother's embodiment of determination in the face of considerable adversity serves as a constant reminder to me that things can get done whilst my father's encouragement to me to question everything has helped shape not only my writing style but also my conception of what political theory is all about. Finally, my biggest thanks must be reserved for the two people who have lived with this book for almost as long as I have: my husband, Andrew Thacker, who, as always, not only debated ideas with me but provided love, affection and excellent cooking to sustain me; and, Daniel, my six year old son, whose passionate curiosity and spirit brighten every day and without whose artwork my study would have been a very dull place to work indeed.

Some chapters are based on previously published work. Part of Chapter Four was originally published as 'The (F)utility of the Feminist Turn to Foucault', in *Economy and Society*, volume 22 (4), 1993, whilst an earlier version of Chapter Seven was published as 'Performativity, Parody, Politics', in *Theory, Culture and Society*, volume 16 (2), 1999.

introduction
the subject and politics

This book began with a puzzle. In the early 1990s, reading about the potential relation between Foucault and feminism, I kept encountering the claim that if I, as a feminist, used Foucault I was 'untrue', somehow, to my feminist politics. I was endangering that politics in some way. Intuitively I experienced this charge as unconvincing. Foucault's idea that resistance to power operates in a multiplicity of local, 'microphysical', and dispersed ways allowed me to explain much of the feminist politics I saw around me and read about. This feminist politics was, to paraphrase Vicky Randall, often ad hoc, based on brief campaigns with a local focus, bolstered by a rough and ready organization, and frequently orchestrated around transient coalitions (1987: 58). This politics was not systematic and it did not simply serve the interests of pre-given groups of women. Instead, it frequently led to the generation of alternative female/feminist identities.[1] So, while it was the case that turning to Foucault compelled me to question vigorously a particular understanding of feminist politics, where politics was construed simply as putting into action the demands of a pre-existing community of women, it did not, to my mind, imperil feminist politics as such. Instead it challenged me to rethink politics and what it does: what it enables and what it disallows. Far from being a tool that could just be used to eradicate all gender conflict and inaugurate, and guarantee, a woman-friendly future, politics in all its guises works, I will suggest throughout this book, as a messy unstable, infinitely reversible, yet generative dynamic. Although Foucault has remained a shadowy companion on my travels, since those early days in my thinking I have ventured beyond him to a wide range of work, both feminist and non-feminist, exploring ideas of what, in this book, I call the 'subject-in-process',[2] a term I use heuristically to capture the idea that subjectivity is constituted (by language, discourse, or power), inessential and thus perpetually open to transformation. For all my theoretical ventures, my initial intuition has, however, been confirmed. Politics is not, I contend, compromised by a turn to the idea of the subject-in-process; it is radically reconfigured by it. This reconfiguration is what I explore in this book.

My argument in what follows is that acknowledging the processual nature of subjectivity does not entail the demise of feminist politics, although it has a number of far-reaching implications for feminism. First, I suggest, it problematizes feminism's assumption that it requires a stable subject in order to justify and ground its politics.[3] This assumption is, I contend, based upon a naturalization of the relation between the subject and politics that is, in fact, itself already political. Next, I argue that recognizing that the subject is politically invested does not impede political engagement; it opens it up. This in turn leads to a proliferation of possible sites of political contestation (from the state to the domestic realm, from bodies and identities to the many places these bodies and identities are reproduced – medicine, the law, and so on). It also multiplies the potential forms of political activity (from parody, to critique, to radical democracy). Finally, I demonstrate how key ideas such as agency, power and domination rightly take on a new shape as a consequence of this radical rethinking of the subject–politics relation and how the role of feminist political theory is thereby transformed.

Interrogating the Stable Subject

To ask questions about the relation between the subject and politics at the start of the twenty-first century is, in some ways, inevitable. Social and political life, in the West, has altered dramatically since the end of the Second World War. The primacy of class in politics was challenged during the 1970s and 1980s, in particular, by the rise of the 'new social movements' (including feminism, gay and lesbian liberationism, the antinuclear movement, and environmentalism). The proliferation of these movements, and the increasing recognition that no subject's identity could be explained exclusively in terms of one axis (race, gender, or sexual orientation) brought forth disquiet with one-dimensional accounts of oppression, such as Marxism (with its sole focus on class). At the end of the 1990s, the relation between formal politics and its informal counterparts became particularly salient. With a turnout of only 69 per cent for the 1997 UK general election – the lowest since the Second World War – and 51 per cent for the US presidential elections in 2000, the indications were that dissatisfied voters were 'boycotting' formal politics (Hertz, 2001: 107). Alongside declining party membership in the post-war period, it seemed that people, and particularly the young, were viewing party and electoral politics as, at best, uninteresting and, at worst, unimportant. At the same time, the aestheticization of daily life, with its heightened emphasis on the cultural and symbolic realms, appeared to be gaining in salience. Changing image (and thus potentially bolstering capitalism), seemed more important (to some) than changing the world – at least, via conventional means.

My point is not that we are witnessing the end of politics. At the same time that disillusionment with party politics set in, there has, after all, been an upsurge in political forms not easily calibrated in conventional terms. These include the politics of ethno-national, linguistic, cultural or religious recognition, ethical forms of politics (including animal rights activism), and the 'anti-political' politics evident in the anti-globalization protests that marked the beginning of this century (Hertz, 2001; Rose, 1999: 1–14). My contention is rather that what these shifts indicate is that the political sphere is not fixed. It changes as dissonant or alternative forms of politics irrupt into it. The same, I propose, is true for feminism. Its conception of the political sphere has also been disrupted by alternative ways of thinking and doing politics. Questioning the nature of the subject–politics relation has been central to this. To use a different idiom, part of the historical present of feminism has been constituted by its claim to need a stable, unified and coherent subject as the basis for its politics. This claim, I suggest, sets a limit to how feminism conceives politics and disguises the power relations that underpin this conception.

It may be objected that feminism has had a persistently interrogatory attitude towards politics from its inception. Throughout its history, it has posed repeated questions about the nature of politics, not least in relation to how politics is gendered. Liberal feminism, while embracing the dominant conception of politics as activities taking place in the formal arena of voting, electoral candidacy, political representation, and so on, argued significantly that women ought to be allowed to participate in them on equal terms with men. This manifested itself not only in the writings of liberal feminists such as Harriet Taylor and John Stuart Mill, advocating equal political rights for women and men, but also in campaigns for women's suffrage and parliamentary representation. It can also be discerned in the emphasis in feminist political science on voting behaviour, female candidacy, lobbying and levels of representation of women in parliaments (at all levels), and in feminist political theory on conceptions of citizenship (a term often used to encapsulate the agential nature of political subjectivity).

Radical feminism, of course, went further: it questioned the very idea that politics could be equated solely with public level, governmental, activity. Authors such as Kate Millett (1977) charged that the realm of the state was a bastion of patriarchal power. Co-opting women into formal politics (as liberal feminists proposed) would do nothing to alter the structure of patriarchy as it spread its tentacles through every aspect of life. Moreover, treating politics as confined to the public sphere obscured the fact that the private realm, far from being immune from politics as conventionally argued, was saturated with gendered power relations, and thus with politics. As the radical feminist slogan put it: 'The personal is political.' In place of the kinds of political activities championed by liberal feminists, radical feminists advocated instead politics as direct action targeted at grassroots power relations. This included, among other things, surrounding army bases believed to contain nuclear weapons (as at Greenham Common, in the UK); establishing rape crisis centres and shelters for survivors of domestic violence; refusing sexual services to male partners and taking up lesbianism as a political stance. Radical feminism not only re-envisioned the sphere of politics (extending it to the private realm). Equally significantly it contested and transformed what could be thought of as a political issue. It *politicized* sexual relations (including prostitution and pornography), sexual orientation, the body, abortion, and reproduction.[4] The effect of this feminist rethinking of politics was to shift the terrain of what could be counted as political. And, of course, Marxist feminism and socialist feminism too added to this contestation of mainstream politics.

The significance of these developments cannot be underestimated. Without them, it is arguable that women would not have the same formal political privileges as men (though the actual ones may remain more elusive) and that politics would have remained confined to a narrower range of activities and issues than it now is. Such has been the change in politics that a student studying its disciplinary form today is more likely to encounter feminist ideas and discourses than one studying 20 years ago. For all this, however, these feminist developments are not quite as radical as they may first appear. The reason, I suggest, is that they still retain the same underlying logic as the accounts they critique in that both feminist and mainstream interpretations assume that politics requires a unitary subject as its guarantor. Although sensibly critiquing the masculinist nature of many conceptions of the individual, this awareness of the *political* contouring of subjectivity has not always led feminists to realize that their own account of the subject (collective or individual) may itself be a *political* construction.[5] Moreover, in these mainstream and feminist accounts, politics is conceived in traditional fashion as a set of practices, processes or policies, tied topographically to a particular realm (public and/or private), which are capable of altering the world in some specifiable way. In Shulamith Firestone's thesis, politics is the means by which when women as a sex-class recognize their subordination they act to liberate themselves from patriarchal structures of oppression by overthrowing the means of reproduction (1970). Or, in the context of liberal feminism, politics refers, for instance, to campaigns that mobilize women to fight against sexual discrimination in the workplace by pressing for legal change. Politics in this sense is intrinsically connected, therefore, to a particular understanding of agency,

4

apprehended as the faculty that enables autonomous actors to transform certain practices or policies or to act self-consciously for their emancipation (political or human). No matter what the ideological position (Marxist, liberal, or feminist – whether it is radical feminist, liberal feminist, Marxist feminist or socialist feminist), the 'politics of the modern era' is, as Diane Elam observes, 'anchored upon the idea of a subject' (1994: 70).

Such is the tenacity of this assumption that, unhelpfully, it seems to have become a 'conceptual necessity' within much feminist discourse (Fraser, 1995a: 69). This particular configuration of the subject–politics relation, that is, has been imbued with a near unquestionable legitimacy. Diane Bell and Renate Duelli Klein thus note that the 'identity of woman' must be 'the basis of political action', for, they inquire, how else 'can we speak if we are fragmented into so many partial and shifting identities?' (1996: xviii; see also Thompson, 1996, 2001; Waters, 1996). Feminist politics cannot exist it seems, without a stable subject. It *alone* gives substance to the feminism that functions in its name. It provides the justification for political intervention, for woman, as a coherent (collective) entity, is the one who has suffered from discrimination/oppression, and who can recall this suffering and act to remedy it. I am not denying that the idea of 'woman' and her pain has mobilized many feminist campaigns including those relating to legal, social, and political change, but did these campaigns act on behalf of a pre-existing subject or did they produce a subject through their activity? Many feminists have contended that interrogating the viability of the traditional subject of feminist inquiry is tantamount to repudiating feminist politics *as such*. For such writers (discussed in more detail in Chapter 1) it de-politicizes women's suffering, compelling them to a collective acquiescence to their situation. But does it?

In 'Eccentric subjects: feminist theory and historical consciousness', Teresa de Lauretis charts three moments of 'self-conscious reflection' within feminism (1990). I am interested in her description of the third of these.[6] This is the moment when four inter-related areas of feminist thought are revisioned. The subject is rethought as multiple and shifting; how to do theory is re-framed in terms of understanding intersecting relations of oppression; there is an increased awareness of 'marginality as location, of identity as dis-identification'; and feminism becomes identified as 'self-displacement'. It slips between the personal and the political, the social and the subjective, 'internal and external' (de Lauretis, 1990: 116).

Chronologically, de Lauretis's description is especially apt for, and prescient about, feminist debates that began to take shape during the 1980s but persisted well into the 1990s. This was a time when, as I discuss in Chapters 1 and 2, feminism was faced not only with insights from postmodern or poststructuralist thought that challenged its theoretical understanding of the nature of subjectivity.[7] It was also the time when the question of how to tackle the differences between women became prominent, differences (of power, privilege, location and oppression) that compromised any attempt to posit a shared history of women's experiences. *Against* and *despite* the hegemonic construction within feminism of politics as an activity in which only a stable subject can engage, then, alternative accounts began to arise to better address the issues just noted. These accounts, in varying ways, positioned the subject as an *effect* of politics; an effect generated in exclusionary and power-invested ways. This is the province of the subject-in-process, articulated by thinkers as diverse as Judith Butler, Chantal Mouffe, Donna Haraway, Diana Fuss, Shane Phelan, and many others.

De Lauretis, in her account, focuses on subjectivity. I intend, instead, to examine the subject–politics *relation*. As indicated already, the claim that politics requires a stable subject operates within certain forms of feminism, as if it has prima facie legitimacy. To question this is taken by them to be both against the feminist subject and against feminist politics, a heresy deemed even more pernicious when those doing the interrogating do so from positions indebted, to some degree, to poststructuralism (or postmodernism, since the two terms are often used interchangeably). This judgement is, in my view, deeply problematic. First, it denies those accounts of mobile subjectivity, which I discuss in Chapters 1, 2 and 8, which have emerged from within feminism itself *without* recourse to poststructuralism. Next, it sets up a dead-end debate between those for the subject and those against by treating the critique of the subject as a dismissal of it. As will become apparent in the next two chapters, exposing the political nature of subjectivity enables us to understand how particular versions of the subject come to be centred while others are denied.[8] Finally, it mistakes the nature of feminism's engagement with poststructuralism. This engagement does not lead to the depoliticization of the subject–politics relation at all but rather to its re-politicization. '"Anti-postmodernist" feminism' (to borrow a descriptor from Sasha Roseneil [1999]), in other words, fails to recognize that the subject–politics relation is *political*: that the subject is a political effect (which helps, as I explain in Chapter 3, to secure other political effects). Politics and the political are thus not negated in this sense by the feminist turn to poststructuralism, I propose, but quite the opposite: they are enlivened by it.

It makes no sense in this context to ask 'what is politics?' if by this a metaphysical response is expected. There is no stable discourse of politics enabling us to say 'this is what politics or the political are.' Instead any answer to that question is itself, I propose, always already *political*; it is an attempt to determine where the boundaries between the political and the apolitical are to be set. Politics, in this sense, may well 'tenaciously resist definition', to borrow words Fuss uses in a different context (1994: 111); it may remain elusive, hard to pin down, altering its markers like a chameleon to fit differing environments. This elusiveness will not be treated, in this book at least, as a problem. It will be regarded as evidence of the effectivity of politics: its capacity to be generative, disruptive, and sometimes transformative.[9]

Examining the work of thinkers who, more or less explicitly, challenge the 'politics of the subject' (Elam, 1994: 70), therefore, facilitates both rethinking politics (and the political) and problematizing the connection that ties feminism to a particular conception of the subject–politics nexus. (This is a nexus that veils the complexity of the relation between elements and that cannot, as such, capture the productivity of feminist politics.) By sketching alternative versions of this relation I aim to identify a route out of a particular aporia within which feminist discourse has become confined: where the recognition of difference or specificity is taken to threaten the foundations of feminist politics. As I explain in Chapter 3, this route does not involve simply reversing the priority between the subject and politics. It requires examining the agonistic interconnections between them. To do this I return to some of the key debates that occupied feminists until the late 1990s, questions about essentialism versus non- or anti-essentialism and identity and difference. My aim is not principally to rehearse these debates, however, but to reframe them. As already indicated, however, *Beyond Identity Politics* is not a book solely devoted to competing conceptions of subjectivity. I am a political theorist by training and, in consequence, many of the concerns I have in this book are with issues traditionally pertaining to that academic discipline. I thus explore how to understand political agency, power, domination, and critique when one begins from a position that emphasizes contingency over necessity and when one sees the relation between the subject and politics as agonistic. I also evaluate how political activism plays out when politics does not require the stable unitary subject to guarantee or authorize it. Here I examine the politics of parody, radical democracy and what Phelan (1994) calls 'nonidentity politics'.

Clarifications and Qualifications

Before I end this Introduction, I want to clarify an earlier remark. This is undeniably a book that explores feminism's utilization of poststructuralist insights (though not all the thinkers I discuss engage in such a use) and I make no apology for this. It is not, however, a book about feminism and poststructuralism if by that is meant a systematic attempt to assess what is at issue in bringing the two together: what feminism loses or gains, what poststructuralism loses or gains, whether or not feminism is derivative of postmodernism, or what politics of authorization may be operating in this conjunction (for recent work on this, see, for example, Ahmed, 1998; Lee, 2001). These are important questions needing careful examination, but they are not my concern. What follows is rather an examination of the effects on how feminists think of politics and the political when the subject is recast as in-process, only certain versions of which result from the importation of poststructuralist insights into feminism. There is, thus, a heavy but by no means exclusive emphasis on feminist work that productively engages with certain aspects of the work of Foucault, Derrida, and to a lesser extent, Lacan. I am not concerned with whether or not these are faithful importations, whether they are loyal to their source or whether they distort it. Indeed, I doubt that they could be faithful for the very reason adduced by Sara Ahmed, that adding gender to the poststructuralist/postmodern pot 'means transforming it' (1998: 15). Forcing questions of gender into theories that conventionally ignore or marginalize them destabilizes those theories, altering their very fabric. But it also subtly transforms feminism and it is these transformed *feminisms* that interest me. Although I am extremely sympathetically disposed towards them, it should not be assumed, as will become apparent, that I offer a blanket endorsement of them.

Beyond Identity Politics is, more specifically, a text concerned with how questions about politics, subjectivity, power and difference were theorized in the Anglophone world (predominantly in North America, the UK and Australia). As such, there is only minimal discussion of the works of, for instance, Luce Irigaray, Julia Kristeva or Hélène Cixous who not only critically engaged with 'poststructuralism' but were also instrumental in its constitution. Poststructuralism has not, however, been the only source of transformation for feminism: psychoanalysis, science fiction and cultural history have also affected its contours and contents. These too have directed feminists away from the idea of a stable subject. In this respect there is a second exclusion in the text and this concerns the interchange between feminism and psychoanalysis, which is covered only partially. The reasons for this are twofold. First, there is a simple matter of space. Second, and more importantly, to ask questions about the intersection between politics and the psyche, while of irrefutable importance, would take this book in a different direction than the one I wish to follow here; hence my limited engagement with psychoanalytic material.

The Structure of the Book

There are two broad areas that concern me in this book. First, the alternative accounts of feminist subjectivity that have emerged as a result of the immanent critique of traditional conceptualizations of the subject in feminism. Second, the rethinking of politics that is contingent upon and productive of these alternative figurations. Obviously, in a single book, I could not hope to chart in detail all the nuances within competing accounts of this relation. So, what I offer is a selective reading of some of the most influential of this material. What this means in practice is that I am evaluating *examples* of how particular issues have been approached without claiming comprehensiveness for what is covered. Bearing this caveat in mind, what follows is a summary of the book's structure.

I begin, in Chapter 1, by mapping various different accounts of the subject-in-process. My aim, as just noted, is not to present a complete chart of feminist accounts of subjectivity or even of the subject-in-process; rather, it is to plot some influential theoretical trajectories within feminist debates about the subject. So, I examine five accounts of subjectivity: the subject as *mobile, lack, deferred, constituted* and *performative*. I then consider what these reformulations of subjectivity portend, in general, for thinking politically. My purpose is to sketch some of the 'new lines of flight' (to borrow from Deleuze and Guattari [1987]) discernible within feminist work on the relation between the subject and politics. One of the impulses behind the idea of subjects as processual, and which motivated, in part, the turn by some feminists to poststructuralism relates to questions of difference and specificity. In Chapter 2, therefore, I consider two broad trends in accounting for difference. The first examines the production of specific differences at particular times in determinate locales; the second revolves around the idea of certain images or concepts that act as metaphors for the plural nature of subjectivity. In this instance, I examine the *mestiza* both as an expression of concrete difference and as an allegory of difference in general. I also consider the question of the politics of identity.

The focus of Chapter 3 is essentialism, an issue that has polarized feminists. In this chapter, I reformulate this debate by rejecting the oppositional logic that *appears* to underpin it and by recasting essentialism/anti-essentialism as an agonistic (rather than binary) relation, and one that is historically inflected. To do so, I deploy the notions of *constation* and *performativity* in considering subjectivity. I begin my examination by exploring the historical conditions of production of subjectivity in its essentialist mode, through a consideration of the work of bell hooks. Re-examining the debate around 'strategic essentialism' (Spivak, 1988), I show that essentialism and anti-essentialism are co-implicated.

The next five chapters take up problems of politics relating to subjectivity. I address questions of power and domination in Chapter 4. I evaluate whether it is possible to offer an account of *global* structures of oppression, subordination and inequality while drawing on poststructuralist ideas. To this end, I consider Teresa Ebert's theory of 'resistance postmodernism' (1993) that conceives of patriarchy as a totality in process. Focusing on the problematic distinction that Ebert draws between the economic and the cultural (and its attendant derogation of the cultural), I offer an alternative account: domination as global strategy. This, I propose, can explain the rationality behind the multiple and complex modes of female subordination without recourse to false generalization.

Critics of the subject-in-process have repeatedly cast this subject as an entity so thoroughly saturated and determined by power relations, that it has no agency. This is my focus in Chapter 5. Here I reflect on questions of agency and resistance through an assessment of the debate between Judith Butler and Seyla Benhabib in *Feminist Contentions* (Benhabib et al., 1995). I appraise the reconfigured account of agency offered by Butler and contend that it can, despite Benhabib's protestations, satisfy feminist demands for agency. This account (centred on such notions as catachresis) is also capable, I suggest, of moving the debate beyond its present terms where the focus is all too frequently on the conceptual inadequacy of resistance as a means for countering domination.

This concern connects with the topic of the next chapter, Chapter 6, which addresses the politics of critique. Knowing when it may be politically expedient or opportune to act often requires a critique of the situation at hand. Eschewing conventional conceptions of feminist ideology and political theory wherein a systematic explanation of women's subordination also provides the motor for political change, by indicating what is to be done, the accounts discussed in this chapter consider critique as a mode of problematization. To this end, I explore the efficacy of such an approach in enabling – though not necessarily governing – political change by considering two different theorizations of critique: one based on a postmodernization of Gramsci and Althusser, the other on Foucault. Since questions of criticism are usually tied in with epistemological matters, I also examine briefly the politics of truth.

Chapters 7 and 8 focus on issues to do with the kinds of politics in which processed subjects can engage. In Chapter 7 I discuss the relation between parody and politics by considering how Judith Butler's ideas have informed the writings of feminist and queer theorists in this area. I contend that by attempting to deduce a politics from Butler's theory, many of her followers not only attribute to Butler a legislative role she wishes to disavow but that they also reinstate the voluntarist subject put in jeopardy by a performative theory of gender. From this reading, I suggest that not only is drag politically ambivalent and its effects incalculable, but that for Butler there is no political programme entailed by her analysis of gender performativity. Politics is a matter of operating and acting within determinate political contexts, taking opportunities as they arise. This raises questions that resonate throughout the book, about how politics is conceived by interpreters of the subject-in-process and how these conceptions differ from those found in much contemporary feminist thought. These debates are particularly germane to the themes of Chapter 8. Each of the writers under scrutiny (Haraway, Phelan and Mouffe) offers a reformulated account of the link between politics and coalitions that takes as its starting point a rejection of identarian logic. Central to this is the assumption that nothing can be assumed about either identities or interests in advance of coalition formation. In this context, therefore, I consider questions about the conditions of possibility (historical or otherwise) for the emergence of inessential coalitions, paying particular attention to Laclau and Mouffe's notion of articulation. In addition, I explore what democracy and democratic citizenship means when politics is seen in terms of the relation between agonism and antagonism.

My argument in this book is that embracing the idea of the subject-in-process, far from depoliticizing feminism, breathes new political life into it. It opens up spaces for political contestation and allows for the flourishing of new forms of politics to sit alongside its more conventional ones. Feminism does not need the stable unitary subject to guarantee its politics. It needs a deeper understanding of the *political* nature of subjectivity and of the dynamism of politics.

Notes

1 For an interesting empirical account exploring how radical feminism, one of the most 'anti-postmodernist' forms of feminism, may nevertheless practise its politics in 'postmodern' style (that is, radically, contingently, pluralistically, deconstructing and transforming gender categories and generating new identities), see Sasha Roseneil's discussion of the Greenham Common Women's Peace Camp of the 1980s (1999).

2 Of course, the term subject-in-process is associated mostly with Julia Kristeva. Like her account, mine makes instability central to it, but unlike her this instability is not taken to be principally a psychic phenomenon.

3 This idea of problematization is derived from Foucault who, in 'Polemics, politics, and problematizations', defines it as 'what has made possible the transformations of the difficulties and obstacles of a practice into a general problem for which one proposes diverse practical solutions' (Foucault, 1984a: 389; see also Foucault, 1985: 11).

4 Arguably other movements were also engaged in politicizing some of these issues at the same time: the gay and lesbian movement being an obvious case.

5 This is somewhat ironic given that radical feminists, especially, reject the use of postmodern theory on the grounds that it is a 'male standpoint' (Bell and Klein, 1996: xiv). Arguably the ideal of the unified subject could also be characterized as a male standpoint.

6 The first moment, dating from the early 1970s, refers to feminism's attempt to define itself in terms of the question 'Who or what is a woman?' The second, brought about

11

by its answers to the first, centred on the paradox of woman as 'a being whose existence and specificity are simultaneously asserted and denied, negated and controlled' (de Lauretis, 1990: 115). Feminism, de Lauretis conjectures, is both within and without the discursive and social factors that determine it; constrained by and yet in excess of them.

7 One of the ways in which the terms postmodernism and poststructuralism have been deployed is as general labels covering a range of thinkers who share certain features in common. All too often, however, such deployment glosses over the considerable differences that exist between authors, not only in relation to how they conceptualize subject formation but also in relation to how they envisage politics. It is important, I think, to address these differences wherever possible. Partly for the reasons noted earlier, and partly because of the problem of over-generalizing postmodernism and poststructuralism, when I want to convey the particularity of the arguments of a specific writer, I name them. I do of course use the general terms at times, normally either when I am referring to a specific critic's own usage of this nomenclature or when I am talking about the broad trend for using postmodern or poststructuralist ideas.

8 This is, in my view, a question that can be turned on those feminists who fear the loss of the stable subject. Just what is the lure for them of this subject? Why do they remain so passionately attached to this regulative ideal given the difficulties of ever adequately defining such a subject? What is at stake in their belief that only such an embattled subject can authorize feminist politics?

9 I am not arguing that everything is political, which would, by making politics ubiquitous, render it a meaningless category. I am also not claiming that anything is either inherently political or apolitical. I am interested here, rather, in how the ways in which politics is defined enable certain phenomena and disallow others.

one

re-imagining the feminist subject

> When I do not see plurality stressed in the very structure of a theory, I know that I will have to do lots of acrobatics – of the contortionist and walk-on-the-tightrope kind – to have this speak to me without allowing the theory to distort me in my complexity. (Lugones, cited in Spelman, 1990: 80)

Maria Lugones's request not to have to fit herself into an oversimplified theory bears eloquent testimony to feminism's recent difficulties with how to acknowledge women's specificity and their differences from each other in terms of geography, culture, ethnic location or embodiment. Second-wave feminism has often assumed that all women share something: a common nature (an ontological moment), common experiences (a narrative moment) or a common developmental trajectory (a psychological moment). It is what women share that is presumed to form the unifying basis of feminist politics. Feminism is, after all, all about women; it speaks of, for, and to them. It has a particular constituency (women), and a particular goal (liberation).

Throughout the second wave, though, feminism has had to respond to various sources of dissension. First were the voices and writings of black feminists and women of colour as they proclaimed their exclusion from, and occlusion by, the terms of predominantly white, middle-class feminist theory with its emphasis on gender. This reaction compelled many white feminists to concede (or, as Haraway puts it, to be 'forced kicking and screaming to notice') the 'non-innocence of the category "woman"' (1991b: 157; see also Flax, 1992: 459). Moreover, it required them to reflect on the epistemic privileging of their own life experiences within feminism and on their participation in structures of domination. Second, and this is my main concern in this book, feminism also had to contend with the cacophonous strains of postmodernist or poststructuralist theory as it problematized the idea(l) of the stable subject. Feminist responses here have been divided between those wedded to the belief that without a stable subject feminist politics is impossible (since postmodernism and/or poststructuralism allegedly disallows truth claims, decentres the subject, and as such destroys the capacity for agency so necessary to feminist politics), and those interested in pursuing some poststructuralist or postmodern insights in order to better understand, acknowledge and resist the power relations which constitute selves in the first place. Together and separately these dual sources of dissent have focused attention on the role that 'identity' plays within feminism and how feminism deals with difference. Does identity imply the eradication or exclusion of difference? Is difference contained within identity? What might be at stake in abandoning the idea of Woman as the centre of feminist practice? Who then might be(come) the subject of feminism? What is the relation of feminism to the subject of feminism? Does it merely articulate the demands of that subject? Or, does it produce that subject in the first place? No small wonder that Linda Alcoff should note that 'for many contemporary feminist theorists, the concept of woman is a problem' (1988: 405). In the rest of this chapter, I explore, thematically, some of the issues raised when feminism adopts the idea of a subject-in-process, by which I mean a subject that has no essential nature but is constituted in various, always incomplete, ways.

Since what follows in this chapter is largely a critical summary of the writings of other feminists also attracted to the idea of the subject-in-process, I will state my position on identity and subjectivity at the outset. I do not reject the possibility that identity, in some form, serves political activity. Instead, I seek to challenge the idea that identity is prior to politics by showing that identities are political effects, generated on the field of power and that part of their production entails their naturalization so that they *appear* to pre-exist politics. Further, I contend that their politicization is required *before* group demands can be articulated. Although identities may be reified, in order to posit a common cause, this is not a safeguard against their inherent instability as performative categories. They are always open, despite appearances to the contrary.[1] Before I outline the different accounts of the subject-in-process that concern me here, let me offer a few preliminary remarks in order further to contextualize my work.

My aim in this chapter is not to examine in detail the arguments of the authors I mention. My concern is with the consequences for feminism of their shared critique (despite many differences between them) of the traditional subject. Many of these accounts borrow at times very freely from the work of key figures in recent contemporary thought (Foucault, Derrida, Lacan) but I am not concerned with how 'true', or otherwise, these borrowings may be. My primary interest is in how *feminists* have *re-articulated* these positions. I thus offer an incomplete map of recent feminist formulations of the subject-in-process.[2] The map is organized around five points: the multiple subject; the subject of lack; the deferred subject; the constituted subject and the performative subject. It should be noted here that several of the co-ordinates used to plot this map derive (to a greater or lesser degree, depending) from more than one source, although frequently one theory takes precedence in a significant way. Bearing this caveat in mind, what I offer is a cartography of the subject-in-process as a starting point for critique, a way of opening up, rather than closing down, a debate about feminist politics. After charting these positions I outline what, for me, are the main ramifications for feminism of the shift to a theorization of the subject as permanently in-process. In particular, I contend that it poses a necessary challenge to the nature of feminist politics as conventionally conceived, thus opening the way to apprehending politics as the messy, conflictual and dissonant dynamic that it actually is.

Before I start to plot these figurations, I want to foreshadow the argument that I make in the coming chapters by signalling how I mean to displace the debate for or against identity that has dominated feminism in recent years. In this debate opponents tend to be ranked according to whether they see identity forming the basis of politics or politics forming the basis of identity. I argue that such a dichotomy reifies one side of the debate at the expense of the other and as such ignores the dynamic relationship between the two sides. Their relation is not one of opposition or negation; it is, as I demonstrate in Chapter 3, an agonistic relation of tension and interplay. The present chapter plots the terrain upon which this debate has taken place. I begin with the multiple subject.

The Multiple Subject

Mestizas, cyborgs, nomads and tricksters: what all these images share is the view that the subject is a coalitional subject wherein various axes of identity (such as gender, race, age, psyche) are perceived as always connected while vying for dominance. All subjects are, that is, produced across, and positioned within, several (sometimes reinforcing, sometimes conflictual) axes. The subject is, thus, in a continual state of flux. This is aptly captured in the image, suggested by Elspeth Probyn, of the self as a combination of acetate transparencies: 'layers and layers of lines and directions that are figured together and in depth, only then to be rearranged again' (1993: 1). Such selves are never fixed; rather, their identity is permanently open to rearticulation, as discursive lines shift along different vectors (as new acetates are added, others taken away, or the ordering changed). Moreover, peeling away the layers reveals no essential self. As Ferguson puts it, these are 'mobile' subjects, who:

> trouble fixed boundaries, antagonize true believers, create new possibilities for themselves ... they are ambiguous, messy and multiple, unstable but persevering. They are ironic, attentive to the manyness of things ... They are politically difficult in their refusal to stick consistently to one stable identity claim. (Ferguson, 1993: 154)

They are both temporal (traversing many axes of power without ever being locked into them) and relational (the effects of aleatory encounters). Mobile subjects, as Ferguson understands them, share affinities with other fluid feminist subjects, including *mestizas*, tricksters and cyborgs.

The cyborg is especially interesting. Familiar from science fiction, the cyborg subverts the theoretical and material binaries of physical/non-physical, human/animal, and animal-human/machine. It is 'a hybrid of machine and organism, a creature of social reality as well as a creature of fiction' (Haraway, 1991b: 149) that transgresses the perimeters separating nature from culture; and, in the process, confusing all modes of identity (particularly gender) categorization. As hybrid, chimera and mosaic, the cyborg is the product of a complex intersection of practices, material artefacts, and heteroglossic discourses. In the late twentieth century, this cyborg hybridity operates both literally through the plethora of engineered devices to elongate life (pace-makers, artificial limbs and joints) or to enhance attractiveness (coloured contact lenses and silicon implants) and figuratively as subjectivity is construed as always and only ever multiple, the effect of *bricolage*.[3] As a figure for feminism, s/he emblematizes the permanent open-endedness of subjectivity, its potential for endless possible (per)mutation.[4]

In a different philosophical idiom, Braidotti, drawing on Deleuze, describes the nomad in a similar way. That is:

> As a figuration of contemporary subjectivity ... the nomad is a postmetaphysical, intensive, multiple entity, functioning in a net of interconnections. S/he cannot be reduced to a linear, teleological form of subjectivity but is rather the site of multiple conceptions. S/he is embodied, and therefore cultural; as an artifact, s/he is a technological compound of human and post-human; s/he is complex, endowed with multiple capacities for interconnectedness in the impersonal mode. S/he is a cyborg, but equipped also with an unconscious ... S/he is abstract and perfectly, operationally real. (Braidotti, 1994: 36)[5]

Thus, the 'nomad has no passport – or has too many of them' (ibid.: 33).

This nomad is a traveller always en route to somewhere else; never anywhere in particular. As such its significance is as a metaphor for becoming-other; for refusing the stableness of a steady, fixed identity. The nomad is only ever 'passing through', in transit to some other place. The nomad's motility occasions, thus, an 'intensive interconnectedness' (ibid.: 5) and the possibility of unusual conjugations and productive associations. Like the cyborg, the nomad is never simply one but always many; and like the cyborg, the nomad is the promise of linkage within, between and through difference. Braidotti observe: 'Nomadic shifts designate a creative sort of becoming; a performative metaphor that allows for otherwise unlikely encounters and unsuspected sources of interaction of experience and of knowledge' (ibid.: 6).[6]

The significance of these figurations of the subject (nomad, cyborg, *mestiza*) is that they capture *metaphorically* the complex interleaving of the multiple dimensions of identity, in imaginative and creative ways. They do not, however, explore the particular mechanisms or processes that generate the subject as unstable and open to rearticulation. To do this, an alternative approach is needed. In the next section, therefore, I examine the idea of the subject of lack.

The Subject of Lack

Derived sometimes loosely, sometimes closely, from the work of Jacques Lacan, the subject of lack is a subject for whom identity closure is impossible. According to this position, the subject is internally divided. Feminists deploying a conception of the subject of lack have tended to highlight one or other of two aspects of this project. Some have followed Lacan closely, though critically, and have emphasized the creation of the sexed subject. Others have explored the production of the subject of lack in a general sense. I begin with the first: the production of the sexed subject.

For Lacan, the constitution of the subject is the result of entry into the Symbolic order, the realm of language that exists prior to the subject and fashions him/her according to its requirements, that is, according to the Law of the Father. Both sexed identity and subjectivity accrue through entry to the Symbolic. The subject can thus only assume its subjectivity as it takes on a sexed identity, determined in relation to the symbolic signifier, the 'phallus'. Further, the subject in this regard is 'actually and necessarily created within a split – a being that can only conceptualise itself when mirrored back to itself from the position of another's desire' (Mitchell, 1982: 5; see also Grosz, 1989, 1990). Any notion of self can *only* be articulated through the positing of an other/Other. As Lacan puts it: 'I is an other' (1977: 23). For Lacan, in this regard, woman necessarily enters the Symbolic as lack; she is what Lacan terms an 'empty set' (1982: 137). This is the point of Lacan's crossed through notation of 'The' in Seminar XX. As Rose observes, '[a]s the place onto which lack is projected, and through which it is simultaneously disavowed, woman is a "symptom" for man.' As such 'the woman does not exist' (1982: 48). She is never fully of the Symbolic. Indeed, as Segal points out, there is only one sex. Woman simply represents that which could, phantasmatically, satisfy and complement the one – Man (Segal, 1990: 85).

According to Fuss, one of the effects of this conceptualization is to 'de-essentialize woman' (1989: 11).[7] Woman is radically other, unknowable in her own right, unthinkable in the terms of phallogocentrism except as the other of man. 'She does not exist, she can not-be' (Cixous and Clément, 1994: 39; see also Cixous and Clément, [19765] 1986). She is the negative element in the economy of sex. For some feminists this claim has been sufficient reason for rejecting a Lacanian approach since it appears to deny women. For others, most notably Julia Kristeva, Hélène Cixous and Luce Irigaray, it has formed a point from which to speculate about the nature of femininity and in particular about the relation between woman and language. Since language structures sexuality in terms of masculinity, the aim of such feminist work has been to thematize the unthematizable, to theorize through concepts such as the semiotic or Plato's notion of the *chora*, that which is unknowable (Kristeva, 1980a, 1984). Moreover, the effect of this claim is to position the feminine as that which disrupts the Symbolic (through catachresis, mimesis, and so forth). Woman is that which resists the closure that the Symbolic attempts to impose. Important as these accounts are, because they do not prioritize the *politicization* of subjectivity I do not explore further the notion of the feminine in this book. Instead, I turn to the second account of the subject of lack, since it is this version that makes clearer the relation between the subject and politics.

As noted earlier, the Lacanian subject is a subject of lack, capable only of generating a sense of self through the positing of an other/Other. This process of identification, which forms the very condition of possibility for the subject, is at one and the same time its condition of impossibility. The dynamic of recognition/misrecognition that structures the mirror phase signals the start of a life-long quest for 'wholeness' (in the Symbolic realm) that is predicated on an identification with the (m)other.[8] This has been taken to mean that individuals identify with historically configured subject positions (Mouffe, 1992a: 372) produced within/by the symbolic order (positions such as worker, gay, or African American). 'The history of the subject is the history of his/her *identifications*' (ibid.: 371, my emphasis). Identification, however, can never secure closure for the subject; that is, subjects can ever actualize their identities. (Subjects can never just be workers, gays or African Americans.) Since lack cannot be eradicated – since it is constitutive of the subject itself – the subject is unable to achieve self-identity (see Fuss, 1989: 102 and Grosz, 1990). This subject is always in-process.

This inability to achieve closure is where, in Laclau and Mouffe's analogous account of lack, ideology becomes pertinent.[9] Ideology attempts to conceal lack, to fill it in and thus to create the impression of closure (Laclau and Mouffe, 1985; see also Mouffe, 1992a, 1993). Labouring, gay or African American subject positions, for instance, are 'constructed by a diversity of discourses among which there is no necessary relation, but a constant movement of overdetermination and displacement' (Mouffe, 1992a: 372). As such, the subject who identifies with a political discourse (say, socialism) is attempting to satisfy its desire for an explanation of its situation and its experiences (that s/he is exploited, say). This attempt to suture over lack is perpetually thwarted. Identity is 'always contingent and precarious', at best only temporarily fixed (Mouffe, 1992a: 372). As Anna Marie Smith comments 'the whole process of identity formation always remains incomplete, for it always fails to resolve the subject's fundamental drive to be "at home" in her given structural positionings' (1998: 68).

How does this theory of the subject work in relation to feminism? Feminist discourse (or ideology) endeavours to generate the kind of 'home' alluded to by Smith, with which the subject can identify. It provides a set of beliefs and explanations that enable woman to understand and deal with her position within the dominant social formation. It makes sense of the category of woman. There is, however, no single discourse that produces woman. As Mouffe observes, woman as subject is produced in multiple, sometimes intersecting, sometimes conflicted, ways (1992a: 382). Sexual difference is generated, for instance, at the level of the family, law, social policy, and culture not through one single mechanism of patriarchy. This does not mean simply that there are multiple subject positions that are all different or 'dispersed'. Rather the ensemble of practices, institutions and discourses that produce the social category woman, reinforce and work on one another in a crucial way. At its most general, this means that woman is always over-determined as inferior or subordinate to man (Mouffe, 1992a: 382; see Laclau and Mouffe, 1985: 114–22). It is this over-determination that generates the apparently systemic dimension of women's oppression as different subject positions are articulated together in such a way as to generate and entrench women's subordination.[10] Given this, for Mouffe the task of feminism is to 'struggle against the multiple forms in which the category "woman" is constructed in subordination' (1992a: 382).

Particular attributes of subjects (or subject positions) may appear natural – women as inherently nurturing – but in reality these meanings are always already social. Their appearance as natural is the result of certain hegemonic processes that attempt to make certain ideas seem commonsensical. Since these meanings are arbitrary and not essential, they are always capable of being subverted. Subject positions are not fixed, therefore, but fluid. Some may endure for considerable periods of time in certain contexts but such endurance is not inevitable. It results from certain political contingencies, not from metaphysical certainty. As I will demonstrate in Chapter 8, one of these contingent factors, for Mouffe at least, is the presence (or absence) of antagonism. It is only in a context of antagonism, she avers, that *political* identities can be formed. It is the fact that the subject is split that enables this politicization to occur. Recall that all subject positions are defined in differentiation from other subject positions. In order to posit an identity, a difference (an other/Other) has also to be posited. The feminist subject thus emerges in differentiation from her Other: the patriarchal other. Where the relation is simply one of differentiation, it remains apolitical but when the relation becomes antagonistic, for Mouffe, it becomes political. So the identity 'woman' becomes political (becomes 'feminist') when an antagonism emerges with men or patriarchy. Given, however, that the subject is inherently alienated, and that any attempt to foreclose identity will fail, the feminist subject woman is herself also necessarily unstable (hence the immanent contestations within feminism around the identity Woman).

Despite significant differences between them, what these twin accounts of the subject of lack share is a dyadic structure (self versus other, man versus woman). Not only does this account explain why subjects are unstable; it explains how subjects endeavour to overcome that instability, through identification. With Laclau and Mouffe, it also becomes clear how identities become politicized. In the next section, I turn to another account of the unstable subject; this is the idea of the deferred subject.

The Deferred Subject

Where the idea of the multiple subject concentrates on the complex nature of identity, and the account of the subject of lack on the inherent instability of all subject positions, the idea of the deferred subject exposes how subject productions are always susceptible to dissolution. In this version of the subject-in-process, which to differing degrees bears traces of Derrida's influence, emphasis is placed on what is prohibited or excluded during the course of subject production. 'Deconstruction', Diana Fuss observes, 'dislocates the understanding of identity as self-presence and offers, instead, a view of identity as difference' (1989: 103). It does not attempt to isolate the particular grounds of identity, therefore. Instead, it undermines the possibility of finding those grounds. It does so, in part, by treating identity as metaphysical and in part by revealing the ways in which every identity 'contains the spectre of non-identity within it' (Fuss, 1989: 103). Like the subject of lack, the deferred subject is regarded as split. Identity, unstable as it is, is bought at the cost of excluding or negating the other. Deconstruction thus implies, what Ellen Feder and Emily Zakin call, a 'critique of consolidated identity'. Although identities may be 'always, already implicated in essentializing ontological claims' (Feder and Zakin, 1997: 21), such essentialist identities are effects based on disavowing difference.

Taking the case of gender, Feder and Žakin contend, that a coherent gender identity is 'an accomplishment', but an uncertain one (ibid.: 23). Successful attainment of a full or proper gender identity cannot be guaranteed to anyone. Gender identities are, at best, naturalized fictions (rather than natural entities), always prone to dissonance and uncertainty. Acknowledging this fictiveness enables gender to be de-coupled from sex. As Feder and Zakin assert, once gender roles are recognized as 'designated', and not natural, any necessary link between women and femininity is broken. Revealing that gender relations are normative allows for their effective subversion (ibid.: 23). It also undermines logocentric discourse. The question is how: what precisely is it that enables this subversion? The answer lies in what Feder and Zakin describe as the 'abyssal structure of any ontological order' (ibid.: 24). In order to examine what this entails for the processual subject, I turn to Diane Elam's discussion of the *mise en abyme* or, as she recodes it, the *ms. en abyme*.

Elam suggests that the metaphor of the *ms. en abyme* is particularly useful in relation to the category of woman. The *mise/ms. en abyme* is a 'structure of infinite deferral' (Elam, 1994: 27). To illustrate this, Elam discusses the image on the Quaker Oats box. Here there is a picture of a man holding a Quaker Oats box, on which box is a picture of a man holding a Quaker Oats box, on which box is a picture of a man holding a Quaker Oats box, and so on, *ad infinitum*. The structure of this image implies that meaning is perpetually deferred in a 'spiral of infinite regression in representation' (ibid.: 27). For Elam, the same structure applies to woman. Asking 'What is woman?' only elicits an infinite number of possible responses to the question, because although women are always determined in specific ways at any one time, there are many other ways in which they may yet be determined. To talk of woman in terms of the *ms. en abyme* is to contend, therefore, that woman is ultimately indeterminate. Not only does she not have a true essence; one can *never* be discerned. As a linguistic construct, woman lacks a proper object and 'an identifiable truth' (Caputo, 1997: 158, n. 2; see also

Cornell, 1991, 1992).[11] Woman is thus a *'permanently contested site of meaning'* (Elam, 1994: 32), where meaning is produced, as Moi notes, in 'an endless process of referring to other absent signifiers' (1985: 106). Elam goes further: woman, she notes, marks a 'point of difference within language itself' (1994: 33). The point is not just that subjectivity is phallogocentric (that is, woman cannot be a subject),[12] but that woman is undecidable.

Feminist (or other) work that charts women's experiences in order to discover the truth of woman is only ever a *representation* of woman – part of the structure of infinite deferral noted above. These representations try to stabilize the meaning of woman in determinate ways, even though such stabilization is ultimately impossible. For this reason, all descriptions of woman are inadequate because they are all susceptible to undermining, and as such can all be (infinitely) resignified. Any ontological claims about women as subjects simultaneously disguise and presuppose undecidability. Woman is thus always in process. For Elam, the task for feminism in this context of undecidability, or open-endedness, is to imagine 'other political spaces – spaces of political otherness' (1994: 84) beyond the myth of the unitary subject.

One of the criticisms levelled at accounts of the deferred subject is that it pays insufficient attention to how particular versions of subjectivity come to be centred and privileged, its emphasis being on the inherent instability of meaning. As such, power tends to disappear from view, since it seems as if all subject positions fail regardless of what they are. Problems of super- and sub-ordination seem irrelevant here. Ideas of the deferred subject on their own are, in my view, consequently inadequate to understanding political change and subversion. They require supplementation by a more historically nuanced, and politically aware, approach. The idea of the constituted subject is one such approach.

The Constituted Subject

What does it mean to talk about a constituted subject? In order to answer this, it is helpful to turn briefly to the work of Michel Foucault. In his 'Two Lectures', Foucault writes:

> it is already one of the prime effects of power that certain bodies, certain gestures, certain discourses, certain desires come to be identified and constituted as individuals. The individual, that is, is not the *vis-à-vis* of power; it is, I believe, one of its prime effects. The individual is an effect of power, and at the same time, or precisely to the extent to which it is that effect, it is the element of its articulation. The individual which power has constituted is at the same time its vehicle. (1980a: 98)

The individual (or the subject) is, for Foucault, produced by power through such mechanisms as: discourses (psychoanalysis, medicine, the law, feminism); objectivizing and dividing practices (case studies, hospital records, classrooms, credit checks); the gaze; and in his later works, technologies of the self (Foucault, 1984b, 1984c, 1985, 1986, 1988a, 1988b). In this respect, there is no pre-discursive subject upon whom power works, only a being produced by power to act in certain ways. This is the being Spivak labels 'a subject-effect' (1988: 204). This subject has no essence; what appears internal to it (a liberal notion of rationality, Marxian idea of species-being, utilitarian conception of psychological hedonism, or a Christian idea of the soul) is the effect of its constitution by power. So, rather than rationality determining behaviour, for instance, rationality is to be understood as the effect of power inscribing the subject. This conception of subjectification leads Spivak to note that:

> that which seems to operate as a subject may be part of an immense discontinuous network ('text' in the general sense) of strands that may be termed politics, ideology, economics, history, sexuality, language and so on ... Different knottings and configurations of these strands, determined by heterogeneous determinations which are themselves dependent upon myriad circumstances, produce the effect of an operating subject. (1988: 204; see Butler, 1992: 10)

This operating subject – or the 'sovereign and determining subject' required by our culture – is nothing more than 'the effect of an effect', a metalepsis comprising 'the substitution of an effect for a cause' (Spivak, 1988: 204). As I show in Chapter 5 this notion of subjectivity has important implications for rethinking agency. Jettisoning the idea that humans have a vital core and, therefore accepting that subjects are constituted, means also jettisoning the idea that human nature is repressed, or alienated. There is no essential self that is distorted or denied by social, economic or political structures, only a variety of subjects constituted by and constituting themselves through the interplay of competing discourses and practices. These subjects may be differentially positioned, such that some are authorized to speak while others are deemed incompetent, and where the knowledge of some is deemed superior to the knowledge of others, thereby creating matrices of inequality and patterns of pathology and normality that encode populations.

Despite certain reservations, this conception of subjectification has been the starting point for a number of feminist accounts of the constituted subject.[13] One of the earliest and most influential is the work of Teresa de Lauretis on the production of gendered (female/feminine) identity. De Lauretis offers a revised understanding of gender 'beyond the limits of "sexual difference"' (1987: ix) within which some feminist theory is confined.[14] She reformulates gender as a political technology. Gender is produced in the interstices between various social practices, such as cinema, and disparate 'institutional discourses, epistemologies, and critical practices, as well as practices of daily life' (ibid.: 2).[15] Gender is the effect of schooling, families, and the media together with art, politics and *feminism*: 'the set of effects produced in bodies, behaviours, and social relations' (ibid.: 3). Gender rethought in this way abandons the idea that the subject is constituted in sex difference alone. In its place, the subject is conceived as engendered in race, class and sexual relations (ibid.: 2). Instead of focusing on how women's natures are repressed or denied by patriarchal institutions, de Lauretis explores how technologies of gender operate to produce multiple, heterogeneous incarnations of gender; what she terms 'variable configurations of sexual-discursive positionalities' (ibid.: 7). This understanding of gender opens the way for a more radical epistemology as the subject is reconceptualized as 'not unified but rather multiple, and not so much divided as contradicted' (ibid.: 2; see also Douglas, 1994 and Flax, 1990). It is in the complex interplay between these contradictions that the subject of feminism operates. Invoking Althusser (to supplement Foucault) she is a subject-in-process, a real historical being that although interpellated by gender, is never only or exclusively that gender (de Lauretis, 1987: 10). Rather, she is inscribed within the 'movement in and out of ideology, that crossing back and forth of the boundaries – and of the limits – of sexual difference(s)' (ibid.: 25); a place, de Lauretis calls (echoing film theory), the 'space-off' or the elsewhere of hegemonic discourse(s).

While de Lauretis recognizes that engendering is modulated by discourses of race and class, she continues to emphasize gender over these other facets by concentrating on the manner in which feminist subjects are 'lived and created within and between the tensions of the [dominant] sex-gender system' (Probyn, 1995: 79). In my view, she stops too soon. I suggest that it is one of the strengths of the idea of the constituted subject that it is capable of exploring how specificity and difference are produced in particular contexts through determinate practices and discourses. For these reasons, in the next chapter, I show how it does so by exploring questions of race and sexual orientation. Before I do so, I need to complete my map by considering the performative subject.

The Performative Subject

In 1999 a tenth anniversary edition of *Gender Trouble* was published, complete with a new Preface by Judith Butler. In this Preface, Butler reflects on her motivations for writing this now classic feminist text.

24

Her primary target was the 'heterosexism at the core of sexual differ-ence fundamentalism' (Butler, 1999: viii). In other words, her starting point was sex/gender and how it was characterized within certain theo-ries as an oppositional pair with the male/masculine subject versus the female/feminine subject. Or, to borrow the words of Janice Raymond, Butler's purpose was to denaturalize 'hetero-reality': 'the ideology that woman is for man' (1986: 11). But it also did more than this. It chal-lenged the idea – a certain feminist orthodoxy even – that certain expressions of gender are original or true, while others are secondary or false (Butler, 1999: viii). It is this, more than anything, that is crucial to Butler's account of performativity.[16]

One of the principal arguments made by feminists has been that there is *something* internal to women which determines gendered iden-tity and that produces female subjects. This could be, *inter alia*, a maternal nature, a specific mode of reasoning, or a specific erotic nature. It is this essence that is given expression in our gendered behaviour. By contrast, Butler argues that gender is performative. As she defines it, this means that 'what we take to be an internal essence of gender is manufactured through a sustained set of acts, posited through the gendered stylization of the body' (ibid.: xv). Butler con-tends that gender is not an expression of what one *is*; it is something that one *does*. As she put it in 1990: 'If the ground of gender identity is the stylized repetition of acts through time and not a seemingly seam-less identity, then the spatial metaphor of the "ground" will be dis-placed and revealed as a stylized configuration, indeed a gendered corporealization of time' (Butler, 1990a: 141). The production of a gen-dered identity relies upon the repetition 'through time' of those acts, gestures, modes of behaviour and so forth that are seen to represent a certain gendered identity. In this regard, gender is inherently imitative, a 'kind of persistent impersonation that passes as the real' (ibid.: x). The gendered self has no ontological status apart from the acts which compose it (ibid.: 139, 140). It has no abiding essence, except as the effect of performative enactment.

Echoing J.L. Austin and Derrida, Butler asserts that a performative is 'that discursive practice that enacts or produces that which it names' (1993a: 13). Moving away from Austin, however, Butler follows Derrida in repudiating the idea that an autonomous agent is the author of per-formative utterances. According to Derrida, the only reason that a per-formative utterance works is because it repeats or reiterates a 'coded' model (1991: 104). It is precisely the practice and possibility of cita-tionality or 'a general iterability' that enables a '"successful" performa-tive' (ibid.: 103). Performative utterances are not singular events; they are the effect of 'citational doubling' (ibid.: 103). In the context of autho-rial intention, this means that intention is the *effect* of iteration (rather than that which governs or determines iteration). What does this have to do with the feminist subject? Butler's own question provides a clue: 'if a subject comes to be through subjection to the norms of sex, a subjection that requires an assumption of the norms of sex, can we read that "assumption" as precisely a modality of this kind of citationality?' (1993a: 13). Her answer is affirmative. Sexing the subject is the effect of the reiteration of a set of inescapable norms. Moreover, it is one that masks the conventions of which it is a re-citation.

So how, simply, does this work? Building on Foucault's observations concerning the productivity of power and power/knowledge (recast by Butler as power/discourse), Butler notes that it is the 'reiterative power of discourse to produce the phenomena that it regulates and constrains' (ibid.: 2). Thus, regulatory and normalizing discourses like biology, psychoanalysis, education and the law effect sexed bodies and gendered subjects.[17] But crucially, they are not produced through a single act of constitution but only through repetition. We are reiterated as female *every time* we state our sex as female on a form, visit a gynaecologist or obstetrician, go to a hairdressers rather than a barber, or buy sanitary products. Performativity, in this respect, adds, I would suggest, a useful codicil to accounts of the constituted subject and subject of lack (as articulated by Mouffe) in particular, insofar as it furnishes a mechanism to explain how particular subject-positions are acquired and sustained, and more significantly can be changed. Gender identity, for Butler, can never be achieved once-and-for-all; rather, the effect of an identity is generated by its continual reiteration on a daily basis.

This has a number of important consequences for thinking about the subject-in-process. First, it indicates that *all* gender identity is imitative in the sense of its being reiterative. There is no original that is copied by imitators, for we are all imitators repeating the acts and gestures that gender us as corporeal subjects. (This, as I demonstrate in Chapter 7, is where the significance of Butler's discussion of drag lies: drag is not, as critics have alleged, the sole exemplar of political practice, although it is one form, but it is a key exemplar of gender identity.) Second, it is in the necessity for reiteration that alterations in gendered identity can be inaugurated. For every reiteration of the norms and practices that produces gendered identity is a reiteration *with a difference*. Butler's theorization of performativity indicates, unlike some other accounts, how the subject's constitutive practices can be the raw material for its own transfiguration.[18] Gender is thus not a fixed or stable category; rather the practices that compose it provide the material for its modification:

> The possibilities of gender transformation are to be found precisely in the arbitrary relation between such acts [i.e. the acts constitutive of gender identity], in the possibility of a failure to repeat, a de-formity, or a parodic

repetition that exposes the phantasmatic effect of abiding identity as a politically tenuous construction. (Butler, 1990a: 141)

Of course, how effective these possibilities for transformation can be in the context of a highly regulated and normalized gendered system – het-ero-reality – is a moot point.[19]

For now, I want simply to stress that the performative subject, like the other figurations hitherto mapped, is a far cry from earlier incarnations of the feminist subject. This subject lacks an essence. The performative subject is an entity produced in the complex interplay of discourse, norms, power relations, institutions and practices. Importantly, like the constituted subject in particular, this theory assumes that politics plays an important productive role in this process.

Conclusion: Destabilizing the Subject

In the place of a stable identity, what is envisioned to differing degrees in the accounts just documented is a version of subjectivity as contingent or provisional. This is a view that correctly resists the idea that subjectivity can be construed as unified. At best, the subject is a composite of 'fragments whose constitutive aspects always include other objects, other subjects, other sediments' (Delany, cited in de Lauretis, 1990: 137). It also accurately exposes the fact that no conception of Woman can stand in for the lived realities of women's plural, multifaceted, and complex lives. As I argue in the rest of the book, feminism cannot afford to hold onto the mistaken idea that it requires a stable and coherent subject for liberation purposes. It needs to embrace an alternative version of the subject, understood as ambivalent, in-process, indeterminate, and terminally open to reinscription; a subject whose identity is always precarious, contingent and ambiguous.[20] Only then can it grasp adequately the nature of the relation between subjectivity and politics. Here I want to sketch briefly some of the contours of this relation.

First, and most obviously, the idea of the subject-in-process refuses the axiom that politics requires a stable or coherent subject: someone 'who persists, who remembers, whose experience and suffering counts', to cite Darryl McGowan Tress (1988: 197). Feminism, like other political ideologies, has assumed that only a stable, coherent subject (perhaps with the benefit of consciousness-raising) can make political demands and act autonomously to challenge the oppressive structures confining women.[21] Further, it has assumed, mistakenly I argue, that critiquing the stable subject jeopardizes the possibility of any kind of feminist politics. Recognizing that the subject is permanently in-process does not mean that politically feminists cannot act, at times, *as if* women share features in common, even an essential, unchanging womanliness. As I argue in Chapter 3, historically there are times when there is no choice but to temporarily reify certain features of identity in order to make political demands: to performatively invoke an identity, which though it may appear to be essential, is in actuality provisional. To argue that subjects are not unified and do not pre-exist discourse, society, or power, is thus to offer a necessary challenge to the idea that the stable subject precedes, and is independent of, politics, but not to deny that feminist politics are possible.

The onslaught on the stable subject is, of course, far from new, although crucially the form that it takes currently differs. Psychoanalysis, for instance, has long argued that subjects are unstable because the unconscious disrupts attempts to present a coherent self. Moreover, feminists have consistently engaged with and adapted these accounts of the role of the unconscious. Jacqueline Rose, for instance, promotes the idea of the unconscious as a form of resistance to identification, such that femininity, for example, is never achieved (1986: 7). Others, such as de Lauretis, discuss the unconscious as a form of 'disidentification' with femininity that signals a mode of female subjectivity beyond phallic representations (1990: 126). Butler, by contrast, surmises that the unconscious is that which exceeds, and thus continuously disrupts but paradoxically enables, identity performance (1991: 28).[22] Outside of psychoanalysis, there have also been attempts to acknowledge the variables combining to produce individuated subjects. One has only to think here about notions such as 'multiple jeopardy' (King, 1988) or the 'inessential woman' (Spelman, 1990), both of which foreground the plural and intersecting nature of oppressions. The problem of accommodating the unconscious or multiple structures such as race and class already put into question the idea of unified subjectivity. Just what, given these variables, provides a subject with stability or coherence? What, if anything, is essential to them and what not? Yet many feminists, even when they accept the thrust of psychoanalytic insights and/or arguments concerning intersecting axes of difference, flee accounts of the subject-in-process when these might be labelled 'poststructuralist' or 'postmodernist'. Take the following passionate intervention:

> the postmodern project, if seriously adopted by feminists, would make any semblance of a feminist politics impossible. To the extent that feminist politics is bound up with a specific constituency or subject, namely, women, the postmodernist prohibition against subject-centred inquiry and theory undermines the legitimacy of a broad-based organized movement dedicated to articulating and implementing the goals of such a constituency. (di Stefano, 1990: 76)[23]

Or, note the comment by Nancy Hartsock that 'postmodernist, post-structuralist dogmas ... inhibit any kind of political activism' (in Hartmann et al., 1996: 938) or that by Denise Thompson that 'feminism is a politics, post-modernism renders its adherents incapable of political commitment' (1996: 325). As Wendy Brown comments: 'deconstruction of the subject incites palpable feminist panic' (1991: 71; see also Elam, 1994: 71), but why? What does this resistance to questioning one of the basic assumptions of feminist theory reveal? Why is it that authors like Hartsock (1990, 1996) and di Stefano (1990) insist, despite everything that has happened within contemporary feminism, on the need for a unitary subject?

There are four relevant factors. To begin with the idea(l) of the stable subject testifies to a strong desire for unity among all women across the many differences that separate us (at times benignly, at other times, acrimoniously). Next, feminism, as a product albeit critical of the Enlightenment, has utilized for its own ends the dominant conception of the subject found in Enlightenment thought. It too has argued for a subject (female rather than human) with certain universal and essential attributes (Nicholson, 1990). Third, some feminists (Bordo, 1990; Brown, 1987; di Stefano, 1990; Flax, 1987; Hartsock, 1987a, 1990) have been sceptical about the alleged synchronicity between the 'postmodern' critique of subjectivity and the attempt to claim agency for women. Men, it is intimated, have once again changed the rules of the game just as women are beginning to play it. Finally, Jane Flax suggests that the feminist repudiation of 'postmodern' deconstruction of the subject may act as a politically acceptable cover for a certain 'racial subtext' within white feminism. Attacking postmodernism may be, that is, an oblique way of dealing with the kinds of criticisms women of colour have levelled against this feminism in respect of difference and the exclusions which white feminism operates. In this regard, she surmises there is significant 'overlap' between postmodernism and the claims of women of colour (Flax, 1992: 459; 1993: 22–8, especially 27). Rejecting postmodernism thus enables white women to preserve the epistemic privilege that goes with holding onto gender discrimination as the *sine qua non* of feminism (Flax, 1992: 458; 1993, *passim*). The refusal of the decentred, ambivalent subject is, on this reading, politically motivated.

To dispose of the stable subject and to embrace subjectivity-in-process, I argue, enables feminists to question, as I think we must, not only the nature of subjectivity but also the nature of the relation between the subject and (feminist) politics. It is not possible, in this context, to hold onto the idea that the subject precedes and is independent of politics and to adequately explore difference and specificity or to attend to questions of the unconscious, though many have tried to do so.[24] This, I contend, is what engaging with poststructuralist insights reveals more starkly than encounters with psychoanalysis or accounts of the multiple intersecting nature of identity. It exposes the degree to which the subject is not simply or necessarily the initiator of politics, but is itself a political effect. Here I suggest we heed Elam's words, that 'the subject is a certain logocentric concept which persists in order to enact specific political effects, and no amount of denying that the subject is political will negate this fact' (1994: 71). So, what kinds of effects are enacted by the claim that the stable subject is, as Hartsock and di Stefano obdurately contend, the guarantor of feminist politics?

To begin with, it constructs as unimpeachable the claim that the subject grounds politics. It puts it beyond political disagreement, as Butler notes, turning it into a necessary truth or analytical *a priori*. To reject the stable subject is, on this count, to reject politics per se. Next, it constitutes what counts as the realm of the political. This political realm does not include questioning the status of the subject. Rather 'the act which unilaterally establishes the domain of the political, then, functions as an authoritarian ruse' that ensures that such questioning is 'summarily silenced' (Butler, 1992: 4). When di Stefano, in the quotation above, merely reiterates, without question, the assertion that legitimacy accrues only to political movements that articulate the demands of a subject-centred constituency, she re-enacts, I suggest, that authoritarian move by once again attempting to depoliticize the subject.

Recognizing the politically invested and unstable nature of the subject-in-process does not, vociferations to the contrary, signal the demise of a relation between a subject and a form of politics. Nor, I argue, does it evince the end of feminist politics specifically. Here I concur with Mouffe that to oppose a politics founded upon the sameness of women against a lack of politics based upon the dissolution of that sameness is illegitimate (Mouffe, 1992a: 381; see also Laclau and Mouffe, 1985: 116). Instead, it compels a rethinking of the *relation* between the subject and politics. Specifically, it asks just what is at stake in the current, hegemonic, form of the relation between subject and politics. It exposes thereby the *political* nature of that relation. This interrogatory stance, I propose, has two effects: first, it draws attention to the historical present within which feminism currently operates. This is an horizon dominated by the politics of identity, where identity has been presented, erroneously I argue, as furnishing the stability required by the subject of feminism. In Chapter 3, by considering the *politics* of identity I show how the idea of the subject as constitutionally open facilitates an understanding of how particular identity claims have been (and may continue to be) made.[25] Second, it necessitates rethinking the relation between the subject and politics so as to reflect more accurately contemporary reality.[26] Not only is the subject recast as in-process, and thus as perpetually open, but politics is also reconceived as a perpetually destabilizing and disruptive, though often generative, dynamic. It poses a challenge, therefore, to the common, and problematic, assumption that feminist politics is *only* a mechanism to secure an end to gender discrimination/oppression, through the elimination of patriarchy, and institute a feminist future. Indeed, I argue later that feminism as a political practice is also one of the regulatory mechanisms whereby the subject woman is produced and disciplined.

As I noted earlier, two sets of dissenting voices have led to the problematization of 'Woman' as the subject of feminism. The first is poststructuralism, and in this chapter I have outlined some alternative conceptions of the subject *qua* subject-in-process drawing on 'poststructuralist' presuppositions. The second is the voices of women critical of the particularism of white feminist theory. In the next chapter, therefore, I demonstrate how ideas of the subject-in-process (specifically the constituted and performative subjects) generate an understanding of how concrete differences between women are produced politically.

Notes

1 In developing my position, I draw critically on the work, in particular, of Michel Foucault and Judith Butler.

2 There is no possibility that I could hope to map all recent feminist reformulations of the subject even those loosely oriented around a refusal of the stable, coherent subject. I plot only those that inform the argument of this book. For an alternative mapping, see Ferguson (1993).

3 See, for example, Balsamo (1996). Haraway also contests any idea of a material boundary to the body, asking: 'why should our bodies end at the skin, or include at best beings encapsulated by skin?' (1991b: 178). This is given a practical articulation through the work of performance artists Orlan and Stelarc.

4 I resume my discussion of the cyborg in Chapter 8.

5 As Braidotti says elsewhere 'In so far as axes of differentiation such as class, race, ethnicity, gender, age, and others intersect and interact with each other in the constitution of subjectivity, the notion of the nomad refers to the simultaneous occurrence of many of these at once' (1994: 4).

6 I return, in the next chapter, to the idea of the multiple subject via my examination of the *mestiza*.

7 There is a debate about the extent to which the concept of female *jouissance* reascribes the very essence that Lacan's relation account of subjectivation unsettles (Lacan, 1977: 151 and 1982: 145; see also Grosz, 1990: 139; Fuss, 1989).

8 Without detailing at great length here with Lacan's ideas and their impact on feminism, suffice it to say that the mirror phase occurs when a child is between six and eighteen months old. During this crucial period the infant, who formerly had no sense of itself, begins to develop an awareness of its own body by seeing it in a mirror or

reflected back in its mother's eyes. The process entails both recognition of itself and mis-recognition of its abilities and capacities. The child presumes from the image in the mirror a wholeness that is, in fact, lacking.

9 There is a question about the extent to which Laclau and Mouffe's thesis in *Hegemony and Socialist Strategy* is Lacanian, hence my denotation of their work, following Smith (1998: 68) as analogous to Lacan's thesis rather than explicitly derivative of it. In her later work, Mouffe focuses far more on Carl Schmitt's notion of the 'friend/enemy' distinction than on the subject of lack (see Mouffe, 1993, 2000). The more general account of the emergence of the subject is displaced by an exploration of the emergence of political subjects. In this chapter, I examine the general account of subject constitution and return to the significance of the friend/enemy distinction in Chapter 8.

10 Here the concept of articulation is central. I return to this in Chapter 8.

11 For these reasons, it has been criticized by a number of feminists for ignoring the historically and socially located 'real' women on whose behalf feminism operates. Participants in this debate include, for example: Ahmed (1998); Braidotti (1991); Coole (1993); Cornell (1991, 1992); Elam (1994); Feder et al. (1997); Flax (1990: 213–14); Fuss (1989); Jardine (1985); Moi (1985); Whitford (1991: 128–9).

12 Through his establishment of a distinction between phallogocentrism and the becoming-woman of philosophy, Derrida is able to launch a particular attack on feminism as a political current on the grounds that it is just another form of phallic logic seeking to instigate another phallic order. For a critical discussion of this position, see Whitford (1991: 128–9). See also Irigaray (1985, 1993).

13 For criticisms of Foucault largely on the grounds that he does not differentiate sufficiently between the bodily constitution of women and of men, see Bartky (1988: 64) and de Lauretis (1987: ix). In order to gauge the wealth of feminist reaction to Foucault, see, for example, Braidotti (1991); Diamond and Quinby (1988); Hekman (1996); McNay (1992, 1994); Ramazanoglu (1993), and Sawicki (1991).

14 For further developments of her idea of subjectivity, see de Lauretis (1990).

15 De Lauretis uses the example of M/F boxes on forms to illustrate the double inscription at work in the production of gender (1987: 12). The first time a woman checks the F box she formally enters the sex-gender matrix, and represents herself as female. At the same time, marking the F box interpellates (or marks) her as female.

16 My aim here is not to trace the development of Butler's account of performativity as it has evolved over the past ten years, but simply to outline her theory as it appeared in *Gender Trouble*, with some attention to *Bodies that Matter*. For an examination of her evolving conceptualization of the relation between gender identity and the politics of parody, particularly in connection to psychoanalysis, see Lloyd (1998–9).

17 These discourses also generate a 'domain of abjected spectres that threaten the arbitrarily closed domain of subject positions', a claim eerily resonant of the idea of the subject of lack (Butler, 1997a: 149, 1993a). I do not explore the notion of abjection here simply because of limitations of space.

18 This mode of subjectification is hinted at in accounts of the constituted subject (say, in Foucault's discussion of the 'sexualized' subject constituted through successive confessions) but the process is not made explicit. Performativity offers a way of theorizing

how transformations – both recuperative and subversive – may occur.

19 I explore this argument in more detail in Chapters 5 and 7.

20 This subject is a fluid, rather than a fragmented subject. This means that the subject is in-process, but not psychologically broken or shattered. For further discussion, see Flax (1993: 93, 101–3).

21 I explore the question of feminist identity politics in the next chapter.

22 It is perhaps because it acknowledges the insecure foundations of identity that psychoanalysis is frequently combined with poststructuralist insights in some recent rethinking of the subject.

23 As noted in the Introduction, the term 'postmodernism' in this quotation conjures up so many different and conflicting impressions that it is, arguably, of little analytical value. Foucault, for example, does not disdain 'subject-centred' inquiry; instead he explains how certain accounts of the subject come to be centred. Butler's call 'for a careful reading' of her own work (against her critics) seems apposite here (1995b).

24 Freud appears to suggest, at times, that the structure of the ego is affected by prevailing social and political conditions such that subjects are always constructs, partially, of history. See Butler (1997a) for an interesting discussion of Freud and Foucault.

25 Here Fuss's question – 'Is politics based on identity, or is identity based on politics?' (1989: 100) – seems apposite. I examine the problems of merely reversing the priority between the subject and politics in Chapter 3.

26 Of course, it might be objected that positing the question in this way presupposes that politics requires a subject of some kind. Could we have subject-less politics? I leave this to others to debate!

two

accounting for specificity and difference

From its very inception, the women's movement has been troubled by problems concerning specificity. When Sojourner Truth, the emancipated slave, walked into a women's convention in Akron, Ohio, in 1851, she was prevented from speaking 'for fear that "every newspaper in the land will have our cause mixed with abolition"'. Unperturbed, she rose to 'a hissing sound of disapprobation from above and below' (Schneir, 1996: 93–4) to deliver these famous words:

> That man over there he says that women need to be helped into carriages, and lifted over ditches, and to have the best place everywhere. Nobody ever helps me into carriages, or over mud-puddles, or gives me any best place! And ain't I a woman? Look at me! Look at my arm! I have ploughed and planted, and gathered into barns, and no man could head me! And ain't I a woman? I could work as much and eat as much as a man – when I could get it – and bear the lash as well! And ain't I a woman? I have borne thirteen children, and seen most of them sold off to slavery, and when I cried out with my mother's grief, none but Jesus heard me! And ain't I a woman? (Truth, 1996: 94–5)

In asking 'ain't I a woman?' (a refrain echoed by many black feminists since), Truth presaged the difficulties feminism was to face in relation the idea of a unitary subject. To those present at the meeting who thought that women should be kept on the proverbial pedestal, women like Truth were incomprehensible. They were not 'real women', for real women were white, and middle class and in need of male protection. It is the question of how to tackle and accommodate specificity and difference that has been the topic of an intense debate within feminism on and off ever since.[1] Difference is, of course, a fraught concept. Within feminism it signifies in, at least, three different ways. First, it stands for the differences between men and women, that is, for sex difference. Second, it refers to the differences between women, that is, to diversity. Finally, difference relates to the inherent instability of categories, not least the category of woman. It signifies what poststructuralists often refer to as *différance*. In this chapter, I outline some ways in which the subject-in-process facilitates a strong understanding of how specific differences between women are produced.

Questions about difference have produced a range of varied responses from within feminism.[2] It is not, however, my intention to survey this vast literature here. Instead I outline how specificity and difference can be understood from the perspective of the subject-in-process, or more specifically in terms of the constituted and performative subjects. For illustrative purposes, I concentrate primarily on the production of racialized and sexual subjectivities. To give the impression that the only way of understanding difference is in relation to the production of specific identities would, however, be misleading. As the account of the mobile subject outlined in the last chapter indicates, feminism needs also to attend to the multiple axes of identity that intersect, and cross-pollinate in order to breed hybrid subjects.[3] I thus also explore precisely how the figuration of the *mestiza* operates to incarnate plural differences. I begin the chapter by considering identity politics. I start by exploring what has been the dominant paradigm for understanding identity, namely where that identity is presumed to preexist politics. I then indicate how this logic mistakes the relation between the subject and politics. My aim is to displace this dominant understanding of identity by demonstrating how the concept of the subject-in-process provides a better explanation of how differentiated subjects are produced.

Critiquing Identity Politics

> Can identity, indeed, be viewed other than as a by-product of a manhandling of life, one that, in fact, refers no more to a consistent pattern of sameness than to an inconsequential process of otherness? (Trinh, 1990: 371–2)

As commonly used, 'identity politics' connotes a form of politics based upon certain characteristics of the individual shared with others. This might be an essential nature or a set of experiences which, regardless of the various differences between members, based on race, age, or sexual orientation, for instance, they all have in common. Identity politics thus operates, according to 'identarian' logic, where unity is sought beneath differences.[4] It is in this common nature or set of experiences that the seeds of a common politics lie: 'we have an identity', Barbara Smith asserts, 'and *therefore* a politics' (Smith, cited in Fuss, 1989: 99;

Brown, 1991; Elam, 1994). On this reading, politics expresses the demands and values of a pre-constituted identity. Identity politics is thus also essentialist, in that it assumes not only that what unites the group is somehow intrinsic to it but that what a group shares transcends history, culture and geography (see Elam, 1994; Fuss, 1989; Parmar, 1990; Schor and Weed, 1994).

In *Fundamental Feminism*, Judith Grant surmises that contemporary feminism is defined by three concepts: 'woman', 'experience', and 'personal politics' (1993).[5] Together these three factors produce the feminist problematic. They determine the questions that feminism asks (What is woman? Who/what is it that is responsible for women's oppression?); the solutions that it seeks (the overthrow of patriarchy); and the ways in which it can achieve those solutions (consciousness-raising and feminist political action). Feminism is an identity politics, therefore. It articulates the demands of a particular constituency (women), united and galvanized on the basis of shared characteristics or experiences. Indeed, it is assumed that this common identity is enough to unify individuals and to lend coherence to policy. Feminist political demands from this viewpoint thus express either women's interests or inherent feminine values.[6] The former can be seen in the politics of abortion or rape, for instance, while the latter is given expression in ideas like the ethic of care (Gilligan, 1982), maternal thinking (Ruddick, 1990), and *écriture feminine* (Cixous, cited in Sellers, 1994).

Clearly, there is political capital to be gained from using the category of identity: where, for instance, would the Israeli state be without the notion of Jewishness based on shared characteristics and a shared history of perceived oppression? Where would Irish nationalism be without a sense of Irishness (grounded in language, culture, and place) at its heart? The notion of identity can underpin the claim to historical continuity, as when a gay subject invokes a history 'that allows us to name Plato, Michelangelo and Sappho as our ancestors' (Gallagher and Wilson, cited in Fuss, 1989: 106). It can ground the possibility of connections across geographic space ('sisterhood is global'). It can serve as a vehicle for self-understanding, explaining why one is discriminated against (because one is a woman, or black, or disabled) and why one wants to act politically (to challenge that discrimination/oppression). In this sense, it furnishes the focal point for collective and thus concerted action (as the feminist slogan 'sisterhood is powerful' suggested). Furthermore, as Pratibha Parmar puts it, identity politics also gives rise to a 'self-righteous assertion that if one inhabits a certain identity this gives one the legitimate and moral right to guilt-trip others into particular ways of behaving' (1990: 107).

As the rallying point for politics, however, identity politics has been beset by a host of difficulties. As feminists of colour pointed out thirty

37

years ago, feminism has not operated all-inclusively to unite women. Because of this, some African-American feminists have rejected the label feminism in favour of alternatives such as 'womanism' (Walker, 1984), while the category 'women of colour' was developed to stress the erroneous, unacknowledged, association of women (and feminism) with whiteness. Both instances illustrate some of the persistent difficulties second-wave feminism has faced with regard to identity in which discord has exposed the myth of feminist unity. Reflecting on these troubled moments within feminism, Butler aptly asks: 'How is it that the very category, the subject, the "we", that is supposed to be presumed for the purpose of solidarity, produces the very factionalization it is supposed to quell?' (1992: 14). Why does attempting to unite women actually divide them? If this divisiveness resulted simply from a poor account of the bases of identity, then it might not be problematic. Remedial action could be taken and a better, more encompassing, conception of identity produced. This, I argue, is not where the problem lies, however. It is how identity is conceived that is the source of feminism's difficulty.

Feminists who deploy the idea of identity have tended to conceive of it in constative terms. Bonnie Honig, following Hannah Arendt, observes that a 'constative' is a necessary truth or expressive condition (1992: 217, *passim*). It represents 'what' we are (the content of what it is to be a woman or a Jew or gay, for instance). It works from what is, allegedly, pre-given about us. Usually this means the ascription to people of particular attributes but it also relates to the description of the experiences that are said to determine their lives. In this sense, identity operates as a 'site of closure' (Honig, 1992: 224): it sets firm boundaries around what counts as an authentic identity or experience. Consequently, identities represented constatively are assumed to be univocal and stable, as well as universal. A central problem with interpreting identity in this way, as Iris Young points out, is that the 'merely different' is turned into the 'absolutely other' (1990: 99). It functions, that is, so as to exclude those who fail to fit with its 'descriptivist ideal' (Butler, 1993a: 221); those whose experiences or natures fall outside the boundaries determining authenticity.

It is precisely the exclusionary nature of feminist theory that has generated much of the criticism of white feminism that appeared during the second wave. Nearly thirty years ago, for instance, Audre Lorde took Mary Daly to task for her exclusion in *Gyn/Ecology* of images of the goddess from non-European non-Judaeo-Christian cultures and for Daly's representation of non-European women as only 'victims and preyers-upon each other' (Lorde, 1984a: 67). At approximately the same time, bell hooks, commenting on Betty Friedan's *The Feminine Mystique*, observed that the 'problem that had no name' emanated from the perspective of Friedan and women like her ('college-educated, middle and upper class, married white women – housewives'). It ignored the lives of 'all non-white women and poor white women' (hooks, 1984: 1–2). In both cases, the lives described in Daly's and Friedan's books failed to resonate with the lives of black women, and in the latter case, with the lives of working-class white women.

At one level, these gaps might be cast as empirical defects with the theories in question insofar as Daly and Friedan generalized from too limited a perspective in their accounts of women's lives. They mistakenly, it might be argued, took their own experiences as coterminous with women's oppression in general and overlooked the experiences of women who were not like them. If this were the case, then, the solution might be to generate more accurate representations of the lived reality of women by formulating representations capable of incorporating the lives and experiences of the excluded. It is my contention, however, that such a strategy is itself deeply flawed. The problem with identity politics is more fundamental than mere empirical inaccuracy. It is that it misreads identity. Identity is not constative (though as I suggest in the next chapter, it may sometimes operate *as if* it is); it is, I propose, performative. Defective accounts of identity, such as those noted above, are defective not only because they are exclusionary (a phenomenon seen by many advocates of the subject-in-process as inevitable).[7] They are defective, on my argument, because they misunderstand the priority between the subject and politics. They present as natural (or constative) something that is a political effect (a performative) secured upon the field of power relations. Here I want to consider Mary Poovey's discussion of the 'metaphysics of substance' (1992).

'The basic assumption of the metaphysics of substance', Poovey notes, 'is that every subject has a substantive being or "core" that precedes social and linguistic coding' (1992: 241). She examines how this works in legal discourse. The legal concept of personhood presumes a subject whose nature incorporates 'the capacity to reason, to exercise moral judgment, and to acquire language'. Additionally, it assumes that the law acknowledges this core, and in turn, recognizes (through a constitutional bill of rights, for instance) its natural rights. Poovey contends, however, that it is the law that 'creates that which it claims to recognize' (ibid.: 241). In other words, the 'core' is actually an effect of legal discourse. It is performatively produced. In the context of certain feminist arguments, a similar operation can be discerned. Features taken to express women's natures are themselves the political effects of discourse (instead of the starting point for politics). This is exemplified well by Judith Butler's critique of feminist psychoanalytic theories based on a model of gender development (1990a, 1990b; Flax, 1993: 56). Butler contends that the assertion common to both object relations theory and some post-Lacanian psychoanalysis, that gender identity is secured via intra-psychic processes, which is expressed in gendered behaviour, relies upon the same (inverted) notion of an inner core that produces certain effects. In this case, the assumption of a psychic core is the effect of psychoanalytic discourse itself, not something that pre-exists it. Far from charting psychosexual reality, these discourses actu-ally prescribe that reality, by among other things, determining what constitutes 'intelligible sex' (Butler, 1990a: 148). What we are does not precede and shape discourse; rather, it is the effect of discourse. Identity is not, thus, an expression of essential characteristics, it is a political construction that presents those characteristics as natural. When feminist discourse proclaims that it has discovered the basis of homogeneity among women, this is not a benign gesture free from power. It is a generative move. It produces the particular feminist – or female – subject that it claims to have discovered. Such discourses are, to borrow a phrase from Gayatri Chakravorty Spivak, 'regulative nar-rative[s]' (1992: 79), establishing what is or is not permissible for women to be and do. They are political.[8] Identities, for this reason, are always saturated with power relations.

So far in this chapter I have argued that it is misleading to think of identity purely in constative terms, as the expression of 'what' we are. Instead, it is imperative that identity is reconceived as a political con-struct that: is productive of subject positions, generates exclusions, and enables the making of oppositional political demands. As I demonstrate in this chapter and the next, feminism needs to attend to the mechan-ics by which identities are produced if it is to apprehend properly both what they foreclose and what they engender. Before I explore how spe-cific identities have been produced around race and sexual orientation, however, it important that I state my thinking here. I agree absolutely that identity constructions operate in regulatory ways, disciplining and possibly even harming those subjectified by them. They also, however, generate possibilities for those same subjects. As the material in the next section indicates, no matter how processed or normalizing 'race' or sexuality may be, or how arbitrary and contingent the historical con-ditions of their production, subjects make sense of their lives in these terms (race and sexuality). They redeploy them, often in subversive and potentially therapeutic ways, in order not just to generate narra-tives of the self but actively to produce themselves as particular kinds of subject, including resistant subjects. As I show in the next chapter, significantly, they also generate opportunities for political engagement. I begin the section with what it means to talk about race and sexuality as ways of producing a self. My purpose is to demonstrate how ideas of the constituted and performative subjects enable one to think more cogently and creatively about specificity and difference and to admit an alternative interpretation of identity politics, where identity politics is seen as producing the very 'we' whose claims it pretends to articulate. While I just hint at what such an identity politics looks like in this chapter, I explore it fully in Chapter 8. Suffice to say at this point, that it does not require identarian logic.

Difference, Specificity and the Subject-in-Process: Thinking about Race and Sexuality

To argue that the subject is constituted is, as I indicated in Chapter 1, to disclaim the idea that there is anything pre-discursively natural about that subject. Like the categories of sex or gender, that of race is fictive. It is a construct both of discourses as varied as nationalism, biology, phrenology, and anthropology and of modalities of power from immigration controls to genetics. These discourses and practices do not represent the truth of racialized identity; they constitute that truth in different ways at different times and in different places. They produce a vocabulary that constrains subjects within certain codes while concurrently and paradoxically empowering them to speak another truth of the self. As constraint, racializing discourses are frequently discourses of racism. This means that racism is not a form of discrimination against pre-constituted races, a 'pathological and aberrant' phenomenon that needs to be vacuumed 'away like so much dust on the carpet' (Carter, 1997: 131). Rather, it is the effect of the mobilization and circulation of certain race truths, truths that have obstructed the advancement of certain races economically, politically, socially, and so forth. As empowerment 'race thinking' generates alternative truth claims. This is captured both in slogans like 'Black is beautiful' and in hairstyles like the 'Afro', posited as the expression of an authentic racial identity. Here, race is the starting point for claiming certain rights or powers as a racialized subject. Like other modes of subjectification, racializing discourses thus both subject and subjectivate. Discourses serving racism may also serve anti-racism (and vice versa) by furnishing a foothold from which to articulate a reverse discourse.[9] The assertion that race is constituted, then, is not a denial that racialized existences are lived; they clearly are. They are not, however, lived only as limited by race but also often as empowered by race. Indeed, race may even offer a means of self-fashioning. As Stuart Hall notes:

> Constituting oneself as 'black' is another recognition of self through difference: certain clear polarities and extremities against which one tries to define oneself. We constantly underestimate the importance, to certain crucial political things that have happened in the world, of this ability of

people to constitute themselves, psychically, in the black identity. (1987: 6, my emphasis)

Hall continues: self-constitution as black could only occur at a particular point in time (the 1970s in Hall's Jamaica). That moment was not a moment of recognition, the time to discover the 'real me' but a '[s]omething constructed, told, spoken, not simply found' (ibid.: 6). In place of the conviction of certain identity politics that there is a moment of consciousness-raising that enables us to discern the real truth about our lives and/or ourselves, the remark made by Hall hints at another way of understanding shifts in the self. They can be regarded as moments in the fabrication of another self; a time of becoming (Fortier, 1999). This indicates, as I demonstrate in more detail in the next chapter, that the projection of a constative identity (a truth about oneself as black or lesbian) is itself a performative effect; it is an identity produced in its articulation (see Phelan 1989, 1993, 1994, 2001). It is exemplified particularly clearly in Shane Phelan's discussion of her own coming-out and the implications of this for the telling of her sexual history, to which I now turn.

Coming-out is usually assumed to be a moment of self-revelation: the unveiling of the truth – formerly hidden or denied – of one's sexual identity or orientation. As Phelan notes, it is seen as 'a process of discovery or admission rather than one of construction or choice' (1993: 773).[10] It is the time when a subject's knowledge of themselves clashes with, and disrupts, the knowledge that others formerly had of them. Coming-out involves more, however, than simply divulging one's innermost secrets; it also requires a reconstruction of one's past in the light of this newly revealed 'truth'. Couched in the language of revelation, this re-inscription of the past seeks traces of one's real sexual identity under the fabrications previously constructed to disguise the 'truth'. As Phelan notes of her own path of 'discovery': 'I looked into my past for the indicators of my true sexuality and gloried to find them … being a tomboy, playing sexual games with pubescent girlfriends, being a feminist, not shaving my body hair' (ibid.: 774). This 'truth', she remembers, was applauded by friends who 'knew it all the time!' despite her decade of sex with men and an ex-husband!

In a culture that assumes that all subjects have a true sexual identity (whether as heterosexual, bisexual, lesbian or gay) and where the truth of that identity is regarded as fundamental to who they are, the recourse to narratives of revelation is inescapable. To proclaim that one has simply decided to be gay for the day would be incomprehensible in terms of this dominant idiom. It would make no sense. Drawing on the work of Mark Blasius, Phelan notes that coming-out is itself the product of a particular historical conjuncture: 'one realizes that one is lesbian or gay by participating in particular historical communities and discourses' (ibid.: 774). Using these discourses within a particular cultural and historical moment, the subject fashions or constructs (albeit unwittingly perhaps) a lesbian self. Lesbian subjectivity is the product of the practices and discourses that name it, not a substance or an essence that exists prior to, or is the author of, those practices and discourses. There is no lesbian self as such to liberate from the confines of heteronormativity, only a self that is a tangible product of that normativity. Self-fashioning is opened up precisely by the kinds of discourses that are mobilized in the establishment and then retrenchment of compulsory heterosexuality. Coming-out is a transgression of the boundary demarcating normal from abnormal sexualities but one that remains imbricated within the historical setting of those boundaries.[11] It is, moreover, performative rather than constative (Sedgwick, 1990: 4).[12]

In a similar way, there is no authentic experience of being black waiting out there to be claimed. It is an experience fashioned in its very articulation. As Patricia Williams puts it, 'black' operates as 'one of a number of governing narratives or presiding fictions by which I am constantly reconfiguring myself in the world' (1993: 256; Butler, 1993a: 247). Rethinking race from this perspective requires relinquishing the notion that there is an essential experience of being black that can be reclaimed from the past (a view shared by some feminists). Rather it involves the revelation of what Drucilla Cornell, commenting on Joan Smith, calls a 'future anterior'; 'a "time" which can never be entirely remembered, because even if read as *already constituted*, the past is being constituted as it is read' (1995: 152). The aim, for both Cornell and Scott, of this mode of doing history is to unsettle those sedimented readings that present the past as 'just "there"' (ibid.: 152). Instead, doing 'black' history from this perspective involves the creation of a past from which critique is made possible, a site of resistance to hegemonic white culture. Politics in this respect appears not to be the by-product of an ontology of the subject: quite the opposite. The ontology is the effect of politics.[13] The question that needs to be asked in determinate historical circumstances is, thus, what are or were the conditions of possibility for the production of racialized subjectivities or lesbian subjectivities? How was it, that at a specific time, a particular racial (or sexual) truth of the self is fictioned as the grounds for a political movement?[14]

The opportunity to 'come out', like the possibility of articulating a 'black' identity, is, I contend, contingent upon the operation of a particular *dispositif*. A *dispositif* is a complex ensemble of, among other things, institutions, laws, discourses, propositions and decisions that relate to one another in a multiplicity of ways. Relations between the various elements are shifting, mobile relations such that particular

43

assumptions may serve contrary ends, and so on. This is not to neglect, however, the fact that any *dispositif* 'has as its major function at a given historical moment that of responding to an *urgent need*' (Foucault, 1980b: 195; see also Deleuze, 1992). It is apparent that despite their considerable differences, 'coming-out' and enunciating a 'black' identity are both underpinned by at least one element in common: the assumption of the historical need for a stable subject as the articulator of a liberatory politics. Despite being performatively enacted (or constituted), these identities *appear* to issue from certain pre-given facts about the individual, and thence group; that is, from their blackness or their lesbianism. It is these features of identity that are cast as those which lend coherence or stability to the subject; as those which centre the subject. I return to the significance of this claim in the next chapter.

Understanding the specification of particular differences from the perspective of their constitution has, I contend, much to recommend it. It encourages exploration of how certain cultural ensembles of discourses, practices, and institutions come to instantiate particular forms of racialized or sexualized subjectivity. It furnishes analyses of these phenomena that are sensitive to specificity, context, and local particularity. While it is possible that explanations of this kind could examine the intersections of race or sexuality with other dimensions of identity (say, with gender or class), for explanatory clarity, they often limit the scope of inquiry to only one such axis. By concentrating exclusively on particularity, however, they may partially mask the intricate operations of discourses and practices, as subjects are constituted *across*, *between* and *within* plural lines of power. It is the relation between these lines (both within individuated subjects and between multiple subjects) that constructs and reflects patterns of domination and subordination within society. These patterns, like the subjects they produce, are themselves fluid and always in-process (and I explain how and why this is the case in Chapter 4). In the next part of this chapter, I indicate how the fluid and processual quality of power relations impacts upon the *form* that feminist theory takes when it endeavours to elucidate the hybrid quality of subjectivity.

Mobile Subjectivity: Figuring (in) Specificity and Difference

I want to acknowledge the ways in which my desires as lesbian but fem, as being black but 'light, bright, and damn near white' (an old Louisiana saying) and as being a feminist but from a particular class and culture reconfigure the politics of reclaiming bodies and pleasure. I want to speak out loud about the complications and contradictions. But which category

addresses which complication? Should I speak to the history of my blackness as a black feminist or as a queer, or do I identify with both because I
am a lesbian of African-American descent? (Harris, 1996: 4)

One of the central tasks facing feminism in relation to specificity and
difference concerns the difficulty of negotiating between retaining gender as *the* central analytic category of feminism (at the expense of
devaluing other facets of identity such as class and race), and producing the kind of analysis Harris wants. This is an analysis that is able to
accommodate the complex braided connections linking, among other
things, gender, race, class and sexual orientation, leading thus to a
more complex and more nuanced analysis of women in their multiplicity. Treating gender as the privileged term within feminism – what
it is really about – poses a particular problem, for it presupposes that
gender can be analytically disarticulated from race and class, etc., for
explanatory purposes. The argument of some black and other feminists
of colour, however, is that it cannot be. Their point is not that, for non-
white women, gender is less important than race in some manner. It is
rather that feminism cannot afford to decouple gender from race or
sexuality when endeavouring to explain and ameliorate women's lives.
Nor can it, as Parmar observes, just collect 'oppressed identities' and
then rank them: 'Such scaling has not only been destructive', she contends, 'but divisive and immobilizing' (1990: 107; see also Elam, 1994:
69–81). For racial, class, sexual orientation and gender divisions traverse contemporary cultural and socio-political formations multiplying
across and *through* one another in a host of elaborate ways in ways that
affect everyone.[15]

In her forceful and compelling book, *Inessential Woman* (1990)
Elizabeth Spelman makes a similar observation. She identifies what she
calls the 'ampersand' problem in feminist theory, where various axes
of identity are treated as entirely separable and where it is assumed
they are only contingently linked via the conjunction 'and'. Ampersand
thinking handles race, class, sexual orientation and gender conceptually, as if these factors are separate atomic particles, metaphorically
speaking, which bump into one another accidentally from time to time
and occasionally stick together. The deficiency with this approach is
that, as Spelman notes, 'sexism and racism do not have different
"objects" in the case of women' (ibid.: 122). That is, black women do
not experience sexism because they are women and racism because
they are black. They experience both simultaneously: that is, sexism
and racism interlock, they modulate and inflect one another. Additive
logic is inadequate precisely because it fails to grasp this; it fails to
acknowledge that sexism and racism work *together* to produce
oppressed subjects. It cannot address the ways in which a discourse of

race is already a discourse of sex and *vice versa*. Significantly, remedying this ampersand or additive approach necessitates jettisoning the claim that feminism can treat gender, politically or analytically, as separate from race (and other like variables). One dimension of existence, Spelman notes, simply cannot be 'subtracted' from others. Feminism, on this count, *has* to address more than just gender.

As Susan Stanford Friedman notes, though, a 'feminist analysis of identity as it is constituted at the crossroads of different systems of stratification requires acknowledging how privilege and oppression are often not absolute categories but, rather, shift in relation to different axes of power and powerlessness' (1995: 7). This necessitates considering how, while recognizing their interactive nature, different dimensions of existence may be more or less significant in particular contexts (see Fraser, 1999). That is, how at one moment an individual may be privileged in respect of her positioning upon the field of power relations, while at another moment she may be marginalized (or worse). This is what Friedman refers to as 'relational positionality' (1995), a theory that relies upon a conception of identity as fluid, hybrid, and syncretic.

Understanding the hybrid subject and relational positionality requires, therefore, a form of analysis that can take account of the shifting, liminal nature of subjectivity and can think about specificity and difference in their complexity. Clearly, it is difficult to envision what such an approach might look like generally speaking. How can feminists identify in advance the convoluted workings of power generating the multidimensional axes of identity that situate female subjects? How can feminists isolate in advance how race will shape gender, for instance, or how class will be modified by sexuality? One way to think through such complexity is, I argue, to think relations of difference *metaphorically*. This is why, I suggest, some feminist theorists have resorted to concept-images such as the cyborg or the nomad outlined in the last chapter, so as to convey imaginatively, if not empirically, the complex and fluid interleaving of class, race, sexual orientation, and so on. They opt for this route, in my view, because it is impossible to theorize ahead of time and out of context how differing vectors of identity will cross-cut and interweave to produce corporeally inscribed subjects. In other words, it is impossible to prefigure analytically how class, race and gender combine in any general sense to fashion specific subjectivities or to position those subjectivities upon the terrain of power. Instead, what is offered is an imaginative representation of those combinations. It is a way of registering that identity is never simple or absolute but rather is always multiple and dynamic.

In the rest of this chapter, I consider how an ethnically particular story of braided identities works: the *mestiza*. This is a term used by

Gloria Anzaldúa to describe women whose genealogy combines Spanish, American Indian and Mexican ancestry, the foremothers of today's Chicanas and Mexican-Americans (1987: 5). I have chosen this image, developed by Anzaldúa, for two reasons: first, because it is written from the perspective of a woman of colour in a very specific geographic locale, namely the US–Mexico border or 'Aztlán' ('with its record of colonization and racial domination' [Phelan, 1994: 70]). It is a direct attempt, therefore, to explore the limitations and potentialities of multiplicity through the contemporary appropriation of a culturally specific idea, the *mestiza*. As an idea, thus, it is deeply embedded in questions of 'race' and ethnicity, though in the way that Anzaldúa uses it, it also implicates questions of gender and lesbian sexuality. Second, I selected it because of the influence it and the idea of new *mestiza* consciousness have had within feminism, as evident in the writings of feminists such as Shane Phelan (1994), Inderpal Grewal (1994), Diane Fowlkes (1997) and Mariana Ortega (2001). In particular, two broad trends are discernible in this feminist work: the first concerns groups of women (such as white lesbians) who have posited their own experiences of marginalization and oppression as analogous to those of the *mestiza*. The second relates to how the image of the *mestiza* has been deployed as a metaphor for female subjectivity understood as processual. Shane Phelan offers a compelling and critical account of the first in her book *Getting Specific: Postmodern Lesbian Politics* (1994). I propose to concentrate on the latter – the *mestiza* as metaphor.

Borderlands/La Frontera, the text where Anzaldúa invokes the life and experiences of the *mestiza*, is both a powerful essay in autobiography and an account of a specific group of women (1987). When Anzaldúa talks about the *mestiza* she talks not only about herself, but also about the difficult existence of the women of colour, particularly Mexican-Indian women, who inhabit the borderland between the USA and Mexico. The *mestiza* performatively embodies the multiple interwoven identities of these particular women. Anzaldúa is not only a *mestiza* because she is Chicana, she argues, she is also one because she is a Chicana lesbian, a difficult identity to occupy within both her own and the dominant culture. 'As *mestizas*', Anzaldúa comments, 'we have different surfaces for each aspect of identity ... we are "written" all over with the sharp needles of experience' (1990a: xv); experiences of race, class, sexuality, hybridity and ghettoization. The *mestiza* thus operates in two registers: narratively, as a way of describing the experiences of a specific group of women *and* metaphorically, as a symbol of blended subjectivity.

Taken as a figuration of female subjectivity in general,[16] then, the *mestiza* symbolizes the ambivalence, contradiction and plurality implicit in all border or marginal identities (Anzaldúa, 1987: 79). It thus converges with a number of other recent tropes of female subjectivity that attempt to theorize the intersection of multiple lines of identity (such as those mobile subjects encountered in the previous chapter). Indeed, it might be further surmised that the *mestiza* encapsulates metaphorically what many poststructuralist accounts of subjectivity attempt to convey often in less elegant ways: that identity is always shifting and incomplete. *Mestiza* subjectivity is not to be thought of simply as a composite of several elements, though; the process is far more complicated than one of addition. The *mestiza* is like the cyborg, whose subjectivity is a movement of shifting 'outsider identities' (Haraway, 1991b: 174); she is a 'coyote', a shape-shifter (on coyote identity, see Phelan, 1995).

Pivotal to Anzaldúa's account is the image of the borderland: 'a vague and undetermined place created by the emotional residue of an unnatural boundary', a place that is a non-place, a site of permanent transition. This is not just the literal geopolitical frontier between the USA and Mexico mentioned earlier, but any invented frontier, between man and woman, gay and straight, or normal and abnormal. The borderland is a frontier space inhabited by *los atravesados*: 'the squint-eyed, the perverse, the queer, the troublesome ... in short, those who cross over, pass over, or go through the confines of the "normal"' (1987: 3). The displacement – or rather lack of place – implied by this existence is frequently daunting, tiring and often excruciatingly painful. 'Petrified, she [Anzaldúa] can't respond, her face caught between *los intersticios*, the spaces between the different world she inhabits' (ibid.: 20). Nevertheless there are 'compensations' and 'certain joys' in this prohibited and forbidden habitation : 'Living on borders and in margins, keeping intact one's shifting and multiple identity and integrity, is like trying to swim in a new element, an 'alien' element. There is an exhilaration in being the participant in the further evolution of humankind, in being 'worked' on' (ibid.).[17]

Borders, whether real or metaphorical, may, but do not have to, confine the *mestiza*. She can move across them, refusing to be contained by them. It is this refusal, and the exhilaration of involvement in change that give rise to what Anzaldúa calls the 'new *mestiza* consciousness'. She evocatively outlines this consciousness in the following poem.

> To survive the Borderlands
> you must live *sin fronteras*
> be a crossroads. (ibid.: 195)

As Anzaldúa writes '[the new *mestiza*] surrenders all notions of safety, of the familiar. Deconstruct, construct. She becomes a *nahual*, able to transform herself into a tree, a coyote, another person' (ibid.: 82–3).

This new consciousness is a disorientating consciousness for it denies the binary thinking and the boundaries designed to contain and define the *mestiza*, that position her as marginal, outside the centre but which also, paradoxically, provide her with a home. This consciousness, however disorienting, is not debilitating; it is positively creative. Its creativity lies precisely in breaking down absolutes (ibid.: 80). This means that the 'new *mestiza* consciousness' is, as Inderpal Grewal comments, 'always in the process of becoming' (1994: 250), never of being. It is never finished, static, or unitary. In this it echoes the 'differential consciousness' discussed by Chela Sandoval. Such consciousness is like the clutch in a car, the 'mechanism that permits the driver to select, engage and disengage gears in a system for the transmission of power'; in other words, 'differential consciousness' facilitates 'movement between and among ideological positionings' (1995: 217–18). By 'being' a crossroads, a site of multiply constituted subjectivity (or what Fowlkes calls an 'intersubject' [1997: 108]), the *mestiza* opens herself up to connections with others and, in the process, both to her own self-transformation and to the transformation of others. At such times, her consciousness changes through her engagement with others as she both gives and receives. Phelan takes up this form of consciousness in her discussion of postmodern lesbian politics. While she counsels against the appropriation of *mestiza* identity by lesbians (on the grounds that it de-recognizes the particular experiences of racial oppression and resistance that govern the actual lives of *mestizaje* in the USA), Phelan suggests that lesbians can nevertheless learn from *mestiza* consciousness. In particular, they can learn to appreciate its 'ability to sustain contradiction and ambiguity' (1994: 74). Hybrid identities require alternative forms of consciousness, ones that refuse dualisms and boundaries, and this is what *mestiza* consciousness suggests, however painful the process entailed in its development.

The *mestiza* is, then, a figuration of the subject that emerges from a very specific geographic location and from a very specific subject position. The materiality of these two things produces an account of the feminist subject, I suggest, as both in process and as hybrid. It speaks both to the idea that the subject is mobile, incomplete and to the consciousness that this subject is always a complex, multiple subject. It indicates that thinking about specificity and difference more adequately requires rethinking the ways in which different vectors of identity intersect, integrate and disintegrate. It also exposes the kind of consciousness that such a form of subjection engenders. Given the qualities of the *mestiza* and of new *mestiza* consciousness, it is easy to see what the appeal of this concept is to feminists interested not only in difference but also in how better to apprehend multiplicity and plurality.

The *mestiza* emblematizes the intricate and heterogeneous nature of subjectivity. In saying this, I am not denying its specificity as a way of thinking about Chicana identities; I am paying testimony to its symbolic purchase as a metaphor for hybrid subjectivity. Here the comment by Ellen Feder and Emily Zakin about the use of another metaphor ('Truth is a Woman') is, I think, particularly apposite; it is, they write, 'only and precisely within ambiguity (rather than identity) that metaphor has meaning' (1997: 29). The *mestiza* is invaluable as a *metaphor* for hybrid subjectivity, in my view, because it captures both the desire for identity and the impossibility of it. One identifies with it expressly because of the impossibility of theorizing generally and in advance *how* different axes of identity mesh with and/or resist others as they produce either an individuated or collective subject. Like the cyborg and the nomad, the *mestiza* works allegorically to convey the ways in which hybrid subjectivity unsettles unitary categories, destabilizes subjectivity and undermines any hierarchization of oppression.

The vibrancy of ideas like the cyborg or the *mestiza* is, as I have indicated, partially due to their efficacy in creatively encapsulating the braided quality of subjectivity, the fact that all subjects are produced across a range of discourses, practices that both fuse and jar. There is no doubt that feminism is in need of such ways of encoding plurality and multiplicity if it is to eschew charges of partiality and exclusion. Moreover, such image-concepts posit the complexity of multiple subjectivity, I hold, in such a way as to avoid the kinds of tortured (because impossible) attempts to unearth *the* underlying reason for women's subordination found in some feminist work. Image concepts are also important for another reason. One of the implications of the *mestiza*, for instance, of 'being' a crossroads is her potential openness to coalitional politics *across* boundaries and differences, to what I refer to in Chapter 8 as 'inessential coalitions'. She signals the potentiality for a feminist collective politics not based on pre-given identities but one that generates its own (enduring or provisional) 'we' through the kind of shape-shifting work that characterizes new *mestiza* consciousness. In turn, this implies the need for more inventive ways of thinking and doing politics, and for new feminist political imaginaries.

Conclusion

My aim in this chapter has been to explore the ways in which specificity and difference have been articulated from the perspective of competing versions of the subject-in-process. I demonstrated that two strategies in particular have been deployed: the first concentrating on the production of a particular identity and its historical conditions of possibility; the second, contemplating the kaleidoscopic nature of identity as multiple fragments intersect to produce individuated subjects, captured in metaphoric representations of subjectivity. Both, I suggest, profoundly unsettle conventional ideas of identity politics. The first does so by exposing how specific and complex identities come to be produced in specific ways at specific times and thus do not pre-exist politics, and the second by thinking creatively about the multiple, open qualities of hybrid subjectivity. Both also entail rethinking the limits and potentialities of politics. I will expand on what this rethinking involves later in the book (Chapters 4 to 8), when I examine in more detail the implications for power and domination, agency, and critique and also such political practices as parody and radical democracy.

Before I do so, however, in the following chapter I continue my interrogation of the relation between the stable subject and politics by reconsidering the debate on essentialism that occupied many feminists throughout the 1990s. In particular, I address the troubled issue of how women as feminists can still make authoritative collective political demands *if* identity is not grounded in a shared nature or experience, if there is no 'we' that can be presumed to precede the claims made on its behalf. Like so many debates immanent to feminism, the one on essentialism has polarized its participants for or against it. It has produced, that is, the kind of oppositional thinking that straitjackets feminism, both theoretically and politically. I argue in the next chapter, therefore, that to make sense of the relation between politics and identity one *must* understand that relation as agonistic. I will show that every identity (essential or historical) is performatively produced *and* that, at the same time, each performative production involves positing a constative claim. Each time, that is, feminists appeal to the idea of woman they performatively invoke her, but each performative invocation produces her anew and differently.

Notes

1 This locution is important. As Shane Phelan notes, to talk only of difference is to suggest deviation from a norm (without necessarily interrogating that norm). Talk of specificity 'acknowledges political location and the construction of self that a given location fosters' (Phelan, 1994: 9) and it also accords some recognition to that self. Specificity is a necessary adjunct to the idea of difference. I say adjunct because it is imperative to consider how the two – difference and specificity – work together.

2 Some writers have argued that certain key feminist conceptions (such as mothering and the family or embodiment) need to be rethought so as to accommodate differences between women (see, for instance, James, 1993 on mothering and the essays in James and Busia, 1993, and by Begum, 1992, on embodiment). Others have tried to

develop theory from the site of difference, articulating such claims often in terms of identity. (Indeed, Diane Fowlkes suggests it is this kind of work that initiates feminist identity politics in the first place [1997: 105].) For examples of black feminist thought, say, see Aziz (1997); Christian (1988); Collins (1989, 1990); Grant (1996); and hooks (1982, 1984). These modes of theorizing also, of course, attempt to displace white feminist theory from its central place within feminism. Additionally, there have been attempts to develop a greater political and methodological awareness of the multiple nature of oppression (see, for instance, Hurtado, 1989; King, 1988; Spelman, 1990). There has also been an effort to better understand the exclusionary nature of difference (see, especially, Trinh, 1989, 1990, and 1992). Amd so on: there are, of course, numerous other examples that could be cited here. Not all feminists, however, actively endeavour to accommodate specificity and difference in their theories, arguing instead that gender is the central category of feminism (Bordo, 1990). Some white feminists, by contrast, have appropriated black feminist theory in ways that allegedly fetishize black women (for a discussion of this, see Childers and hooks, 1990: 60–81; and Martin and Mohanty, 1986: 199).

3 I should perhaps stress that the term hybrid subject can be taken to apply to all subjects, since all are produced through and by gender, race, sexual orientation, etc.

4 Identarian logic works by reducing diverse phenomena to a single point, subsuming therefore everything under one universal norm, turning the 'differently similar' into the 'same' (Young, 1990: 99; see also Phelan, 1994: xiii).

5 For Grant, this means radical feminism since it is the only feminist theory and practice deriving exclusively from the experiences of women. All other accounts (liberal, Marxist, or socialist) take their starting-point from preceding masculinist theories.

6 For a sample of the debate on 'women's interests', see Diamond and Hartsock (1998); Pringle and Watson (1998); and Sapiro (1998).

7 As noted in the last chapter with regard to the subject of lack, this is because there is an inherent gap within subjectivity that needs tracing over in order to generate an identity (much in the way that heterosexuality is constructed through a repudiation of homosexuality). Or, as Papusa Molina in non-Lacanian vein observes, it demonstrates how '[e]verything around us tells us that in order to affirm who we are, we need to negate the other or define it as the opposite' (1990: 330).

8 In *States of Injury*, Wendy Brown offers the provocative claim, which I do not explore in detail at this time, that not only are identities power-laden but they may also be injurious (1995; see also Butler, 1997a; and Lloyd, 1998–99). Arguing that the identities upon which oppositional movements such as feminism are based usually begin life as part of a strategy to subordinate or marginalize those groups, she suggests that when women articulate an emancipatory politics based on such identities, they continue to invest in this injury (Brown, 1995: 73–4). They develop what she terms 'wounded attachments'. 'Politicized identity thus enunciates itself, makes claims for itself', Brown notes, 'only by entrenching, restating, dramatizing, and inscribing its pain in politics' (ibid.: 74). It thus reifies those identities. See also Hekman (2000a).

9 I return to the efficacy of reverse discourses in Chapter 5.

10 To remain closeted, on this logic, is to deny one's sexual truth to others.

11 Transgression only makes sense when there is a boundary to cross. This further

suggests that without such boundaries, there could be no transgressive counter-practices in the first place. The boundaries, therefore, generate the potential for transgression.

12 Sedgwick cites the case of 'a T-shirt that ACT UP sells in New York bearing the text "I am out, therefore I am"' that, she proposes, is 'meant to do for the wearer, not the constative work of reporting s/he *is* out, but the performative work of coming out in the first place' (1990: 4, original emphasis).

13 The account of race proposed here, like that of gender discussed in the last chapter, can operate in two ways: as the location for genealogical analyses and as the site for the generation of new forms of subjectivity.

14 The same kind of analysis can be applied to feminism. One can examine the specific historical conditions of possibility that generated it as a particular social and political movement and that produced its determinate terms of reference. See Showalter's point about the emergence of hysteria in the 1920s (1987: 145).

15 The fact that several black feminists advocate what might loosely be termed humanist visions of social progress is due, in part, to their reluctance to view the end to oppression as anything less than the end of all oppressions (Collins, 1990; hooks, 1982, 1984; Walker, 1984).

16 There is some ambiguity about Anzaldúa's own position of the legitimacy or otherwise of utilizing the idea of the *mestiza* as an account of female subjectivity in general. Compare Anzaldúa 1987 and 1990b.

17 Pages in the Preface are unnumbered.

three

essentialism
a risk worth taking?

In the previous two chapters, I have demonstrated ways in which the subject-in-process entails a different understanding of identity and difference than that discerned in other feminist writings. This understanding challenges the idea that there is such a thing as a stable, unified, universal subject. There are, rather, historically and culturally differentiated subject positions. Every subject is a fluid, multiple subject. As I indicated in Chapter 2, these subject positions operate both to regulate and inhibit as well as to empower and enable those (self) constituted by them. Given all this, it might be supposed that my position on subjectivity is resolutely anti-essentialist since I prioritize specificity and difference, the naturalization of identity claims and the abandonment of a pre-discursive foundation to subjectivity. (Indeed, for some time it was.) In this chapter, however, I want to revisit the feminist debate about essentialism in order to scramble the easy connections that have congealed between identity (understood constatively) and essentialism, on the one hand, and identity (understood performatively) and anti-essentialism, on the other. I want to rethink the opposition between essentialism and constructivism. This is necessary if the relation between the subject and politics is to be interrogated fully.

Let me first re-plot, briefly, the debate within feminism about the relation between identity and politics since this is one of the fields upon which essentialism versus anti-essentialism has been played out. For many poststructuralist critics of identity politics, as we have seen, there is a basic confusion in the arguments of their opponents about the ways in which the relation between identity and politics operates. To make political demands on behalf of a group presupposes that the group – and its identity – have already been politicized. The traces of the operation that secure this politicization may be hidden but, nevertheless, they exist. For feminists opposed to the use of poststructuralism, this logic misses the basic point, which is that without a shared experience of oppression – an identity – political demands cannot be articulated in the first place. Is it possible to reconcile these two positions? Are they diametrically opposed or are their exponents simply talking past each other because they focus on only a part of the whole? Certainly the opposing camps do take up vehemently articulated positions. For the likes of Butler (1991, 1992), Elam (1994), Fuss (1991) and Honig (1992), identity politics (apprehended as the proclamation of some form of homogeneity among women) is not simply an attempt to describe certain crucial characteristics or an 'authentic subjective experience' (Parmar, 1990: 107), it is inherently prescriptive and normalizing. As Biddy Martin and Chandra Mohanty put it: 'stable notions of the self and identity are based on exclusion and secured by terror' (1986: 197). It is a matter of power. Implied in this argument against the stable subject as the grounds of identity politics is the contention that any mode of identity politics is doomed to failure. That is, it is bound to divide and shatter any 'liberation' movement because those constitutively excluded by the production of the identity in question will come back to haunt it. For those such as Tress and Hartsock, as we saw in the first chapter, however, it is the very absence of stability and the challenge to the unitary subject that are politically stultifying. This means that there are no criteria for determining whether the demands of certain groups are legitimate; indeed, there are no grounds for making any demands since nothing can be assumed about women's experiences at all.

It is here that the question of essentialism emerges. It is charged that the presumption that feminism requires a stable subject relies on essentialist claims – the idea that there is something authentic transcending culture, history and geography that all women share. As noted in the previous chapter, however, what that something is has been a point of contention. Indeed, a number of different possibilities are run together when essentialism is generalized as it has been within feminism. It has meant: an essential nature (predicated on mothering, sex, sexuality, a feminine mode of reasoning); women's reality, understood as a particular set of experiences – potential or otherwise (the ability to be raped, for instance or the sexual division of labour); 'Woman as general conceptual form, or Woman as a set of identifiable properties which define her unique being' (Cornell, 1991: 4). This blanket use of the term essentialism disguises, *inter alia*, the conflation of essentialism with universalism (Lee, 2001: 40) and naturalist or biological accounts of female sexuality with accounts of feminine reality (Cornell, 1991: 4). Moreover, it masks the different forms that essentialism takes in feminist work. Thus, for instance, Lee, drawing on de Lauretis, differentiates between strong essentialism and weak essentialism. Citing philosophical antecedents, Lee points out that Plato's theory of the forms, which relies on the idea that essence equates with 'absolute being', represents a strong essentialism whereas Locke's 'nominal essence' operates as a weak essentialism in that it 'enables us to name and sort things by way of attributing an "artificial constitution" to objects' (Lee, 2001: 39–40; see also Fuss, 1989; Spelman, 1990). Although Lee dismisses the idea that feminists have subscribed to strong essentialism on the somewhat spurious grounds that if they had 'we would probably have witnessed a much more coherent and unified political movement' (2001: 51), it is clear that certain forms of feminism are close to it. In particular those which when they define what women are annul the specificities and differences between them. Rather than see strong and weak essentialism as either/or positions, it would be better in my view to recast the relation as a continuum that enables us to see a plurality of essentialisms. My intention, however, is not to try to plot which feminisms fit where on this continuum (although this is important work). It is to consider the political purposes served by essentialism.

As Diana Fuss noted of essentialism: 'Few other words in the vocabulary of contemporary critical theory are so persistently maligned, so little interrogated, and so predictably summoned as a term of infallible critique' (1989: xi). For anti-essentialists (or constructionists), the term has been one of rebuke and tart dismissal. Even thinkers more inclined to see potentiality in essentialism speak in a language which signals the precariousness of using essentialist ideas – a language of 'risk' (see below). Essentialism, it appears, has become a dirty word. To be an essentialist is to be positioned as theoretically naïve, and blind to specificity and difference. The opposition between essentialism and constructionism, if we follow Fuss, however, is itself unsustainable; constructionism in her account is simply a 'more sophisticated form of essentialism' (ibid.: xii). Instead of reprising Fuss's incisive and convincing arguments here, I want to take up the challenge that her book poses by considering the effects that are secured politically when essentialist claims are made. I do so, in this chapter, by revisiting the question of identity politics since identity is so often figured as an essentialist category. My central question is thus: what should feminism's relation to identity be?

It certainly appears from the vehemence of anti-essentialist arguments that all identity categories, whether those generally accepted as 'normalizing' (the good woman) or those charted as 'liberating' (gay, lesbian or feminist), act in a regulatory fashion. They discipline those subjected to them by establishing the parameters of what counts as normal or authentic behaviour. Moreover, hegemonic constructions of identity often operate constatively, insofar as they reify or naturalize specific features of identity. But if Judith Butler is right, that each invocation of an identity claim is always a recitation and thus non-identical to former citations, then this suggests that even in a context where an identity appears to have become reified, each of its subsequent articulations is distinct from those that precede it. They may, that is, be twisted appropriations, subversions, or even perversions of previous claims (a theme I return to in Chapter 5). Since performativity makes difference elemental to identity, it implies, I contend, that the politics of identity is never entirely constraining or negative. Arguing for an understanding of identity production as performative entails acknowledging that all identity is contingent. The fact that identity is performatively produced should not, though, obscure the fact that this production usually secures constative effects, which in turn create the impression that these effects precede (are causative of) political demands made on their behalf. As I indicated in the last chapter, performative productions of the self such as '(be)coming out' involve the postulation of 'truths' of the self – that is constative claims that are seen as expressions of what we are – even as those 'truths' may be revealed to be historically generated constructions. Constation and performativity are thus each implied by and implicated in the other.

I contend, first, that to focus therefore on only one side of the equation (constation or performativity, essentialism or constitution) is detrimental to feminism. It locks it into a binary framework that rigidifies debate into an either/or structure that forces feminists to make a decision about which side is 'right'. (This is indicated all too readily by the way that feminists are polarized into two competing camps by this debate.) Indeed, as Susan Hekman points out in a different idiom, 'contrasting the foundational subject with one lacking any foundation at all perpetuates the dichotomy that we are seeking to displace' (2000a: 301). Against this dichotomous logic, I argue that we have to think about the dynamic, 'undecidable', relations between these bi-polar terms. We have to understand, for instance, that to invoke a stable subject as the active agent of politics is *not* to refer to a subject that precedes discourse or politics; it is to performatively enact that subject as the initiator of politics. It is to understand the political effects this mode of subjectification generates. Similarly, to say that identity grounds politics is *not* to refer to identity understood metaphysically or universally; it is to performatively invoke that identity as organizational of politics. Instead of deciding which camp I wish to join, I propose to treat the gulf between the two as an agonistic space; a space, that is, for strategic thinking (see Owen, 1998: 306–7). I also have a second task. I aim to demonstrate that historically and politically, the injunction to think essentially has been unavoidable; it was imperative if feminist political claims were to be treated as rightful. One of the reasons for feminism's 'passionate attachment' (Butler, 1997a; cf. Brown, 1995) to the idea of a coherent unified feminist subject is, thus,

historically contingent. That is, to accrue legitimacy for feminist political demands these demands had to be couched in terms of the needs
of a distinct constituency, women. I propose that to understand the
richness and complexity of the debate on essentialism, it is necessary
to contemplate the historical conditions of possibility in which claims
are articulated in essentialist or constative terms.

I begin the chapter by considering a debate between Diana Fuss and
bell hooks about experiential thinking in order to consider the ways in
which essentialism and historical context interact. I then move on to
consider the trajectory that hooks's work has taken over the last
decades in order to demonstrate the agonistic relation between essentialism and anti-essentialism in determinate historical conditions, in
this case in the production of black subjectivity. This leads me onto the
question of 'strategic essentialism' as formulated by Gayatri Spivak in
her account of the Subaltern Studies Group. Deploying the idea of
'strategic essentialism', I argue that feminism cannot and should not
avoid essentialism. Instead it needs to interrogate what political effects
essentialism enables. This does not, as my earlier comments indicated,
mean abandoning the turn to the subject-in-process. Instead, it means
recognizing that the relation between the subject and politics is often a
complex, circular, one.

Essentialism in Context

At the end of her book *Essentially Speaking*, Diana Fuss contemplates
the ambivalence of the category of experience as the grounds of authoritative knowledge claims (1989: 113–19). Discussing experiential thinking in a classroom context, Fuss notes the way that it simultaneously
empowers some as it silences others. It empowers insofar as students
perceive themselves to be the same as others in the group and thus feel
comfortable with speaking out. It silences by establishing boundaries
between those with a specific set of experiences and those without, dis-
allowing the latter from intervening authoritatively in debate.[1] Her
point is that recourse to experience as an explanation relies upon essentialism. Not only does it set up certain essences as 'more *essential* than
others' (ibid.: 116) since experiential reasoning works through the institution of hierarchies within and between identities, but it also presumes the immediacy of experience to interpretation and
understanding. In a critical response to this chapter in *Teaching To
Transgress*, bell hooks observes that Fuss's chronicle of experiential
thinking in the classroom vilifies its use by marginalized groups while
ignoring its use by those in positions of privilege (1994a: 82). As she
notes: 'the very discursive practices that allow for the assertion of the

"authority of experience" have already been determined by a politics of race, sex and class domination' (ibid.: 81). They are drawn on by the dominated (in their plurality) in situations that are themselves patterned by 'structures of domination' (ibid.: 83). They represent a strategically chosen survival response to these structures, empowering those who are marginalized to speak in relative safety. Consequently, for hooks, they are not harmful practices as Fuss allegedly claims (though I disagree with hooks's reading of Fuss on this point). The important point for hooks is that experiential speaking is a necessary tactic both in the construction of standpoints from which to critique domination and in the development of purposive political struggle (ibid.: 88–9). Although I believe that Fuss is much more sensitive to nuances in the use of, or appeal to, experience than hooks allows,[2] hooks is, nevertheless, right to situate the pedagogical practice of experientialism on a broader terrain than does Fuss. Despite the apparent differences between them, there is nonetheless also an important point of affinity. They both recognize the necessity to eventalize specific political or linguistic practice, such as the 'authority of experience'. That is to say, they both see the need to attend to the historical conditions of production of specific practices.

Feminists regard experience as offering privileged access to the truth or the realities of oppression. It is precisely this notion underpinning consciousness-raising or standpoint theory that, purportedly, enables women to speak authoritatively about their lives. This in turn generates feminist analyses of specific experiences: harassment, rape, domestic abuse, and so on. Once experience is conceptualized as always already discursive, however, the relation between knowledge and politics changes. Narratives of experience are seen to *produce* rather than reveal reality. So, to take an example, let's look at sexual harassment. On my reading, sexual harassment is neither revealed nor discovered by feminism. It is feminist discourse(s) that produces the concept of harassment. That is, that names as harassment certain male actions and attitudes that women experience as sexual approaches that are unwanted and unwarranted.[3] There is no such thing as a prosecutable offence of sexual harassment until feminists generate the concept and, more significantly, the law instantiates it.

This eventalization of harassment connects with one of the points that Fuss makes. Talk about experience should involve a double move: the theorization of the 'essentialist spaces from which we speak' (as women, say) and the opening up to scrutiny of the *historical processes and practices that shape these narrative spaces into particular scripts*. For Fuss, this legislates a 'responsibility to historicize' (1989: 118). It requires, that is, the simultaneous admission of the constitutivity of essences and the essentialism of constitution. Translated into a method for the sorts of 'race' talking considered in the last chapter for instance, this implies the concurrent acknowledgement that race is a fiction that is lived, sometimes painfully and sometimes joyously, as reality. Contrary to the claims of those who regard the historicization or deconstruction of race as negating or destroying black identity and the specificity of black history,[4] such a move emphasizes the continuing significance of 'race' for those black subjects inscribed ('racialized') by it. The aim of an approach like Fuss's in the context of race, is to expose the historical underpinnings of racial essentialism, which subtend cultural racism (hooks, 1990a: 86), *and*, I would add, made possible movements such as Black Power in the USA or Black Consciousness in South Africa.[5]

Fuss's doubled injunction to consider essentialist spaces while at the same time historicizing those spaces is an important contribution to the debate on essentialism. It counters the claim that essentialism is necessarily ahistorical. Critics need to consider when and where essentialist claims are invoked. In the next section, I borrow Fuss's framework in order to consider the work of bell hooks over the past 20 years or so. I do so for a particular purpose that relates to my interrogation of the link between the subject and politics. I show that the developments in hooks's approach reveal the ways in which the need for a stable subject as preceding politics is itself historically configured. That is, articulating a constative account of black identity is seen as necessary in order to legitimate a black feminist politics.

bell hooks: Towards a Radical Black Subjectivity

If one wants to chart the debate on essentialism versus anti-essentialism one has only to compare hooks's writing in her first book *Ain't I a Woman: Black Women and Feminism* (1982) with her later collections of essays (1989, 1990a, 1992a, 1994a, 1994b, 1995). In her earlier writings, hooks endeavours to expose the uncritical dependence of white feminist thought upon discourses of race and class. Her diatribe against Betty Friedan in *Feminist Theory: From Margin to Center* (1984) and her construction of a history of 'black womanhood' under slavery in *Ain't I a Woman*, both seek to illuminate the interdependence of gender, race and class for black women, and to query any universal experience of oppression. Commenting some time later on her first book, hooks remarks: 'The book emerged out of my longing for self-recovery, for education for critical consciousness – *for a way of understanding black female experience that would liberate us from the colonizing mentality fostered in a racist sexist context*' (1989: 151, my emphasis). Her motivation was to redress the exclusion of black women from feminist accounts of oppression by developing an account of *their* experiences of oppression as *black* women.[6] She was engaged in what Clough terms 'engendering African-American criticism': the production of a form of criticism growing out of the experiences of being black (1994: 86–113). *Ain't I a Woman* was, hooks says later, an expression of 'the deep and passionate longing for change in the social status of black women, for an end to sexist domination and exploitation' (1989: 152).

Like Patricia Hill Collins in *Black Feminist Thought* (1990), hooks in *Feminist Theory* argues for the need to re-evaluate the lives of black women from their own perspective and insists that this perspective offers a 'special vantage point' that makes black women's conscious-ness into a privileged site of consciousness (1984: 15).

> To be in the margin is to be part of the whole but outside the main body ... Living as we [black Americans] did – on the edge – we developed a par-ticular way of seeing reality. We looked both from the outside in and from the inside out. We focused our attention on the center as well as in the margin. We understood both ... This sense of wholeness, impressed upon our consciousness by the very structure of our daily lives, provided us with an oppositional world view – a mode of seeing unknown to most of our oppressors, that sustained us, aided us in our struggle to transcend poverty and despair, strengthened our sense of self and our solidarity. (ibid,: ix)

As with Collins's idea of the 'outsider-within', marginality offers a particular epistemological stance emphasizing the experiences of the marginalized subject over those of the dominant. To cite Collins: 'Domestic work allowed African-American women to see white elites, both actual and aspiring, from perspectives largely obscured from Black men and from these groups themselves' (1990: 11). As a conse-quence '[t]he result was a curious outsider-within stance, a peculiar marginality that stimulated a special black women's perspective' (ibid.: 11).[7] Side-stepping questions about either the reliability of, or indeed the viability of, experientialist epistemologies, the purpose of both hooks and Collins is to highlight the diversity of female experi-ences of oppression by speaking for and of black women's specific experiences.[8] While Collins concentrates upon the development of *an* alternative African-American tradition of thought – symbolized by story-telling – hooks turns her attention to dealing with the differ-ences of black women both from white feminists and within black communities. So, in these early works, hooks's approach can be seen as an exploration of the 'essentialist spaces' from which Black women speak (to echo Fuss above). In this, it accords with the needs of resistant groups to assert identity politically as a means of reclaiming agency and as a process of self-empowerment (see Aziz, 1997: 76; Trinh, 1992: 157).

The direction taken by hooks in her later work, however, suggests a critical distancing from such essential-experiential claims. This direction is one that is assimilated to a critical suspicion of traditional identity politics. Thus, in 'Postmodern blackness' she writes: 'The critique of essentialism encouraged by postmodern thought is useful for African-Americans concerned with reforming outmoded notions of identity'; in particular, because it can 'open up new possibilities for the construction of the self and the assertion of agency' (hooks, 1990b: 28). Similarly in 'The politics of radical black subjectivity', hooks eschews 'essentialist notions of identity' in favour of fashioning new selves, of constructing 'radical black subjectivity'. Here again she highlights the importance of sites of marginality in the development of critical spaces (1990c: 20). So, why does hooks appear to move away from identity-as-essence to identity-as-self-fashioning? hooks, herself, provides the answer: 'we all recognize the primacy of identity politics as an important stage in the liberation process' (ibid.: 19). In other words, making essentialist claims is of political utility at certain historical moments. It is politically important at such times to contend that a marginalized group has a specific identity denied or denigrated by the dominant order of the day. I'll return to this below.

Instead of claiming that hooks has merely swapped one position for another here, however, I contend that what we can see at work in hooks's writing is the agonism between constation and performativity, essentialism and constructivism. Feminism has set up the debate between essentialism and anti-essentialism by construing the former as entirely about constative claims (what we are) and the latter as entirely performative or constituted (what we are made into). The story is much less simple. I want to make two points here: first that the choice in terms of identity is not between identity-as-essentialism and identity as the production of forms of subjectivity (including self-fashioning). Identity, understood as an essence, also involves identity-production. As we saw in the last chapter, it is the idiom of a sexed nature or a racial past that furnishes the vocabulary from which to fashion a self. An essentialist identity is thus itself a fabrication. hooks's work implies that the relations between essentialism and constructivism and, I contend, between constation and performativity, are not simple ones of opposition. Theories of identity that are regarded as essentialist operate performatively: they are constructions that enact (or re-enact) subjects as they name them. Theories that are seen as constructivist also rely on moments of constation when the self-fashioning subject expresses 'truths' about him or herself based on historically specific discourses.

The second point is that identity understood in essentialist terms operates in certain historical instances as the only authentic mode of political address. (This takes us back to Stuart Hall's comment above: that being 'black' was only possible in Jamaica in the 1970s.) As I demonstrate below, the reason for this is that the domain of the political regulates what counts as legitimate terms of intervention. Claiming the rights that exist for non-white female, feminist, subjects by using a similar mode of address (experientialism) to that underpinning white claims, opens up a point of entry for black feminist intervention in political debate. Essentialism in respect of identity claims has strategic political import. At a time when the idea of a subject (be that an individual agent, woman, or a collective national subject, the British) dominates politics (Elam, 1994: 70), hooks's desire to construct an account of authentic black identity is entirely logical. The shift in her position may be taken, then, to reveal a change in priority: between the need to articulate identity in constative terms in order for it to secure political legitimacy and the impossibility of ever fully and completely determining that identity. It is this latter situation that opens up the opportunity to think of identities as new forms of open subjectivity to be fashioned and posited anew. In her early works, by contrast, the dominant political idiom required that she discuss what it was to *be* a black female subject.

In the next section I examine the debate on 'strategic essentialism'. I do so for two reasons. First, to develop further my claim that essentialist theories of identity are historically situated by arguing that strategy should not be understood as an expression of free choice but as an effect of how the domain of the political is configured at a specific time. Second, I explore this debate to reveal more about the intricate intercalations between essentialism and constructivism and between performativity and constation.

Strategic Essentialism

Reflecting on the difficulties with the concept of identity, Judith Butler makes reference to the work of Gayatri Spivak. She notes:

> Gayatri Spivak has argued that feminists need to rely on an operational essentialism, a false ontology of women as universal in order to advance a feminist political program. She concedes that the category of women is not fully expressive, that the multiplicity and discontinuity of the signified rebels against the univocity of the sign, but she suggests that we need to use it for strategic purposes. (1990b: 325)

Butler's worry about this operational usage of the signifier woman centres on the 'political matter of setting who gets to make the designation and in the name of whom' (ibid.: 325). Driven by a concern about the normalizing thrust of identity claims, Butler, at this point, queries all operational or strategic uses of essence.[9] This critique of strategic or operational essentialism suggests that the process is volitional; that there is a conscious positing of a 'false' essence by feminists for their own ends. In other words, feminists decide when and where to make particular essentialist claims. Indeed, it might also be taken to imply that somehow they can control or limit the usage of such terms. This analysis obfuscates the co-implication of essentialism and construc-tivism one in the other. It presents an essence as something that can be manipulated at will by someone who stands before or outside of it.[10] In its place, I would maintain that it is *the summoning of an identity that performatively produces the essence in question*. Those who 'deploy' an essentialist model of identity are themselves the products of that model. This bears out Spivak's own claims, I propose.

Spivak's discussion of 'strategic essentialism' occurs in a review of the work of the Subaltern Studies Group (1988: 197–221). Spivak notes the group's appropriation for themselves of the Marxist idea of con-sciousness, producing the idea of a 'subaltern consciousness', a con-sciousness at once historical and essentialist. Reading against the grain of their Marxist writings, Spivak deconstructs this idea of subaltern consciousness. Observing that the group does not wittingly manipulate the term consciousness at all, Spivak proposes to *read them as if they do*. Thus it is possible to see them as '*strategically* adhering to the essen-tialist notion of consciousness' (ibid.: 206). It is their 'subalternity in claiming a positive subject-position for the subaltern' that Spivak regards as 'strategic' (ibid.: 207); that is, refusing their actual historical subordination by appropriating for themselves the role of *the* subject of history. Cautioning against the alignment of strategic essentialism with the assumption that only the personal, and not the collective, is politi-cal, Spivak notes that strategic essentialism is not a theory. Rather, 'strategy suits a situation' (1994: 154).

It might be argued that feminists, in claiming subject-status for women, exhibit a similar subalternity to the one Spivak describes. This appears to be echoed by Rosi Braidotti when she notes of feminism that 'the feminist today cannot afford *not* to be essentialist' (1994: 177). If feminism wants to retain the 'positivity of female subjectivity' even while questioning that subjectivity then, she avers, essentialist claims 'may be a necessary strategy' (ibid.: 175, 177). One reason for feminist declarations about women's real natures initially (in both first and sec-ond waves of feminist activity) was to counter the illusory notions about women and femininity circulating within the political and socio-economic spheres. Feminists intervened to challenge misperceptions about women. That intervention consisted in positing 'truer', more accurate accounts of women's natures (see also Oliver, 1998: 70–1). This too could be cast as strategic, not in the sense that it is a wilful deployment of essentialism but because it establishes women as specific kinds of subject by its invocation. That is, the declaration that women shared qualities that are transcendent, unitary and stable and, thus, common to them all generated a notion of womanhood with which women came to identify and believe in and around which feminist activity was galvanized. As in the case of the Subaltern Studies Group who appropriated the role of the subject of history, so feminists appropriated the version of the subject sanctioned by the language of the dominators (albeit one corrupted by feminist vernacular), that is a subject bearing particular attributes deserving recognition. Political credibility, in other words, accrues to particular subjects to the degree that they exhibit the 'right' qualities. The appropriation of the terms of legitimacy – even as that appropriation is a subtle reconfiguration of those terms – has thus been a *necessary* moment in political struggle when its aim has been to garner similar rights for the excluded as those enjoyed by the included.[11]

Strictly bifurcating essentialism and anti-essentialism into two separate camps, I propose, bogs feminism down in an impossible debate where one must be either for or against essence. Concentrating on the agonistic space between essentialism and anti-essentialism opens up the debate by exposing one vital site of political activity. While the political realm is conceptualized as the realm of advocacy where parliamentarians and political activists speak on behalf of others, then politics requires that demands be couched in terms of the needs of particular constituencies. This is politics organized around interest representation, constituencies and parties. In this context, there is a need (often desperate) to make demands on behalf of women (or in hooks's case, African Americans). At this time, essences (based on experience or identity) are posited and the assumed facticity of womanhood or blackness or lesbianism prioritized over other factors. These essences are nevertheless provisional in the sense that they are fabrications always amenable to change and contestation. The field of politics is precisely a field of such contestation.

It may, however, only be possible to discern them as 'strategic' forms of essentialism from a position of critical hindsight since naturalizing (essentializing) such identities has been crucial, historically, to their formation and to the functioning of collective political movement. Given the exclusionary nature of identity claims, the fact that solidifying 'what we are' is, at such moments, more significant than addressing 'what we are *not*', feminism must continually reflect upon the dangers of the demands it makes on behalf of women, particularly in the face of resistance to them. It must weigh the cost to individuals and groups of postulating a 'coherent identity position' when that position hides difference and specificity (Butler, 1997a: 149; Butler, in Rajchman, 1995: 131). Or, even more problematic, when as Butler contends, it produces a realm inhabited by 'deauthorized subjects, presubjects, figures of abjection, populations erased from view' (1992: 13), figures 'living under the sign of the "unlivable"' (1993a: 3). As Spivak perceptively observes, strategy implies 'persistent critique'; a process oriented to destabilizing essentialist claims (see also Trinh, 1992: 157). While a provisional return to essence might be successful in certain contexts, there is the issue, which Fuss worries about, concerning the long-term effects of a 'temporary' intervention: that it might retrench a more reactionary form of essence. Since the repeated reiteration of constative identities may secure their longevity and guarantee them legitimacy, it may also reify them in regulatory ways. Hence Fuss's question 'at what point does this move cease to be provisional and become permanent?' (1994: 107).[12] The answer, unsatisfactory as it may be, is that it is not possible to predict what will happen. The social is a realm of indeterminacy and uncertainty. There is no way of predicting in advance when or if an essence (or which essence) may acquire hegemonic status. As I have articulated it, even when an essence becomes hegemonic, it is never simply locked down. It remains performative – producing that which it names as it names it through reiteration and re-citation. For this reason, performative identities are always susceptible to subversion, transgression and even transformation. They are always insecure in certain ways. This does not, however, vitiate the need for feminist vigilance: feminism, like other political movements, needs to reflect on the strategies it deploys and to constantly engage in (self-)critique.

Conclusion: The Circular Logic of the Subject and Politics

In this chapter I have addressed the question of essentialism. I challenged the claim so prevalent within feminism that one must be *either* for *or* against essentialism. Instead, I contended that the only way to operate is to see essentialism and constructivism as held in an agonistic relation. The focus needs to be on the space between the two. It is here that the interplay between them is most visible. Species of feminist thinking that have been assimilated to poststructuralism, as discussed earlier, have been accused of decentring the subject or of denying subject-centred analysis. As I have shown in the last two chapters, this denies the interest of such work in the mechanisms whereby certain incarnations of the subject come to be centred (see, for instance, the discussion of Phelan in the last chapter). One of those mechanisms has been the positing of an essence. I am not suggesting, as should be clear, that there exist essences that are independent of discourse, whose nature is simply revealed in an unmediated way through critical analysis (such as the idea of an essential feminine out there awaiting admission). I am arguing rather that essences are posited; that they are effects projected and secured through discourse. This does not mean that essences are manufactured at will, however. 'Strategic essentialism' occurs not through choice but because of the way that the political is configured at certain historical moments; that is, when legitimacy accrues to those who can speak on behalf of the 'real' needs and desires of specific peoples. At such times the domain of the political recognizes only constative claims. It is the attempt to fix the debate on essentialism at this point (where what *we really are or need* is privileged) that is problematic. Set up against a concern with specificity and difference, essentialist claims have been roundly castigated as always already excluding certain groups. This is undeniable but not necessarily always as problematic as it has been presented. I contend that it may be the generation of essentialist claims that paradoxically makes possible the production of resistant subjectivities and that allows for a certain dialect of difference to be enunciated in the first place. It is in the shifting ground between constation and performativity that politics works. They are not separate poles, rather, they are moments in a dynamic, in a moving field of power relations.

In Chapter 1 I argued that the turn to the subject-in-process was particularly contentious within feminism for what it meant about the nature and grounding of feminist politics. Here I contend that what the foregoing debate about strategic essentialism reveals is that the choice between the subject Woman as the ground of feminist politics and the idea that this very subject is herself a political effect, may be no choice at all. Women are born inserted into particular languages and cultures, interpellated into specific sexed, gendered and racialized subject positions. These speak women just as effectively as women use them to speak (for) themselves. Acting as women is not being 'true', however, to a particular definition of women; quite the contrary, in the process of feminist politics the category of women is itself produced anew and differently. (A feminist is not simply a woman; if she were, so many women would not refuse the category of feminist for all that they believe it negatively implies.) In its efforts to reveal the processed nature of identity, radical anti-essentialism has often failed to acknowledge the importance for women's self-definition and ability to act, of the very discourses that constitute them and their potential for re-appropriation and resignification (I explain what I mean by this in more detail in Chapter 5). Conversely, to assume that there is a unitary definition of woman that can satisfactorily accommodate all women in their diversity and whose interests are merely represented by politics is also mistaken. The very need to reiterate the scripts that produce women and the very impossibility of those scripts ever containing women means that feminist politics is never about the mere representation of pre-existing demands. Rather, feminist discourse produces that which it then claims to represent, and whose representation retroactively authorizes its claims. What does this say about the relation between the subject and politics?

It indicates that the relation is complex. There is no simple opposition between the claim of those who argue that identity precedes politics (indeed, that it is the rationale behind political intervention) and the claim of those who see all identity as the effect of politics.[13] As I demonstrate, every declaration of what woman is, is simultaneously a performative production of that being and every time that demands are made on behalf of women (as a whole or specific groups of them), there is a provisional reification of what it means to be a woman ('the victim of rape', a 'mother', and so forth). There is no stable subject that pre-exists discourse, rather her (temporary) stabilization is the effect of discourse and it is this stabilization that creates the base from which certain claims are made. The relation between the subject and politics is thus dynamic, unstable and messy as it moves between the impulse to fix identity and the impulse to unsettle identity. Feminism thus needs, in my view, to jettison the idea that identity must be thought of *either* as constative *or* as performative. Retaining this binary merely stalls the debate.[14] Constation and performativity are conjoined in identity politics. Accepting this agonistic relation implies that feminist politics must both make demands on behalf of women, as it always conventionally has, *and* must seek to de-determine identity (for all the reasons noted above to do with exclusion, its reification, and so on).

In the last three chapters, I have focused principally on the relation between politics and subject constitution. In what remains of the book, therefore, I turn my attention to what feminist politics looks like from the perspective of fluid, open, subject positions or identities. As I indicated in this chapter and as I establish more fully in the remaining chapters of the book, the political is a site of contestation. It is subject to attempts to foreclose what counts as politics. The 'domain of the political' (to borrow Butler's phrase, 1992: 4) is open to normalization (and pathologization) in terms of the *political* identities it recognizes, the kinds of claims that can be made *politically*, the sorts of activities that count as *political*, and in the modes of *political* analysis that are validated. This is just as true of feminist accounts of politics as of non-feminist or anti-feminist accounts. Over the next five chapters, therefore, I examine some of the resources open to the feminist subject-in-process to change the world in which she lives.

Notes

1 Fuss uses the example of the student in a class on postcolonialism who asks about the 'social and structural forms of non-Western homosexual relations' only to be confronted with the retort: 'what on earth does sexual preference have to do with imperialism?' (1989: 116).

2 Indeed, a central component of Fuss's critique is that positions of marginality are also constructed within the classroom through a process of ranking identities *within* individuals. The identity feature that is prioritized tends to depend upon the issue under discussion.

3 It is not that women invent harassment *ab initio*. It is that feminism has named as harassment a certain cluster of male actions and attitudes, which it can then act legally to curtail and punish.

4 This is captured, for example, in Joyce A. Joyce's remark that '[i]t is insidious for the Black literary critic to adopt any kind of strategy that diminishes ... or negates his blackness' (cited in Fuss, 1989: 77; see also hooks, 1990b: 23, 28).

5 Recall all subjects are 'racialized', though in different ways and with different consequences in terms of patterns of authority and domination.

6 Importantly hooks claims that her aim was not to 'explain black women to white feminist women' but rather to understand her own experience.

7 For a different perspective on the relation between the inside(r) and the outside(r), see Trinh (1990, 1992). Her conception of the 'inappropriate(d) other' challenges both the mutual opposition between the inside and the outside and the idea that epistemic privilege can accrue to the outsider within.

8 Interventions of this kind have offered important insights that have brought about significant changes within feminism, politically and theoretically, however, a more encompassing account of 'racialization' must go beyond them. What 'needs', and is given, explanation in these works is exactly 'blackness' (or colour) as a specific and unique set of experiences distinct from white experience(s). This leaves intact the 'racialization of whiteness', as Abel calls it (cited in Clough, 1994: 107–8), and the ways in which the relations between blackness and whiteness are mapped on the field of power relations. This alone can explain how certain modalities of the racialized subject come to be positioned as superior to other modalities. I am not contending, however, that black feminists or feminists of colour must do this plotting. It is the duty of us all.

9 The vehemence of Butler's rejection here seems to be tempered in her later work where she allows for the possibility that identity categories, such as woman, can be resignified (1993a: 191, 221; 1995a: 50; 1999: xxiv). That is, she takes the idea that identity is unstable to be the source of its political productivity. The language that she uses here – resignification rather than strategic essentialism – may suggest continued suspicion of the latter for what it posits rather than what it disrupts. See Chapter 5.

10 See the contribution by Laclau to the debate on identity covered in Rajchman (1995: 131) and, in particular, Laclau's point that the word strategy is problematic.

11 Significantly, in the moments when an essentialist identity is deployed, its advocates will likely believe that it is real. They will experience it as authentic. Indeed, as Appiah

notes, 'the demands of agency seem always – in the real world of politics – to *entail a misrecognition of its genesis*' (1995: 106).

12 To worry about this suggests that Fuss retains some sense of essentialism as a bad thing, echoed in Braidotti's refrain that '[t]aking a priori an antiessentialist stand may be politically right' (1994: 185). My sense is that we only know when essentialist claims become constraining when they produce resistances to them.

13 I see the two as philosophically indissociable, although I recognize that there is heuristic value in separating them analytically in order, for instance, to excavate the conditions of possibility for the emergence of certain kinds of political subjects (as discussed in Chapter 2 of this book, say).

14 For an alternative account directed at overcoming the dualistic logic noted here, see Hekman (2000a). Her solution consists of, first, incorporating a sense of stability for the subject through recourse to object relations theory and, second, by endeavouring to displace the reliance on identity for political claims in the liberal polity by arguing for politics as the identification with particular causes (ibid.: 304). The latter is certainly a potentially productive strategy, one that is already empirically familiar from the politics of environmentalism, for instance.

four

power and domination

Resistance to power is resistance to specific strategies by which power relations are patterned. Gendered power relations are specifically organized according to the interplay among the traditional discourses which have controlled women's bodies. (Faith, 1994: 58)

Not always sure whether to castigate it or to desire it, feminism's attitude towards power has been an ambivalent one. Liberal feminists keen to acquire equality with men argued for a share of men's power, seeing this as the route out of sex discrimination. Radical feminists and some materialist feminists, by contrast, saw male power as domination, the power over things or other human beings that had resulted historically in the subordination of women. They argued for its repudiation and overthrow. Rejecting a virile, masculinist form of power in favour of a specifically female conception, some of these feminists reconceptualized power as the ability to do things, to create, and to generate. Power as capacity betokened freedom from exploitation, and the promise of a new ethically oriented society. Others reacted critically to the idea that there could be a specifically feminine or feminist conception of power that arose from women's experiences, challenging the essentialist imperative that underwrote this claim. For many of these authors, power was seen as generative of both liberating and constraining aspects of human life and identity. Reconfiguring the field of power would bring about change, but a world in which power relations were non-existent was a utopian fantasy.

My aim in this chapter is not to explore the variant ways in which feminists have conceptualized power; the limitations of space preclude this. Instead, I evaluate how to theorize domination when one rejects the framework within which the stable subject is embedded; one that, in its radical and materialist feminist formats, has often couched women's subordination in terms of a reductive narrative of domination. My focus is thus on the ability of feminist theories influenced by poststructuralism to account for broad patterns of super- and subordination in society. One of the primary features of feminist politics, as Denise Thompson reminded readers, is the analysis of male domination of women (2001). A common complaint of poststructuralist theories is that because they rely on a 'social logic of contingency' they cannot account for systematic domination (Hennessy, 1993). In the first section of this chapter, I set out in more detail the nature of this charge. This is followed by a critical examination of an account, self-styled 'resistance postmodernism', which attempts to retain systematicity (through an emphasis on economic materialism) while also embracing some postmodern insights. Arguing that 'resistance postmodernism' merely reproduces the structural problems that bedevilled earlier materialist and radical feminist accounts of women's oppression by rendering gender relations as primary and all other axes of identity as secondary cultural effects, I argue for an alternative account. Utilizing the idea of 'global strategy' to trace relations of domination, I demonstrate that this anti-determinist, contingent understanding of relations of power provides a preferable framework for apprehending widespread and persistent configurations of domination. In this it continues the project of earlier feminist work in charting the subordinate status of women but it does so in a way consonant with the need to acknowledge difference and thus it resonates with the idea of the *mestiza as metaphor*. It recognizes, that is, that all aspects of identity are moderated and modulated (perhaps, over-determined) by others but that there is no single, unique cause of this inter-twining.

Patriarchy and Domination

How is feminism to understand the nature and extent of women's oppression? Over the years there has been much debate within feminism about this question both concerning what women suffer from (oppression, discrimination, inequality [Phillips, 1987: 1–2]) and its extent (local, national, global). In the course of these discussions radical feminists developed the concept of patriarchy to capture the apparent all-pervasiveness of women's oppression at the hands of men. As Kate Millett noted in the early 1970s, sexual domination is one of, if not the most, ubiquitous ideologies of western culture. It is so because of patriarchy. As she asserts: 'The fact is evident at once if one recalls that the military, industry, technology, universities, science, political office, and finance – *in short every avenue of power within the society*, including the coercive force of the police, *is entirely in male hands*' (Millett, 1977: 25, my emphasis). Patriarchy is a *system* of male power that permeates *all* aspects of life at all times and in all places.

The conceptualization of patriarchy as a unified, monolithic system of male power with a transhistorical and global reach has been severely criticized. Feminists challenged the homogenization of women's oppression implied by it and the concomitant presentation of male power as universal and identical across historically and culturally differentiated states. Furthermore, radical feminists in particular were castigated for neglecting factors such as class or race in the operation of male power, seeing them as, at best, epi-phenomenal to patriarchy.[1] As a result, current attempts to understand women's oppression tend rightly to conceive it as operating in multiple intersecting registers. Attention has therefore turned to exploring the dense network of structures that converge to produce women's subordinate place in the world. Accompanying this shift in how to analyse oppression has been a rethinking, in some quarters at least, about how to understand society itself. Society has often been presented within feminist work as a totality, that is, as an integrated whole amenable to knowledge and analysis in terms of an underlying (patriarchal) structure. Here one has only to think of Shulamith Firestone's account of patriarchy as founded in male control over the means of reproduction (1970). Because men controlled these means, they were able to control women, thus securing men's own interests as the ruling sex-class. The structure of society was knowable in terms of the laws of technological development relating to reproduction. Seizing control over the means of reproduction (once they had reached a sufficiently advanced stage) was the only way to secure an end to male domination over women. Once this revolution occurred, society could be recreated in non-patriarchal fashion. Society, for Firestone appears, I suggest, to be 'an intelligible structure' (Laclau and Mouffe, 1985: 2) whose nature can be apprehended. It is this intelligibility that promises a diagnosis of the prevailing social condition (patriarchy), an excavation of the roots of this condition (male control of the means of reproduction) and a set of remedies for its problems (revolution and rebuilding a new future). The problem with such accounts, laudable as they are in terms of generating feminist political imaginaries, is that they fail adequately to account for the multiple forms of oppression that exist. So, how else could society be understood so as to more accurately capture its multiple oppressions?

The answer, I think, is to see society as 'impossible', to borrow from Laclau and Mouffe (1985), in the sense that the divisions within it (which are quite real) are neither fixed nor organized around a single principle (such as patriarchy). Instead of having an essential or particular character, society is inessential or incomplete. It is not governed by a particular logic. The ever-increasing proliferation of differences that cut across society cannot all be construed, therefore, as various aspects of the same structure. This means that all explanations of society (including feminist) that endeavour to define a single point uniting such differences as class, race and gender will inevitably fail (Laclau and Mouffe, 1985: 112). For these reasons, society is at best understood, at any one time, as contingent and unstable and explanations of it as always partial and open to rearticulation. It is in this context that we need to locate feminist work influenced by poststructuralism, and its capacity to understand domination and subordination.[2] Is there a way of understanding the connections between relations of subordination that are actually disparate and aleatory? What does domination mean if it is not apprehended in terms of a unified system of power? What might be gained or lost by a strategic apprehension of domination that concentrates on how women are positioned in relation to, and upon the field of, power? I begin by looking at the criticisms levelled *against* the idea of feminist accounts of domination drawing on poststructuralist ideas.

Domination from a Poststructuralist Perspective: The Case Against

In her book, *The Female Body and the Law* (1988), Zillah Eisenstein argues that the deficiency of a Foucauldian analytic of power for feminism is not that it involves discussion of the heterogeneity of power, the variety of micropractices engendered thereby, or the dislocation of power from a central site. The deficiency stems from the fact that it 'carries deconstruction too far'. In other words, an *exclusive* consideration of the 'disparate sites of power ... privileges diversity, discontinuity, and difference while it silences unity, continuity, and similarity' (ibid.: 18). While there is value in Foucault's pluralist conception of power in that it enables the exploration of the specific conditions for the production of different discursive formations, there remains a fundamental problem. It is inadequate to an understanding of the continuities and connections between dispersed manifestations of power. It does not offer a way of analysing either the unities that may be established through discourse or the production of sites of concentrated power. As Hennessy observes, 'Foucault's social logic cannot ... allow for any necessary relation between the multiple registers in which the modalities of difference circulate' (1993: 21). This means that it is possible to explore the relays of power generating gendered subjects but without positing any necessary link between them (ibid.: 21–2). While the insights that emerge from an examination of the local functionings of power should not necessarily be rejected out of hand, feminist work requires something additional. It must be able to 'focus on how power is both concentrated in its dispersion – how multiple sites articulate a unity – *and* dispersed in its concentration – how sites of power are heterogeneous and contradictory' (Eisenstein, 1988: 16, my emphasis). Foucault is criticized, thus, for failing to reconnect the various dispersions he illuminates and for neglecting to consider their organization within various 'hierarchical system(s) of power(s)', such as the gendered state (Eisenstein, 1988: 19; Hartsock, 1990).[3] This is not only a problem for feminists borrowing from Foucault.

Nancy Fraser and Linda Nicholson, reflecting on feminism's engagement with postmodernism in general, take a different tack (1990). They explore the possibilities of 'social criticism without philosophy', that is without foundational underpinnings, through an account of the (f)utilities of a feminist turn to Lyotard. Fraser and Nicholson make the observation that Lyotard's rejection of an overarching theory of justice in favour of a 'justice of multiplicities' precludes, among other things, 'identification and critique of macrostructures of inequality and injustice which cut across the boundaries separating relatively discrete practices and institutions' (ibid.: 23). It is not possible, from this Lyotardian position to criticize large-scale relations of subordination and domination such as patriarchy, racism, etc. Furthermore, it is not possible to understand the social field by way of general categories such as gender or class, since from a Lyotardian stance these are 'too reductive of the complexity of social identities' (ibid.: 24). Criticism has to be local, for Lyotard does not recognize that there may be systemic factors that cannot be addressed via local, ad hoc criticism. So, while there is much to be gained from a feminist engagement with postmodern analyses of the Lyotardian variety, not least a critique of feminism's own tendencies towards essentialism and reductionism, Fraser and Nicholson conclude that such an engagement does not provide the tools to explain systemic patterns of inequality and power.

For several critics, therefore, the crucial inadequacy of feminist work influenced by poststructuralism is that it operates with what Teresa Ebert and Hennessy both call the 'logic of contingency' (Ebert, 1993: 7; Hennessy, 1993).[4] This means that it apprehends power as operating in a diffuse, and non-systemic, fashion. In other words, it assumes that there are no necessary connections between various power effects. It thus belies, according to its critics, the possibility of explaining the 'general structural tendencies' by which, as Lois McNay notes, 'difference becomes inequality' (1992: 155), or by which oppression is produced. As such it stands in opposition to the 'logic of social necessity' (Ebert, 1993: 7), a mode of thinking that emphasizes 'a systemic understanding of power as exploitation' (Hennessy, 1993: 32) and that posits necessary relations between multiple differences. Indeed, Ebert regards analyses that deploy a contingent logic, therefore, as being inherently 'post-political' and ludic.[5] They are post-political insofar as they mask the need for collectively organized socio-political transformation and, in its place, highlight a plurality of local points of resistance. They are ludic because instead of examining the material reality of oppression, they emphasize cultural politics, dismissively described by Ebert as a mode of 'textual practice ... that has no reliable reference "outside" itself' (1993: 15). This is politics 'as a language-effect, a mode of rhetoric aimed at changing cultural representations' (ibid.: 6) or, as she continues, a *'process* without a *product*; it is a mode of semiotic activism' (ibid.: 15). It is playful, oriented towards textuality, pleasure or *jouissance*, and is over-focused on the body. It offers, for her, no means of intervention in the realities of oppression and has no capacity to radically transform the state of things although it may problematize practices.

The criticism of ludic postmodernism appears, I suggest, to have currency in respect of some writers but crucially not all. For instance, critics have frequently and reasonably, in my view, castigated Derridean-influenced accounts of the subject for their neglect of the concrete historical or somatic experiences (such as race or class) of those subjects. Within this paradigm, there appears, as Flax observes, to be no prospect of accounting for differences that are 'nontextual' (1990: 214). This is an important criticism. An emphasis on textuality and on the free play of signification certainly suggests a social realm that is contingent and provisional. However, the claim is not in itself sufficient to explain how certain kinds of hierarchy are produced, how certain conditions become congealed in certain ways, such that, for instance, one account of reality comes to be privileged in the world while another is discounted. Indeed, deconstruction seems to lack a grammar of power and, therefore, an adequate conception of politics (Hennessy, 1993: 5–6; Said, 1978), though not all would agree on that.[6]

In relation to other modes of thinking the subject-in-process discussed in this book, the plausibility of this interpretation is highly debatable, as I show below. Whatever the merits or demerits of Ebert's reading of ludic postmodernism and the plausibility or otherwise of applying this reading to the collocation of authors she constructs, the core of her criticism is that without consideration of the systemic nature of oppression, feminist work is meaningless politically. She assumes thus that only an account that posits necessary connections between elements is able to explain the organization of social and political life. As I indicate in the section after next, I disagree. It is possible to understand social and political life as the result of contingent connections between otherwise dispersed elements, when patterns of domination are interpreted as global effects or strategies. What, then, is at stake in Ebert's claim that feminists must hold onto the logic of necessity in order to explain oppression and power? In order to explore this, I first set out her version of 'resistance postmodernism' before demonstrating that it devalues non-gender-based differences by treating them as immaterial.[7]

'Resistance Postmodernism': Patriarchy as a Totality in Process

Resistance postmodernism turns on the idea that it is possible to blend postmodern insights with a critique of the 'systematicity and global relations of oppression' (Ebert, 1993: 18). 'By postmodern', Ebert declares, 'I do not mean a monolithic discourse', rather 'the ensemble of conflicting discourses produced in late patriarchy in which capital and the sexual division of labor are deployed in new ways' (ibid.: 14). Ebert offers therefore a version of materialist feminism that takes into account the condition of postmodernity. Her account is thus both materialist in that it moves beyond the Marxist problematic that emphasizes class through its incorporation of an analysis of the primary role of the sexual division of labour, and postmodern in that it deals with a particular phase of patriarchal capitalist development.[8] As I show below, combining materialism and postmodernity in this way ultimately renders profoundly problematic Ebert's attempt to address difference.

Ebert offers resistance postmodernism as a superior alternative to ludic postmodernism, which, on her interpretation, has a number of deficiencies. The first concerns its rejection of the idea of totality (that is, the idea that anything can be conceived of as general or universal). Ludic postmodernism, Ebert argues, confuses totality conceived in terms of the systematicity of 'regimes of exploitation' with totality understood as totalitarian (ibid.: 20). This compels it to occlude systematic inequalities in power. In turn, this means that ludic postmodernism cannot account for patriarchy as a general or universal phenomenon. The second deficiency refers to ludic postmodernism's emphasis on local or microphysical instantiations of power. This, for Ebert, is politically counterproductive. It accords only the possibility of destabilizing meaning and liberating the libidinal impulses of the individual. In the place of ludic postmodernism, Ebert offers resistance postmodernism, a postmodernism that is, for her at least, actually, materially, political. As Ebert formulates it, '[r]esistance or materialist postmodern politics insists on *politics as the practice aimed at "equal" access for all to social, cultural and economic resources*' and 'an end to the exploitative exercise of power' (ibid.: 18). This accords more emphatically with the needs of feminism, for feminism requires patriarchy as a 'struggle concept' (Mies, cited in Ebert, 1993: 20). It is this concept, in Ebert's view that, despite the charges of reductionism levelled at it, lends coherence to feminist political struggle.

Resistance postmodernism can thus be differentiated from ludic postmodernism on the grounds that it conceives of oppression as systemic. So, what are the grounds of this system? Recognizing that a reductive notion of patriarchy has been the subject of consternation within feminism and that Marxists have been critical of the class-blind nature of certain conceptualizations of patriarchy, Ebert proposes the following, materialist feminist definition. Patriarchy is:

> [a] regime of exploitation that produces gender difference in order to construct asymmetrical, unequal divisions of labor, accumulation, and access to social, economic, and cultural resources, guaranteeing not only the privilege of one gender (male) over the other (female) but, more important, the subjugation and exploitation of the 'other' gender as the very grounds of wealth and accumulation. In other words, patriarchy is a historically diverse, ongoing, and unequal system of gender differences and exploitation: one that is 'necessary' to the very existence and prosperity of the majority of socio-economic systems in the world and is fundamental to the global expansion and colonization of capitalism. (Ebert, 1993: 20)

Patriarchy is thus predicated on the economic organization of gender difference. This means that it is a totality but a totality with a difference, the difference being that despite Ebert's emphasis on the socio-economic, patriarchy is not presented as a unified or homogeneous system. It is thought of as a combined system of relations with 'an *overdetermined structure of difference*' (ibid.: 21; Hennessy, 1995: 170–1).

For Ebert, patriarchy is a system that is historical, dynamic, crossed by social contradictions and as such, diverse and internally differentiated. Despite the fact that it is differentiated, even 'traversed by ... différance', there is nevertheless a 'logic of connection' (1993: 21) that runs through it. This is provided by the ideological construction of gender differences (particularly in relation to the division of labour) as natural and inescapable. This process of naturalization is on-going and, changes over time and in different contexts. Patriarchy itself is seen, then, as '*a totality in process*' (ibid.: 21) although it may not appear as such to those observing it, for ideology presents patriarchy as inevitable, universal, transhistorical and coherent.

From Ebert's postmodern materialist perspective, patriarchy achieves continuity in terms of its differential organization of gender but is discontinuous in that its practices are historically and conjuncturally specific. It produces identical effects in terms of male–female opposition and hierarchy in all its contexts in that women are *invariably* positioned as oppressed, excluded Others, subject to economic exploitation and denied full social rights. But these identical effects are, she avers, different insofar as they depend on the level of economic development of the society in question (see ibid.: 21–2 for examples). In other words, a woman in a late capitalist patriarchy such as the USA experiences her oppression and exploitation in ways that are unlike the experiences of a woman in a European feudal state. She also experiences it differently than a woman of another class or race in the same context. But they are all subordinate to men. Ebert's reconfiguration of patriarchy centres thus on the idea of 'difference-in-relation' (ibid.: 22). Difference is established micropolitically at the level of culture wherein oppression manifests itself in various competing and altered ways. Relation or connection is cemented through the economic organization of gendered labour relations. It is these latter relations that are, for Ebert, determinant in the last instance, since they operate in 'macropolitical' fashion to establish the underlying structure of oppression (ibid.: 22).

How satisfactory is this postmodern account of patriarchy as a totality-in-process? It certainly satisfies the demand expressed by Ebert and Hennessy for an account of patriarchy that acknowledges its systematicity. Moreover, it apparently allows for the articulation of a differentiated account of oppression, capable of accommodating multiplicity since it recognizes, for instance, that women may be positioned variously in respect of factors such as race. So far, so good! The problem for me is that in casting multiplicity ('the different and contradictory manifestations of oppression') as primarily *cultural*, Ebert renders difference epiphenomenal to what she perceives as the underlying gendered organization of labour (ibid.: 22). In stating gendered labour relations are primary, this makes all other aspects of identity secondary or immaterial. In this, her position is redolent of that much-contested claim from the early days of second-wave feminism that 'male supremacy is the oldest, most basic form of domination' and that all 'other forms of exploitation and oppression (racism ...) are extensions of male supremacy' (Redstockings Manifesto, in Schneir, 1995: 127). A claim, that I think it is important to recall, alienated many women for whom male supremacy was neither the sole nor necessarily the most important mode of oppression. Ebert, despite declarations to the contrary, fails to take difference seriously enough.

It is, therefore, a deficiency of postmodern materialist feminism (resistance postmodernism) that, although claiming patriarchy is differential, it nevertheless regards the dominant mode of 'organization of differences' in terms of 'the gender opposition of male/female' (Ebert, 1993: 22). Or, as Hennessy puts it, where 'all women as a group are positioned the same (as subordinate or other) in relation to men' (1995: 171). As I demonstrated in Chapter 2, for feminists of colour and other feminists critical of the solipsistic concerns of white, middle-class heterosexual feminism, the idea that gender is more important or more basic than other axes of identity is simply not tenable. Ebert simply repeats this move in modified form when she makes ethnicity and sexuality, for instance, inessential compared to gender. Ebert is surely right, however, that questions of political economy get eclipsed in debates on identity and difference, achieved in part, as Wendy Brown perspicuously notes, by a 'certain renaturalization of capitalism' (1995: 60). This preservation of 'capitalism from critique' (ibid.: 61) undoubtedly needs redressing since capitalism remains a potent factor ordering social and political life (see also i ek, 2000: 90–135). Doing so, however, does not mean according it primacy. The passionate attachment Ebert displays towards the isolation of a *necessary* 'logic of connection' underpinning women's subordination may successfully centre issues of political economy but, I suggest, in so doing, it relegates questions of difference to the wings once again. It takes feminism right back to the point when the unity that it offered was exposed as an exclusionary fiction grounded in ignoring the diversity of women's lives.

It is the division instituted by Ebert between the economic and the cultural that is central to the problems this mode of theorizing encounters. By bifurcating the economic and the cultural Ebert establishes a hierarchy between the properly feminist political task of securing emancipation to be achieved through the transformation of the material (socio-economic) base, and the tangential, even trivial or ludic concerns of cultural politics (see also Hennessy, 1995). This dichotomy between the economic and the cultural thus produces a ranking of political forms: the serious or 'real' concerns of labour-based politics versus the secondary concerns of cultural politics construed as 'changing cultural representations' of 'gender, sexuality and race' (Ebert, 1993: 5). Indeed, the implication is that, for Ebert, cultural politics only has legitimacy when analyzed from a materialist paradigm that posits 'patriarchal-capitalist labor relations' as fundamental and culture as the effect of 'socio-economic arrangements' (ibid.: 9, 14). As Judith Butler notes, reflecting on trends in Left criticism, the effect of characterizing non-labour-based movements as cultural or, rather 'merely cultural', is, however to reduce their importance and thus to stigmatize cultural political struggles as 'factionalizing, identarian, and particularistic' (1998: 33).[9] Ebert's position, in my view, echoes this trend and, as such, involves a number of questionable assumptions. First, it assumes the possibility of a materialism based on an objective examination of economic relations. Second, it appears to conflate the economic with the material. Finally, it assumes that when 'ludic' postmodernists talk about culture, they do so in a way that divorces it from materiality. This in turn presupposes too easy a separation between the two for, as Nancy Fraser rightly observes, cultural (or symbolic) phenomena are 'materially instantiated – in institutions and social practices, in social action and embodied habitus, and ... in ideological apparatuses' (1998: 144). It is deeply problematic, therefore, to argue that 'cultural' phenomena are 'immaterial'. Indeed, such an interpretation, I would suggest, compels us to ask what is at stake in this derogation of the cultural, a question to which I will return in Chapter 6.

As I noted earlier, the social is an indeterminate realm, traversed by plural differences. Any theory that endeavours to prioritize the primacy of one realm as determinant of society not only offers a potentially totalizing account of oppression but must also be questioned as to the political interests that motivate it. In relation specifically to Ebert's account, therefore, we need to interrogate which political movements and kinds of activism are being demoted to the 'cultural' sphere and which are being prioritized as material and transformative. While it is possible to understand the impulse behind postmodern materialist feminism, the desire that is to integrate the problematic of difference into the analysis of overarching social totalities, its degradation of cultural politics and its insistence on the re-subordination of race and sexuality (inter alia) to gender and labour considerations is profoundly troubling. Ironically, its very aspiration to generate unity is, I suggest, more likely to produce division.

In the next section, therefore, I offer an alternative account, which can elucidate both patterns of domination and the production of irreducible differences, and which acknowledges the indeterminacy of the social realm. It is an account that can, when necessary, take into consideration the significance of capitalism in the reproduction both of identity and inequity but which does not accord primacy to the economic sphere. Moreover, it is one that avoids treating 'cultural' (or noneconomic) factors as immaterial.

Domination as Global Strategy

Nancy Fraser in a critical rejoinder to Judith Butler in *New Left Review* comments that 'historicization represents a better approach to social theory then destabilization or deconstruction' (1998: 149). Fraser's judgement rests on the fact that to historicize is to focus on specificity; it is to be precise. Deconstruction may have benefits in terms of the politics of recognition, where Fraser commends it over 'standard identity politics' for its emphasis on transformation over affirmation (1998: 149, n. 8; 1997: 11–39), but not when it comes to understanding the structural effects of domination. Fraser's adjudication raises a number of questions (not all of which I will pursue at this time): why is destabilization transformative when limited to questions of subjectivity but not when talking about institutions and structures? Is it not important

to historicize identity? Fraser's own position is interesting for it strad-
dles the division that Lois McNay observes within feminist accounts of
change. Here McNay contrasts work on the 'symbolic construction of
the subject', which emphasizes indeterminacy and absolutizes change,
with materialist accounts concentrating on structural and institutional
forms of domination and which are more cautious about transformation, since it invariably entails 'new forms of dependency and subordination' (2000: 155, 156).[10] In what follows, I pursue Fraser's
injunction to historicize (though not necessarily in the manner she
might advise). I do so, however, in a way that endeavours to re-connect
questions of sociality and subjectivity and thus to re-join – in some
fashion – the two modalities of change discerned by McNay. I draw my
inspiration from the work of Foucault, although my aim is not to be
faithful to him but to develop an analysis of domination that does not
mistakenly treat interconnecting oppressions as if they are all part of a
seamless, monolithic system.

It is incontestable that an account of domination starting from
Foucault's analytic of power and genealogical approach will not presuppose the 'logic of social necessity' (Ebert, 1993: 7). First, genealogy is predicated upon a rejection of the kinds of linear or
teleological theories of historical development that have often underpinned such logic. Emphasis is placed instead on the discontinuities
that govern historical change. 'Effective history' (to use the
Nietzschean term) concentrates on the accidental, chance elements
that produce certain historical effects. Second, repudiating the
search for the *origins* of specific historical phenomena necessitates
attention to the multiplicity of disparate factors that haphazardly
converge to produce them as particular events. Totalities are consequently fragmented. This means quite simply that there are no necessary or predetermined connections between elements. Next, one of
the most salient characteristics of genealogical analyses is that they
are not usually focused on large-scale phenomena such as capitalism
or patriarchy. Rather specific genealogical inquiries have examined,
for instance, such molecular concerns as sexuality (Foucault, 1978),
punishment (Foucault, 1977), social insurance (Defert, 1991), families (Donzelot, 1979), education (Hunter, 1988, 1994), poverty and
insecurity (Dean, 1991), or child abuse (Bell, 1993). Despite this particularistic focus, I contend that a genealogical approach can nevertheless elucidate ways in which specific elements converge in
contingent historical fashion to produce women's oppression in its
variety and persistence. An analytic of power, that is, can be
deployed that enables us to explore how specific force relations
intersect and, crucially, where there are gaps or contradictions (and
there will be many) in this intersection.

The account I present below, building on earlier work (Lloyd, 1993), indicates the directions that feminist work *might* take using this approach. It does not, as such, provide a substantive explanation of women's oppression in its generality or its multiplicity. This is both because of constraints of space and because as I have claimed before, it is impossible to offer a total explanation of women's oppression. This is not, however, to decry the prospect of investigating how, to use Eisenstein's words, 'multiple sites articulate a unity' (1988: 16), that is, how women's subordination is produced across a range of discourses and practices (including economic, cultural, political factors). The way of understanding large-scale operations of power that I offer does not, however, counter the macro to the micro (say, the public to the private). In my view, how power circulates through institutions (such as the state or government) is not ontologically distinct from how it circulates through subjects, though it may require the use of different technologies in order to generate its effects (Rose, 1999: 5). These caveats aside: how might we rethink domination?

Foucault himself, of course, provides no account of power's gendered asymmetries. He does nevertheless offer an example of a large-scale (or joined-up) operation of power that can serve, I suggest, as a template for understanding the connections between other discrete instantiations of power. This is the phenomenon of 'bio-power', developed in *Discipline and Punish* (1977) and in the first volume of *The History of Sexuality* (1978). Bio-power can be seen as a *dispositif*. To recall from Chapter 2, a *dispositif* is an 'apparatus' consisting, *inter alia*, of laws, discourses, institutions, ideas and decisions that connect in various complex, mutable, open-ended and, importantly, confrontational, ways (Foucault, 1980b: 194). A *dispositif* is a 'system of relations' between diverse elements (ibid.: 194). Thus, bio-power emerges from the coalescence of two broad sets of techniques: those for population control (demography, public health, housing and migration) and those of discipline (exemplified in schools, hospitals, factories and the army). Together they generate a 'form of concrete arrangements' (Foucault, 1978: 140). Elsewhere Foucault calls this a 'global strategy' (1980a).

The essence of a global strategy is that it neither inheres in nor issues from a central point (the state or patriarchy). Instead global domination emerges from the ways in which 'infinitesimal mechanisms [of power], which each have their own history, their own trajectory, their own techniques and tactics' are 'invested, colonised, utilised, involved, transferred, displaced, extended etc. by ever more general mechanisms, and by forms of global domination' (ibid.: 99). To apprehend a pattern of global domination, then, necessitates tracing the actual connections (of investment, colonization, utilization, and so forth) that have been established between otherwise disparate elements. That connections will be made is assured by the fact that any *dispositif* responds (in determinate historical circumstances) to some kind of strategic imperative. It is this 'strategic function' that generates the matrix of intelligibility within which heterogeneous factors are assimilated, deployed, and coordinated. The logic of social necessity is thus replaced by the practice of strategy.

How, then, might domination be apprehended strategically? First, it requires accepting that domination is the effect of the mobilization and transformation of a multiplicity of dispersed, localized, polymorphous mechanisms of power. Further, it necessitates the idea that these sundry relations of power converge to produce a 'hegemonic effect' (Foucault, 1978: 94). A system of relations between elements is created not out of necessity but through the accidental confluence of discrete, often conflicting, modalities of power. Further, since any 'global strategy' is always in the 'play of power' (Foucault, 1980b: 196), it is incessantly working both to generate and organize the distribution of these modalities. In other words, it spawns its own peculiar rationality through a process of 'double conditioning' whereby that rationality is both constituted by and constitutive of various dispersed micropractices (Foucault, 1978: 100). There is thus *'functional overdetermination'* as the constitutive elements of an apparatus are constantly re-adjusted and re-worked as they resonate with or contradict one another, and *'strategic elaboration'* where unintended effects are integrated into a changed (and changing) strategy (Foucault, 1980b: 195).[11] The apparent systematicity (or rationality, as Foucault talks of it) of any persistent pattern of domination is the effect of these twin processes and *not* the motor that drives them. Domination cannot be explained, therefore, in the terms of a single theory (say, materialism). It must be understood, rather, as a particular historical configuration of power relations, without common origin or necessary determining logic. This is not to negate the material existence of gendered, racialized or other asymmetries of power. It is to caution against elucidating these asymmetries in terms of a reductive theory, such as a universally applicable narrative of patriarchy. If there is continuing talk of patriarchy at all, it must be, as Sawicki observes, talk of a 'particular and not universal historical phenomenon' (1991: 24).

If we are to understand women's subordination in its multiplicity, then I propose, we need to attend to the multiple discourses and mechanisms of power historically that effect that subordination. These could include forms of 'protectionist' legislation that traditionally disallowed working women from entering certain occupations through fears for their health, thus reinforcing unequal treatment between the sexes and reinscribing women as the weaker sex. It could cover the gendering of material spaces, such as buildings such as cafés, restaurants or the UK

House of Commons constructed with inadequate facilities both for women in general and for nursing mothers in particular. We could examine how reproductive medicine operates differentially, through compulsory sterilization of African-American women compared to (restricted) access to abortion for middle-class white women in the USA, to generate racialized accounts of sexuality and gendered embodiment. We could also explore the construction of the feminized discourse and practice of 'retail therapy' in the developed world, and the role this plays in reinforcing inegalitarian capitalist economic practices as well as in constituting gendered consuming subjects. We could, that is, excavate how different techniques of power, ranging across the law, architecture, design and construction, medicine, and capitalism, function to produce women as subordinated subjects. We could also examine how practices developed in one field are colonized elsewhere and how larger-scale forms of global gendered domination emerge and are embedded. Thus, we could demonstrate how the law has appropriated biology in order, for instance, to construct pre-menstrual syndrome as a mitigating factor in women's crime, a move that identifies women more emphatically with their biology (Smart, 1992). Similarly, we could show how similar understandings of women's biology were used historically to justify their exclusion from education on the grounds that it would harm their capacity to bear children. By tracing how the two are articulated together within an ever-more global strategy, we could plot the course of women's multiple and disparate subordinations.

The instances I cite are not to be regarded as inherently patriarchal; they did not necessarily originate as part of a system organized to subordinate women. For instance, the law has functioned – through equal opportunities or sex discrimination legislation – to advance women's interests as well as to restrict them. Feminists, as well as conservatives, have promoted the idea that the biological differences between men and women matter. Medicine has developed techniques enabling gay and lesbian (and other non-normative) couples and individuals to have children. To understand women's oppression in the manner I suggest is thus to abandon the idea of necessary connections between elements and is instead to embrace the idea of a contingent convergence between them. Charting, through a series of interlocking genealogies, the actual ways in which molecular practices of power have been appropriated or displaced by ever more general mechanisms, and how those mechanisms in turn have generated specific discursive practices, enables us to demonstrate exactly how women have been subjectified (in their plurality).[12] It facilitates the kinds of feminist demands noted in Chapter 2, for the recognition of the variegated forms of subordination across, within and between gender, class, race, and geographic location. It is, moreover, an approach consistent with

Fraser's injunction to historicize. Finally, it offers a way of thinking through the intersections between institutional forms of domination and the production of subjectivities.

Conclusion

In this chapter I considered the question of how to apprehend the apparently 'rational' or co-ordinated nature of women's subordination. I contended that the only account presented here that can accommodate the theoretical premises of the 'subject-in-process' and society as indeterminate is one that understands domination in contingent strategic terms. Here, relations of domination are the effect of tactical alignment, in which the distribution of elements is constantly modulated and rearranged. This interpretation of domination alone allows us to recognize how historically constituted incarnations of gendered subjectivity may be appropriated and modified for 'patriarchal' ends. It will, of course, offend those who argue that despite women's differential positioning within, between and across competing axes of power, feminism requires attention to social totalities (such as patriarchy or capitalism) assumed to function according to the logic of necessity. In the account I offer, 'patriarchy' can be understood as a system of relations but not as a system of necessary relations.

I indicated earlier that it is a feature of global strategies that they are shot through with contradictions and fissures. In the next chapter, therefore, I want to consider what my reformulated account of domination indicates about the opportunities for resistant political activity. In order to do this, it is necessary to look at the question of agency: what it means, what challenges the subject-in-process poses to existing accounts of agency, what a reconceptualized version may look like, and whether such a reformulated version enables meaningful, political *transformation* of the world we inhabit. This idea of transformative change is frequently predicated on the kinds of dichotomies discussed earlier in this chapter: between the cultural and the material, and by implication (if not assertion) between subjectivity and social structures/institutions. However vital it is to alter subjectivity, such alteration is often seen as less important than transforming wide-ranging social patterns of domination. In this chapter, I indicated that treating subjectivity and sociality as separate or even separable, however tempting this might be, needs to be resisted. They are intertwined. The most effective way of showing this is to explore the historical specificity of the interconnections between particular modalities of subjectivity and the socio-political mechanisms (structures, institutions, discourses and practices) that produce them. In this chapter, I offered an account of how this might be achieved through a non-reductive account of domination.

In the next chapter, I consider an account of agency that does not rely on a voluntarist subject, what McNay describes as 'performative agency' (1999: 177). Central to my discussion is a debate between Butler and Benhabib. I will argue that reconceptualizing agency as (re) iteration opens up space for action (and for an alternative conception of autonomy) but also that it overemphasizes linguistic 'vulnerability' (Butler, 1997b) at the expense of considering *why* it is historically that particular areas (discourses, practices and so forth) and not others that become the locus of agential activity. In Chapter 6, therefore, I consider various approaches to the diagnosis of potential sites of transformation when I look at the politics and critique. My purpose is to further substantiate the contention that historicization is essential to change. This is not simply because historicizing furnishes an understanding of the present but rather because such an understanding is predicated upon the revelation of a set of questions and problems that can expose the gaps, fissures or contradictions where change, of a necessarily indeterminate and inchoate nature, is possible.

Notes

1 See Chapter 2.

2 Here once again terminological inexactitude raises its ugly head. In what follows there is an uneasy shifting between the terms postmodernism and poststructuralism. This is a consequence of the variable uses of those terms by the authors under discussion. As in earlier chapters, I have followed the terminology of those that I am discussing.

3 For a response to both Hartsock and Eisenstein that addresses the issue of the (f)utility of Foucault's analytic of power for feminism, see Lloyd (1993).

4 Eisenstein is a bit of an exception here. Her focus is less on the necessity of the connections between elements and more on the very fact of making some kind of connections between them.

5 These include *inter alia* Lyotard, Foucault, Derrida, Irigaray, Jardine, Haraway, Butler, and Laclau. There is the usual difficulty (noted in the Introduction) in lumping together willy-nilly such diverse writers and projects as different as deconstruction, genealogy, performativity and cyborg politics. Ebert makes little attempt to discriminate between these distinctive projects despite significant differences between them methodologically and politically, thus her criticisms have more or less validity depending on whom they are applied to.

6 For an alternative reading that champions the politics of deconstruction, see Elam (1994).

7 Hennessy (1993) offers another version of resistance postmodernism that shares much with the version discussed here, but is also significantly different in that she

conceives of materialism as a way of reading the world. I examine this account in detail in the next chapter.

8 For general discussions of materialist feminism see Ferguson and Wicke (1994); Hennessy (1993); and Landry and MacLean (1993).

9 On the question of the 'merely cultural', see also M. Fraser (1999); N. Fraser (1998); McNay (2000); and Sheridan (2002).

10 Again note the opposition between the 'symbolic' and the 'material'.

11 There is a parallel here with the idea of articulation as espoused by Laclau and Mouffe (1985), highlighted in Chapter 1 and considered later on in Chapter 8.

12 Butler's account of the normativized production of heterosexuality in *Gender Trouble* (1990a) is an instance of just such a genealogy.

five

agency and resistance

Commenting on the work of Sandra Bartky, Lois McNay states that an over-emphasis on the disciplinary nature of power leads her 'to make the problematic assumption that women are simply passive victims of systems of patriarchal domination' (1992: 36). Women's agency is effaced; their negotiation of gendered identity and practices of femininity occluded; and they are presented, instead, as creatures upon which gender stamps its imprint. '[N]o explanation of how individuals may act in an autonomous and creative fashion despite overarching social constraints' is offered here (McNay, 1992: 12). Similarly, discussing the 'Death of Man'[1] Seyla Benhabib observes that 'Along with this dissolution of the subject into yet "another position in language" disappears of course concepts of intentionality, accountability, self-reflexivity, and autonomy' (1995: 20). This thesis is, she asserts, incompatible with feminism. 'Not only feminist politics, but also coherent theorizing become impossible if the speaking and thinking self is replaced by "authorial positions", and if the self becomes a ventriloquist for discourses operating through her or "mobilizing" her' (ibid.: 110). So, is it possible to retrieve a concept of agency that makes sense for the subject-in-process? A concept, that is, 'that does not ground itself on the possibility of a stable or coherent subject free to make its own political decisions' (Elam, 1994: 71)? If so, what would it look like? I begin this chapter by sketching out the parameters of agency as conventionally understood in political theory. I then turn my attention to the recent debate between Seyla Benhabib and Judith Butler concerning the agency of the performative subject. This debate crystallizes many of the issues at stake in feminist discussions of agency and is, in this way, a representative rather than comprehensive overview of them. I claim that Butler's reformulated account of agency allows her to circumvent the criticism that constituted subjects are merely passive ciphers of power. I show that it allows for both resistance and change by considering examples of reverse discourses and political catachresis.

I caution, however, that this is not the same as arguing that such a re-conception of agency provides sufficient grounds for understanding political intervention, although it does furnish necessary conditions for it. In the final part of this chapter, therefore, I isolate some of the limitations of performative agency. I do so in order to highlight the need not only to explore *how* change is possible but also *why* it occurs where it does and when (Chapter 6) and why it might fail (Chapter 7). I start by tracing in brief what the concept of agency traditionally stands for.

Agency and the Individual

Since the seventeenth century the concept of agency has been tied to the idea of action. As Anna Yeatman points out, 'Freedom to be an actor ... is understood as freedom to be one's own agent' (1994: 59). This is exemplified in the work of Hobbes, Locke and Rousseau, three seminal figures in the history of social contract theory. The contract is the ultimate expression of men's ability to create, through their own will, a political society. These agents of political genesis – aptly termed by C.B. Macpherson 'possessive individuals' (1962) – own a number of vital characteristics: rationality, freedom, intentionality, and free will. Indeed, these characteristics are seen to accrue to all men as men. Importantly, for Hobbes and Locke at least, these men are pre-constituted subjects (endowed, in Locke's case, with natural rights) fulfilling their potential as men through this act of collective creation. Central to this historically and culturally dominant idea of agency is the opposition of freedom to power. Hobbes's famous formulation of freedom or 'Liberty' as the 'absence of externall Impediments' to motion (Hobbes, [1651] 1991: 91) encapsulates this exactly. The subject described above is thwarted when faced with external operations of power. To overcome the operations of power is to act agentially. Put another way, it is to act freely. While Hobbes talks of freedom or liberty, others, such as Marx, talk of liberation and emancipation. Here the focus is on throwing off the shackles of oppression and alienation in order, among other things, to cultivate a world according to one's desires, goals or needs. In this context, the development of class-consciousness plays a role in illuminating the structures of oppression. Agency on this formulation exceeds the idea of freedom of choice, since our choices may be structured by any number of ideological, political and cultural forces. Rather, it consists in the capability of actually structuring choices in the first place. Whatever the quite substantial differences between them, Hobbes, Locke, Rousseau and Marx all regard some form of agency as central to any political intervention in the external world.

Historically, of course, these attributes of agency were seen to accrue to men only (or rather to men of a certain kind). Feminists, nevertheless, appropriated this conception (sometimes in partially revised form) for themselves. They argued strongly for women to be recognized as agents capable of acting on and thus transforming the world.[2] Indeed, this notion has been central to the emancipatory thrust of much feminist writing such as, for instance, when authors such as Hartsock and MacKinnon argue that feminist consciousness-raising empowers women not only to recognize the sources of their oppression but also to create women-friendly environments (Hartsock, 1985, 1987a, 1987b, 1990; MacKinnon, 1987, 1989). Or, in a different context, when Dorothy Leland, evincing criteria for the usefulness of psychoanalytic ideas for feminist work, notes that an 'adequate political psychology must be non-deterministic'; it must enable the 'transcendence' of oppression (1992: 114).

The idea that the feminist subject-in-process is an unstable fiction (even a multiple, cyborg or trickster), compromises this understanding of agency, particularly when the pervasiveness of generative power or language is recalled. There is no pre-existing subject here with innate rights, traits, experiences or features. Ideas like rationality and freedom are now regarded as products of particular discourses not metaphysical realities. There can, as a consequence, be no creations *ab initio* and no chance of transcendence. Assuming that the subject is an effect thus undermines the idea of a possessive notion of agency, that is, one where agency is regarded as a capacity held by individuals that enables them to self-consciously change the world. As I demonstrate in this chapter, agency per se is not rendered meaningless as a consequence of this undermining; rather, we need to reconfigure how agency is thought. To explore what such a reconfiguration looks like, I focus on the exchange of ideas between Judith Butler and Seyla Benhabib that was published in *Feminist Contentions* (Benhabib et al., 1995). Clearly, the positions adopted by Butler and Benhabib do not represent or exhaust all possible feminist positions on agency.[3] Nevertheless, this discussion does forcefully capture some of the main issues at stake about agency in contemporary feminist political theory. Since Benhabib's two essays in *Feminist Contentions* draw on an earlier piece of work (1992), I will also make reference to it whenever appropriate.

Butler and Benhabib: Determination versus Constitution

In a comment on *Gender Trouble*, Benhabib remarks that the thrust of Butler's work is:

[to] bid farewell to the 'doer beyond [sic] the deed', to the self as the subject of a life narrative ... If this view of the self is adopted, is there any possibility of changing those 'expressions' which constitute us? If we are no
more than the sum total of the gendered expressions we perform, is there
ever any chance to stop the performance for a while, to pull the curtain
down, and let it rise only if one can have a say in the production of the
play itself? Isn't this what the struggle over gender is all about? ... [I]s such
a challenge only thinkable via a complete debunking of any concepts of
selfhood, agency, and autonomy? (1995: 21)

Leaving aside Benhabib's misreading of performativity as a kind of theatrical performance (see Chapter 7) and her misquotation of Nietzsche
(who refers to a 'doer *behind* the deed'), the crux of her objection to
Butler is that it is not enough for feminist emancipatory purposes to
reduce 'female agency to a "doing without the doer"' (1995: 22). Her
point is that to construe the subject as linguistically constituted is to
erase any conception of intentionality or agency. If the subject is itself
a position in language, it is unable to distance itself from the language
in which it is embedded so as to reflect upon it and to 'creatively alter'
it. The implication here is that the subject is determined by language
to such an extent that it cannot act. There are a number of issues here.
Does performative constitution disallow agency? Or, does it reformulate it? Is language the same as discourse? All in all, does Benhabib
offer an accurate interpretation of Butler's account of agency?

The best way to assess this is to consider the essay, 'Contingent
Foundations', which forms the twin with Benhabib's essay above
(Butler, 1995a).[4] As I have already shown, the chief aim of Butler's
essay is to challenge the idea that politics presupposes a stable subject
by demonstrating the contingency of all foundational claims. Her claim
is that the assertion that politics requires a stable subject is itself a *political* assertion. It sets or naturalizes the boundaries of the political by
determining in advance what counts as politics and what doesn't. It is
a ruse of power. By deploying such a notion, we are led to believe that
the context in which the subject operates is absolutely external to
them; that they can intervene at will in that context and that they can
legislate for the outcomes of their actions. They can produce what they
intend to produce; they are instrumental actors or agents. The idea of
the stable subject entails, therefore, particular consequences for a theorization of agency.

This presumption of the subject as prior to politics is the condition
of possibility for the idea of agency outlined above. If, however, we
assume another account of the subject – a version of the subject-in-
process – what happens to agency? An integral feature of such accounts
of subjectivity is that they displace the intentional subject. Instead, the

subject is seen to be the effect of discourse or power or language. Formulated another way, s/he is 'the instituted effect of prior actions' (Butler, paraphrasing Foucault, 1995a: 43). Far from miring the subject in a bog of determinism from which she cannot escape, Butler contends that it is the very constitutivity of the subject that enables her to act. The context or field in which subjects act is not simply an horizon that is external to them; it is the constitutive possibility of their acting in the first place. Significantly, while subjects can act, they cannot guarantee the direction of their actions, the outcomes, or the effects. The effects of any action will exceed the stated intentions of the actor. Although this might undermine agency as apprehended by Benhabib, it does not undermine agency as such but instead recasts, as I show in Chapter 7, what we understand by it.

The main implication of this for Butler is that political transformation, change and alteration are all possible *without* the presumption of agency as the mechanism that *enables* these changes. Conceptually, agency can be recast as the political *effect* of these changes. To summarize: if we reject the idea that agency only accrues to instrumental actors facing an external political reality, and accept that subjects and their agency are constructed and made possible on a political level, then agency cannot be thought of as something that has a 'formal existence' as such (Butler, 1995a: 46). It is not an attribute or property that subjects can be said to possess. Like Foucault's conception of power, it would appear, it only exists in its operation. (At least, this is how I would construe Butler's claim that agency has no formal existence.) This shift in thinking about agency requires a shift in approach. Instead of assuming the a priori necessity of agency for political practice, Butler commends us to consider questions concerning the kinds of possibility for mobilization and reworking of power relations on the basis of their current organization, questions about how to reconstitute and/or resist regulatory matrices. '[A]gency is always and only a political prerogative' (ibid.: 46–7).

Benhabib's response to Butler is to draw attention to three perceived areas of difficulty with her thought, two of which concern me here.[5] They are, first, what it means to say that language is constitutive of gendered subjectivity; and next, whether it is possible to read *constitution* as anything other than *determination*. Beginning with the first, Benhabib inquires 'Are linguistic practices the *primary* site where we should be searching for an explication of gender constitution?' (Benhabib et al., 1995: 109). Or are there other key areas, such as 'family structures, child-rearing patterns, children's games, dress habits, schooling, cultural habitus' (ibid.: 109) as well as other non-verbal factors (gesture, body language, and so on)? Focusing, for Benhabib, solely on language occludes the other factors that enable a helpless infant to become a linguistically competent and gendered adult. Now, Butler certainly puts a premium on language in the generation of subjects – after all her account of performativity derives from a speech-act theory (which I explore below). To speak of performativity as *only* a linguistic phenomenon is, however, to ignore Butler's debt to Foucault. When Butler explains what it means to be 'constituted by language' she defines it in the following way: it is 'to be produced within a given network of power/discourse' (1995b: 135). If this is read through a Foucauldian lens, then implied in the linking of power/discourse are the acts and practices that are constituted by and constitutive of the discursive. In other words, 'language' as Butler uses it (perhaps not entirely consistently) implicates and is implicated by gestures, acts, and practices. Moreover, the account of identity formation that she proffers is, as Webster notes, 'precisely a theory about structural and developmental processes ... (such as identification and repetition)' (2000: 20). In this respect, the version of performativity developed by Butler can take account of those elements that Benhabib sees as necessary to an account of gender constitution (see Butler, 1997a, 1997b).

Part of the confusion in this debate stems from the different ways in which the terms language and discourse are mobilized and the differing aims of that mobilization. Benhabib, drawing on Habermas, conceptualizes language and discourse in terms of inter-subjective communication and the validity claims implied in that communication. Moreover, such an approach concentrates on the procedures of communication: who speaks and who is silenced, who can raise issues and who cannot, who can make proposals and who cannot. That is, this mode of understanding language and discourse 'puts ethical questions at the center of feminist concerns' (Fraser, 1995b: 160). It is thus essentially normative. Allied to this is a bracketing off of forms of communication not oriented towards mutual understanding (such as poetry or non-verbal practices). It is this attention to the inter-subjective context of communication that prompts Benhabib to read Butler in this way. So, although both thinkers are concerned with the performative and how utterances do things, their respective understanding of what counts as an utterance and what can operate performatively differ. Further, the aims of their work also differ. Butler is not concerned with the procedures underpinning undistorted communication; rather, her focus is on the content of power/discourses (and this locution is important) and the historically specific material effects of those contents. In essence, then, Benhabib's criticisms miss the point here insofar as she is working from a different perspective on language and discourse. For the non-linguistic elements to which Benhabib draws our attention are elements of the discursive regimes that Butler is exploring. Benhabib's objection would, thus, seem to be refutable.

This leads us on to Benhabib's second observation concerning the viability of agency conceived as a performative effect. As Fraser notes:

> critique delegitimate[s] received significations, [and] it also opens space for the production of alternatives. The latter do not emerge *ex nihilo*, however, but through what Butler calls *resignification*, acts of iteration that are also innovations. Paradoxically, these acts are performed from, and indeed enabled by, subject positions that are themselves constructed by the very discursive regimes they contest. (1995b: 162)

The question this raises is how innovation is possible if subjects themselves are the effects of discourse. Butler, as we have already seen, contends that it is the very fact that utterances have to be reiterated that creates the space for change, transformation and resistance. Benhabib is more sceptical. She returns to one of the concluding passages in *Gender Trouble* where Butler, discussing debates on agency where agency is linked with the viability of the subject, comments that 'this kind of reasoning falsely presumes ... that to be constituted by discourse is to be determined by discourse where determination forecloses the possibility of agency' (1990a: 143). Benhabib remarks: 'how can one be constituted by discourse without being determined by it?' (Benhabib et al., 1995: 110). According to Benhabib's assessment, Butler's theory of performativity is unable to explain the human capacity for self-determination. It cannot, that is, explain what it is that enables subjects to resist or to change. In short, it has no understanding of the creative resources that humans need in order to alter circumstances. It is too deterministic. As such, agency has no place. In making this claim, Benhabib is reiterating her earlier point that deeds require doers and is refusing to differentiate between constituting the subject and determining it.

Determination implies that subjects are programmed to operate in certain ways and, consequently, that they are unable to act freely to change things, so thoroughly saturated with power, discourse, or language are they. In this, it is the opposite to the idea of the Cartesian autonomous agent carving its own way in the world. As Hekman reminds us, the Enlightenment sets up an antinomy between determinism and free will that occludes, or even precludes, the possibility of a position that may displace this antinomy (Hekman, 1990: 72–3). This is where constitution in Butler's terms would appear to fit. That is, the constituted subject is subjected at the same time as they are resistant and active at the same time as they are passive (Butler, 1997a). The performative production of the subject is dependent upon reiteration of the norms and practices that generate the subject; it is this requirement for reiteration that 'enables' the subject to act. In Chapter 2, for instance,

I discussed how the lesbian subject produced herself through the appropriation of particular historically contingent discourses: this process enabled her to act as a lesbian. It is this possibility of recon-figuration (itself an effect of reiteration) that underpins Butler's refig-ured notion of agency. Recalling the argument made in Chapter 1, despite the language that is often used (the subject as a *product* of x or y), the subject that Butler is discussing is very much a subject-in-process. It is never actually completed. Rather, the subject is in a state of perpetual constitution; subjected time and again. It is in this condi-tion because of the nature of re-iteration. Second, and significantly, the performative subject is not the autonomous author of their constitu-tive performances; instead intentionality (or autonomy) is bounded by the iterability of the elements making up the performance.[6] The repetition with a difference that 'grounds' gendered identity operates both as a mechanism of constraint (the reiteration of sets of norms that define us as normal/abnormal) and, importantly in the context of the present discussion, as a locus for productive activity (see also Butler, 1997a: 12). It is precisely the instability of the subject that generates agency.

It would appear from her criticisms that Benhabib adheres to an underlying conception of what constitutes a human subject, albeit one that is sensitive to particularity and difference as her championing of the 'concrete' other reveals; that is, a being that is self-reflexive, self-determining and autonomous (see also Weir, 1996: 124). In this regard, Benhabib 'clearly equate[s] agency with subjective capacities for choice or *self*-determination' (Webster, 2000: 10). This prevents her from see-ing how agency could operate without the (stable) subject as its guar-antor. For it is Butler's contention that agency is an effect of action and not a cause. That is, while an utterance may appear to declare a prior intention, the prior intention is actually the effect of the utterance.[7] As noted above, performativity works through reiteration; it draws on his-torically sedimented conventions and recites them. It is here that change occurs and the effect of agency is produced. '"Agency" is to be found', Butler proposes, 'precisely at such junctures where discourse is renewed.' And, as she continues a little further on, 'Discourse is the horizon of agency' (1995b: 135). A subject is not determined because the possibility of change resides in the very process of its constitution. This does not mean that deeds express the will of doers, nor that doers can control the extent or effect of deeds, rather that there are possibil-ities in the resignifying process that produces doers that create scope for resistance and change. Agency is contingent. The challenge is to find the possibilities, to work out how change could be or has been effected. In this respect, reprising a claim made by Butler in *Gender Trouble, discontinuities* in performance are a good place to look. For they reveal the contingency of gendered identity and, as such, are indicative of productive – agential – activity.

I noted above that Butler regards agency not as the possession of the subject but as a phenomenon that exists in its operation; that can be located at the site where discourses are renewed. In the next section, therefore, I endeavour to put more flesh on these ideas by considering examples of its operation. I begin with the idea of reverse discourses before exploring instances of political catachresis. I end by considering their effectiveness.

Reverse Discourses

According to Foucault, from whom the idea of reverse discourse originates, discourse works by making culturally intelligible certain relations between elements.[8] Other combinations of these same elements come to appear unnatural, even impossible. So discourses of sexuality posit a relation between sex, gender and desire such that man = masculine = desires a woman; woman = feminine = desires a man. Subjects that conform to this ordering of elements are considered to be 'normal', while those who do not are constructed as pathological or unnatural. Even the most hegemonic of discourses is, on Foucault's account, nonetheless always open and polyvalent. Discourses, for him, are 'a series of discontinuous segments whose tactical function is neither uniform nor stable' (Foucault, 1978: 100). They neither uniformly serve the interests of power nor uniformly resist them; rather they are more complex and volatile than this, working at once both to consolidate hegemonic power and to resist it. 'Discourse transmits and produces power; it reinforces it', Foucault observes, 'but also undermines and exposes it, renders it fragile and makes it possible to thwart it' (ibid.: 101). Indeed, such is the nature of its operation that within any field of power relations, not only do discourses contain contradictory elements but, as noted in the previous chapter, contradictory discourses may circulate within the same overall strategy. This is where 'reverse' discourses are significant. Here the terms of a discourse are reversed in order to signify in a different way, perhaps to affirm that which in another mode is negated or proscribed.

This process may be seen at work in the production of radical feminist discourses of motherhood and sexuality. Throughout the eighteenth and nineteenth centuries, a number of (patriarchal) discourses emerged that constructed female sexuality and femininity in very specific ways (see, for instance, Bland, 1995; and Bland and Doan, 1998). The effect of these discourses on middle-class women, in particular, was to attempt to confine them to the domestic sphere of hearth and

99

home, fit only for reproduction and mothering. Ultimately, of course, the influence of the values embedded in these discourses extended beyond the middle class, becoming a standard (however unrealizable) for all women. Suffice to say that such discourses forged and reinforced a connection naturalizing women's role as mothers. This connection continues to resonate to this day. Women, such as Myra Hindley, who commit crimes of violence against children are reviled and demonized for their 'unnatural' behaviour (to the point, in Hindley's case, where she is seen as far more evil than Ian Brady who actually committed the murders). Psychologists, social policy experts, conservative politicians and the media pontificate repeatedly about the harmful consequences to children's development of mothers who work outside the home. Indeed, in the early days of second-wave feminism, many feminists vilified the norm naturalizing motherhood for how it constrained women's choices by pressurizing them into having children, sometimes against their will.

Some feminists, however, took a different tack. Feminists, such as Adrienne Rich and other maternalists, appropriated the discursive link between women and mothering, rearticulated – or reversed – its claims and valorized nurturance and motherhood. They reformulated and redeployed several of its constitutive elements in order to argue a very different case, seeing motherhood (outside of patriarchy, at least) as a joyful and fulfilling experience for women. Recognition was demanded by feminist activists for the dissimilar career patterns of women compared to men. Governments and employers were petitioned in light of the importance of child-bearing and child-rearing for enhanced maternity benefits, paternity leave, family-friendly policies, and career breaks. Writers such as Sara Ruddick contended that women's different experience opened them up to a distinct, more co-operative, ethical and pacifist way of thinking (1990). The factors that had allowed for 'the reconstitution of the social norms of femininity' (Weedon, 1987: 108) in one century thus acted as the catalyst for a similar, though more resistant, phenomenon in another century.[9] The normalizing apparatus that initially endeavoured to control the behaviour and impulses of middle-class women was transformed into a mechanism, a hermeneutic, to affirm this behaviour and these impulses in women in general. A resistant discourse was born that in turn produced an alternative, resistant, subject position for women.

As noted at the start of this section, reverse discourses enable those delegitimized within dominant discourse to reverse its terms in a way that affirms their existence. It enables them to turn around a discourse in order to argue for a position or behaviour that is originally condemned or pathologized by it. Often this entails expropriating assumptions that have been 'naturalized' by a specific discourse and utilizing them in surprising or challenging ways. Later in this chapter, I consider the efficacy of such a strategy. For now, however, I want to consider what may be thought of as a 'radicalization' of this notion of reversal by returning to the idea of the performative subject and to the idea of citationality underpinning performativity. In particular, I explore the idea of political catachresis, that is, the appropriation of particular terms and their recitation in formerly inappropriate contexts.

Political Catachresis

In *Excitable Speech*, Butler turns her attention to the concept of 'words that wound' (Matsuda et al., 1993), that is, words that do harm as they are spoken (1997b). Her purpose is to cast doubt on any simple alignment between linguistic utterance and effect by exposing both the 'excitability' and 'uncontrollability' of all utterances, that is their inherent capacity for resignification, and the conventionality of all utterances. As noted in Chapter 1, Butler's account of performativity is indebted to Derrida's reformulation of Austinian speech act theory. In *Excitable Speech*, she explores further the distinction between perlocutionary and illocutionary speech acts. Perlocutionary speech acts 'produce certain effects as their consequence; by saying something, a certain effect follows' (Butler, 1997b: 3). There is thus a temporal gap between the utterance and the effect. Illocutionary performatives, by contrast, do what they say at the moment of saying. That is, there is no temporal gap between saying and doing. This is the implication behind the charge of 'words that wound'; saying wounding words is simultaneously to wound. It is this idea of instantaneity that Butler contests. Following Derrida, she contends that if performatives rely upon the existence of prior linguistic conventions or rituals for their force, then it makes no sense to claim that illocutionary speech acts operate by simultaneously saying and doing or uttering and effecting, since the 'moment' of the utterance is 'never a single moment. The "moment" in ritual is condensed historicity.' It draws on prior invocations and implies future ones, both of which 'escape the instance of the utterance' (ibid.: 3). They are perlocutionary, then, not illocutionary. As McNay comments: 'In Butler's view, Austin's understanding of illocutionary force rests on an untenable conflation of utterance with effect, speech with conduct' (1999: 179). By according them simultaneity, Austin fails to recognize the existence of the structures and conventions that precede and outlast the performative utterance.

For the subject named injuriously in speech, this means that the effect of wounding words differs from a slap in the face – where the injury occurs at the same time as the deed – rather it implies that regarding such words as wounding or injurious is predicated on them already having acquired the status of derogatory or demeaning speech (Butler, 1997b: 160, 161). Recognizing the temporality of the linguistic structure governing all speech, including hate-speech and wounding words, thus requires acknowledgement that every utterance recalls prior utterances. It also, significantly, points to the need for future reiteration if such speech is to continue in existence and to continue to have effects. It is this injunction to repeat that is crucial to agency. For it is Butler's contention that repeating the terms of such injurious speech has the capacity to undermine rather than consolidate hegemonic power relations. Moreover, since all language is vulnerable (Butler, 1997b: 87), this means that all of it is open to resignification.

Butler goes further than this. Richard Delgado discussing 'words that wound' notes that 'Words such as "nigger" and "spik" are badges of degradation ... *these words have no other connotation*' (cited in Butler, 1997b: 100). While conceding that the repetition of these words retains their injurious connotation, Butler contends that they do connote differently depending on where they are circulating. Thus, repeated in a court as testimony or in psychoanalysis as part of a discussion of trauma, they are re-contextualized. In effect, their becoming part of other discourses reveals their reproducibility and resignifiability as terms. If these terms can be reproduced in court or in psychoanalysis, why can they not be reproduced in other more positive or more subversive ways? Instead of appropriation, why not expropriation? That is, why not a form of resignification that contests, head on, dominant or authorized discourse, that challenges its legitimacy thereby?

Two examples should suffice to show the potential here. The first is from *Excitable Speech*. Here Butler draws on the incident that allegedly set in motion the Montgomery bus protests of 1955, when Rosa Parks refused to yield her seat to a white passenger. Butler writes:

> When Rosa Parks sat in the front of the bus, she had no prior right to do so guaranteed by any of the segregationist conventions of the South. And yet, in laying claim to the right for which she had no *prior* authorization, she endowed a certain authority on the act, and began the insurrectionary process of overthrowing those established codes of legitimacy. (Butler, 1997b: 147)

By occupying a bus seat while a white passenger was forced to stand, according to Butler, Parks expropriated the terms of the dominant segregationist discourse and authorized her resistant act. 'The effects of catachresis in political discourse are possible', Butler surmises, 'only when terms that have traditionally signified in certain ways are misappropriated for other kinds of purposes' (ibid.: 144). Thus, Parks 'misappropriates' the notion of 'rights' when she demands they be extended to her (an African-American) in defiance of hegemonic norms and values. She takes the discourse of rights and uses it to empower herself. It is the iterability of the performative (or citational doubling) that is crucial in allowing her to do so. The performative has the capacity to 'break with its prior context and ... to assume new contexts' (ibid.: 147, 157–8). It is this that allows for this public moment of subversion or catachresis. (And, of course, somewhat contestably, in Butler's reading the effectiveness of Parks's act is to begin an insurrection.[10])

The second example is taken from *Antigone's Claim: Kinship between Life and Death* (Butler, 2000a).[11] 'I began to think about Antigone a few years ago', Butler writes in the opening sentence of the book, 'as I wondered what happened to those feminist efforts to confront and defy the state' (ibid.: 1). Butler turns to Antigone, the incestuous progeny of Oedipus and a character in Greek tragedy, because Antigone puts into question the politics of representation.[12] 'As a figure for politics', Antigone gestures, 'not to politics as a question of representation but to that political possibility that emerges when the limits to representation and representability are exposed' (ibid.: 2).

Butler is not, of course, the first person to draw on the story of Antigone; Hegel, Lacan, and Irigaray all precede her in this vein. Indeed, she claims that these prior interpretations all share one common feature: they position Antigone's opposition to the state and to Creon as a mode of 'pre-political opposition to politics' (ibid.: 2) because they present Antigone as a liminal figure. She is located at the threshold of the social; the site, that is, where kinship is separated from and even suppressed in the inauguration and maintenance of the state. Kinship functions, therefore, as the sphere that conditions politics but that does not enter it. It is apolitical. This strict bifurcation of kinship and the state poses a problem for representation. Casting Antigone as the representative of kinship and Creon of the state fails because the state and kinship are co-dependent; they cannot be treated as entirely separable. When Antigone buries Polyneices and when she refuses to deny this to Creon, Antigone takes on – or 'expropriates' – the language of the state: she speaks a language of entitlement that she is barred from. Recall that Creon, King of Thebes, expressly forbids the burial of Polyneices (Antigone's brother). His edict is an act of sovereign agency. He expects it to be obeyed; such is his authority. Not only does Antigone disobey the law but also she publicly refuses to deny her disobedience. She thus asserts her own sovereign agency against Creon. 'Her agency emerges precisely through her refusal to honor his command' (ibid.: 11). For the sequestered Antigone to speak publicly and to grieve her brother publicly, is to appropriate (or to follow the earlier discussion, to 'misappropriate') the language of sovereignty and of public discourse. '[T]o the extent that she occupies the language that can never belong to her, she functions as a chiasm within the vocabulary of political norms' (ibid.: 82). Antigone's defiance of Creon and the law is not one of pure opposition in the sense that it derives exclusively from the language of kinship (as has been contended); rather it is 'scandalously impure' because Antigone utilizes the language and prerogatives of sovereignty (ibid.: 5). Antigone's act, thus, symbolizes the deformation of both *idealized kinship and political sovereignty* (ibid.: 6). The example of Antigone's resistance to Creon and her resignification of the language of entitlement thus resonate with the earlier example of Rosa Parks. In both cases, the indications are clear: Rosa Parks and Antigone, both prohibited from certain rights, nevertheless catachrestically appropriate those rights. They act where they should not. They trouble the vocabulary of a law that attempts to constrain them. They disrupt hegemonic political norms. The question that remains is, in what senses are these activities politically transformative?

Transformation and Change

Both reverse discourses and catachresis, in different ways, redeploy terms – most often hegemonic terms – already circulating in debate. Because of this, there is the potential for these actions to remain caught within the web of the discursive or linguistic formation they appropriate. Reversals, as indicated, tend to be implicated in the same mode of thought that they are labouring against since one of the ways they operate is by accepting the legitimacy of certain key elements of a discourse. Being able to turn a discourse around in order to argue for a position or behaviour that is initially condemned or pathologized, or deploying certain 'naturalized' assumptions against the grain, does not necessarily displace the discourse in question. In the feminist discourse on mothering, the implied natural connection linking mother and child found in anti-feminist discourses remains, leaving open the possibility that women who do not want or cannot have children may be seen as unnatural both by feminists and anti-feminists. Similarly, when the Subaltern Studies Group (discussed in Chapter 3) appropriated for themselves the role of the subject of history, they accepted the legitimacy of the idea that there was a subject of history. In this sense, it may be contended that agency understood in this way does not necessarily or inevitably dislodge the relations of domination within which particular terms operate even as it partially reconfigures them.

This process, what Bernard-Henri Lévy calls 'a double détente' (in Foucault, 1988c: 116), recognizes that reverse discourses – and catachreses – are imbricated within particular discursive configurations just as they attempt to liberate themselves from them. In a sense, of course, this imbrication is unavoidable. As Ann Ferguson notes, contestatory cultures such as lesbianism are *'potential* cultures of resistance *within* historically specific patriarchal cultures' (1990: 84, my emphasis). Movements of reversal are culturally embedded because there is no place outside of their historical location from which to work, which means that the discursive formations that structure those locations also inform the kinds of resistance that are possible. It might also be argued that it is because there is no outside from which to operate politically that such extraordinary labour is required to delineate and sustain all contestatory movements, since they can be all the more easily reabsorbed. As Shane Phelan puts it, although 'it is possible for lesbian sex and sexuality to present possibilities not comprehended by heterosex(uality), *this is not a given but an achievement'* (1993: 776, my emphasis).

A number of points are worth noting here. Many of the examples that Butler cites in *Excitable Speech* concern, as noted previously, injurious words or hate-speech, that is, words and speech that are 'tainted' (Butler, 1997b: 160). Re-invoking them, albeit for different ends, may appear resonant with their former oppressive uses. Does this mean therefore, that reversal or catachresis should (as if it could) be avoided since in some sense it perpetuates conditions of harm (see Brown, 1995)? Or are these 'sullied' words open to 'unexpected innocence' (Butler, 1997b: 161)? Obviously each case needs to be examined as an event in itself. Different instances of catachresis or reversal will result in more or less radical change depending on context, and will thus have more or less meaning in the lives of specific marginalized subjects.[13] As Iris Young has shown, the ideal of universal citizenship, in both theory and practice, was predicated on the exclusion of all difference from the norm of white, male, and middle-class values (1990). In effect, this ideal de-recognized women, people of colour, lesbians and gays. Does this mean that marginalized groups should repudiate altogether the aim of universal citizenship? Or, does their appropriation of the ideal allow for its resignification in new terms? It would certainly appear, for instance, from the breadth and tenor of debates on citizenship that the meaning of the term can be (and has been) resignified in more 'innocent' directions, not all of which have led to the 'simple assimilation and accommodation of what has been excluded into existing terms' (Butler, 1997b: 161). Rather some have produced a subversion of those terms from within in such a way as to open up the term to different uses in the future.[14] Accordingly, it would be misleading to contend that under no conditions can reversals or catachreses ever operate in unsullied ways, since potentially they can.

Two issues remain: what kinds of material political transformation do reversals and catachreses engender? And, while it is undoubtedly the case that Butler can evince a non-voluntarist account of agency, is this account sufficient on its own to offer all the resources that feminists need in respect of political action? It is impossible to theorize in the abstract about whether reversal and catachreses per se constitute modes of social and political transformation. Attention needs to be paid to concrete instances of both. On Butler's reading of Rosa Parks, the implication is that widespread social and political change does result from a 'moment' of expropriation (with moment understood in terms of condensed historicity). Parks's action on this count sparked the protests that brought Martin Luther King to greater public attention and thus helped launch the Civil Rights movement. In its turn, this movement managed to secure legal change from a sympathetic regime (via the Civil Rights Act of 1964). Although it wasn't the moment of catachresis per se that achieved this, but was rather the momentum that it generated and the repercussions that ensued from it, nevertheless, the example is useful in indicating what Butler intends by the political efficacy of misappropriation. While these changes are not of the same order as the utopian calls for overthrowing patriarchy found in some earlier forms of feminism – with their implied construction *ab initio* of a gynocentric society – they do portend far-reaching change. What Butler's curt treatment of the Parks example masks, however, are the historical conditions of possibility of this insurrectionary act. How did the bus boycotts come about? What were the wider political circumstances that enabled Parks to resist segregationist policy? Why did she, in particular, refuse to give up her seat? Was her act spontaneous or was it pre-planned? Was she chosen to commit this act of defiance? It is here that my second question becomes important.

Resistance, as Wendy Brown observes, does not itself 'contain a critique, a vision, or grounds for organized collective efforts' (1995: 49). Just so, but I want to contend that it needs to be supplemented by at least some of them. That is, although resistance itself might not 'contain' any specific directions for political intervention, feminist activists cannot eschew entirely the task of identifying particular strategies of resistance or 'subversive repetition' (Butler, 1990a: 147), even if those strategies are not directly determined by or deduced from feminist theoretical inquiry. Critique, even if it is non-normative and anti-prescriptive – is, I suggest, vital to feminist politics. As I contend in the next chapter, it offers a mode of political intervention that acts to denaturalize what is taken for granted (norms, modes of behaviour, modalities of sexed embodiment, and so on), even if what results from critique remains contingent. As Brown notes: 'whether or not resistance is possible is a different question from what its aim is, what it is for, and especially whether or not it resubjugates the resisting subject' (1995: 64). The same is true of agency. In this chapter, I have explored whether agency is possible from the perspective of a processual subject. In Chapter 7 I consider what agency means in terms of political activity.

Conclusion

The debate between Butler and Benhabib that I outlined above testifies to some of the ways in which the dominant conception of agency has come under scrutiny in recent years. Significantly, it also reveals differing modes of articulating and situating theoretically and conceptually the question of agency. For Benhabib, agency is an attribute that inheres in humans. Linguistic interaction merely facilitates its operation. By contrast, for Butler, agency is not related to a theory of the self but is an effect of the operations of discourse–power through which subjects are produced. Here agency cannot be separated from context. From being presented as a robust phenomenon that transcends context, agency is reconceived here as a more frangible potentiality generated in the process of performative constitution. Here, I would endorse McNay's conclusion that 'by expanding on Foucault's remark that the autonomous subject emerges from constraint, Butler has outlined a non-voluntarist conception of agency that breaks out of the dualisms of domination and resistance that sometimes hamper feminist thought' (1999: 190). But, of course, is it not merely the opportunity to become other or to do things differently that is at stake in feminist discussions of agency, for both Benhabib's and Butler's respective accounts of agency could, in their own ways, accommodate these possibilities.

Central to feminist accounts of agency has been the idea of *transformative* change. The material covered in this chapter reveals that a reformulated account of agency can produce change but not necessarily sweeping transformation of the kind envisaged in some more utopian forms of feminist theory, where the aim is to eradicate in one fell swoop the structures producing sexist oppression. Instead, however, of rejecting out of hand a theory that cannot guarantee revolutionary transformation, we would be better advised to think again about what it means to *transform* society. Part of this rethinking depends, I suggest, on our ability to consider opportunities for change at source; that is, to ask when and where it is possible to bring about alterations in the systems of domination that structure the world we inhabit (see Chapter 7). For while it is certainly the case that some forms of reversal or catachresis occur spontaneously, even unconsciously, not all either can or do. Lots result from analysing and *critiquing* the myriad power relations that instate and reproduce inequality and marginalization for subjects through discourses and practices of race, class, gender, sexuality, and so forth. Indeed, feminism's vitality as a political movement is allied intimately to its capacity for critique both in itself for what it exposes about society, and as a prelude to collective endeavour. The question is: can feminism influenced by poststructuralist ideas deliver this? The answer, I think, is yes, but as I suggest in the next chapter, only if it is recognized that in order to avoid reductive accounts of oppression the mode of critique to be practised must be attentive to contingency, to the convergence *and* divergence of the operations of power and to variations in the intensity of power across its many fields of operation.

Notes

1 According to Flax (1990), this is one of the three prongs of postmodern theory – the others being the 'Death of History' and the 'Death of Metaphysics', which Benhabib explores (1992, 1995).

2 On some of the psychological implications for a gendered account of agency, see Meyers (1992).

3 Lois McNay's *Gender and Agency* (2000), for instance, explores a range of feminist (and social theory) writings on agency. See also McNay (1999) for an alternative reading of Butler's interpretation of agency. I explore the question of the psychic dimension of subjectivity and its implications for political change in Lloyd (1998–99).

4 This essay is also a reprint of an earlier essay (Butler, 1992). In this chapter, my references are to the 1995 version since my focus is the debate in *Feminist Contentions*. Elsewhere my references are to the original publication.

5 The other concerns the normative imperatives entailed by a performative conception of agency.

6 This, I show in Chapter 7, has a bearing on the capacity of parodic recitations to produce transgressive effects, raising the question of which differences make a difference.

7 Saying 'no', for example, may suggest a previous intention to refuse something but, on Butler's reading, it is the 'no' alone that generates the effect of this previous intention.

8 For a brief consideration of reverse discourses by Butler, see her 1991 chapter, highlighting the differential discursive treatment of gays and lesbians.

9 This is not to suggest falsely that the two bear a continuous relationship to one another, merely that because discourses are polyvalent, they work in many ways. In addition, it should be remembered that practices that serve strategies of domination can be co-opted into practices of resistance (see Sawicki, 1988: 185; Lloyd, 1993).

10 Butler does not consider, for instance, the fact that Parks's act itself reiterates the terms of the emerging Black discourses of the South that were already challenging the authority of the segregationist laws and ordinances of Alabama (see Disch, 1999; Lovell, 2003).

11 Constraints of space prevent me considering this book in detail at this time. I address them in 'Butler, Antigone, and the state' (Lloyd, forthcoming).

12 In short, Antigone is one of the incestuous progeny of Oedipus' liaison with his mother. Her two brothers (Polyneices and Eteocles) fight, and the former kills the latter. Creon, King of Thebes, honours Eteocles with a military funeral while ordering that Polyneices shall not be buried. Rather his body is to lie unburied on a hillside. As Jean Elshtain puts it, 'Creon issues an order in the higher interests of state that violates the sacred familial duty to bury and honour the dead' (1998: 369). Antigone, in defiance of Creon, buries Polyneices, not once but twice. What is more, she does not deny it when Creon asks publicly. For her 'crime' Antigone must die.

13 Whether or not reiteration operates as a mode of strategic essentialism is an open question. There appears to be no reason why the expropriation of categories might not lead to the projection of a form of provisional reification that allows for collective action, though Butler does not examine this. The language that she uses – resignification rather than strategic essentialism – may suggest her continued suspicion of the latter for what it posits rather than for what it disrupts. See Chapter 3.

14 Thus, instead of trying to expand the terms of citizenship to include women on equal – the same – terms as men, feminists such as Carole Pateman have endeavoured to develop gynocentric forms of citizenship designed specifically for women, thus resignifying what is meant by 'universality' away from identical treatment to differential treatment (1988, 1989). This is not to suggest, however, that there are not problems, now well documented, attaching to these specific reconceptualizations.

six

the politics of critique

A feminist practice can only be ... at odds with what already exists so that we may say 'that's not it' and 'that's still not it'. (Kristeva, 1980b: 137)

Kristeva's intuition about feminism captures one of its most important dimensions: that it is an insistent practice of critique rejecting what is unsatisfactory in the present. Feminism is a radical oppositional project in the sense that it is both inherently critical and political. This is not to claim, however, that feminism offers a monolithic theory or stance on any topic. A brief glimpse at the range of positions feminists adopt in relation to women's subordination indicates otherwise: where liberal feminists concentrate, by and large, on the legal and institutional impediments to equality, Marxist feminists expose the class nature of women's oppression; where radical feminists see patriarchy at work, socialist feminists see patriarchal capitalism understood in a number of different ways. Feminism suggests, rather, what Butler and Scott call in a discussion of poststructuralism 'a field of critical practices that cannot be totalized' (1992: xiii). While individual versions of feminism may, as highlighted in previous chapters, attempt to totalize, feminism in general does not. Rather, it interrogates in multiple ways the many and varied mechanisms, local and global, molecular and molar, that produce and define women and shape their lives. From engagements with 'malestream' political theory to reflections on its own corpus of work, feminist writing has been characterized by its critical contestation of claims, explanations, premises, and postulates.

A number of recent feminist writers, however, have expressed doubt whether feminist work that draws upon poststructuralist writings can ever be truly critical. For feminist work to be critical, these exponents contend, it must be explanatory, not descriptive and it must, as indicated in the last chapter, open the way to social transformation (Ebert, 1993; Hennessy, 1993). In this chapter, therefore, I explore the politics of criticism. Specifically, I examine forms of critical work responsive to poststructuralism and challenge the claim that this critical work can neither be explanatory nor potentially transformative. I argue that what marks this work out is that, unlike the feminist positions noted above, it raises questions about the field upon which criticism is practised. Instead of endeavouring to present an internally consistent and coherent ideology that drives criticism and determines its focus, this mode of feminist critique emphasizes problematization: questioning, among other things, the setting of limits and the positing of positivities. It necessitates examining the exclusions and erasures that define the critical field, determining what 'counts' and what does not. '[T]o question a form of activity or a conceptual terrain is not', as Butler remarks, 'to banish or censor it; it is, for the duration, to suspend its ordinary play in order to ask after its constitution' (2000c: 264).

In Chapter 4, I argued for an analytic of domination understood as the effect of multiple, sometimes interlocking, processes. The question for this chapter, is how this analytic operates. Minimally, I suggest, it implies that feminist critique must operate in several registers at once, for as Susan Hekman rightly points out, '[t]he subordination of women cannot be eradicated by reforming the political and/or economic structures alone'; that is, by attacking some 'centre' of male power (1990: 186; see also Martin, 1988: 9–10). It must rather recognize the interconnections of practices and discourses and the 'multiplicity of positionalities concurrently available in the social field seen as a field of forces' (de Lauretis, 1990: 131). Appreciating the tangled web of power relations and sites of resistance that traverse the social not only undermines, as noted earlier, the idea that domination is comprehensible in terms of a fully coherent single, omnipotent, system of power but it also necessitates an approach capable of engaging multiple strategies of struggle *and* critique. The 'question is not *whether* to become involved', as Honig remarks of de Lauretis 'but *how*' (1996: 266); *how*, that is, to interrogate and resist. If agency is, as indicated in the last chapter, partly concerned with the potential to appropriate and rework power relations and partly with how to reconstitute and/or resist regulatory matrices, then political critique must be able to understand how those power relations and/or matrices come to be what they are. If the domain of the political is reconceptualized as a process of boundary setting, then politics as an activity must be identified, partially, in terms of their transgression. This raises a number of questions about feminist criticism: how is it to challenge limits? What are the presuppositions that underpin critique? How is it related to the broader question of political struggle?

This chapter is divided into four sections. In the first, I return to the debate begun in Chapter 4 concerning the distinction found within postmodern materialist feminism between ludic postmodernism and resistance postmodernism. Then I concentrated on Ebert's contention that if postmodern feminism is to have any political purchase, it needs to be grounded in a 'logic of social necessity' (making it a resistance postmodernism). Here, I turn to what constitutes, for materialist feminists, the proper grounds and range of critique. Subsequently, I explore the nature of critique from a resistance postmodern perspective by examining the work of Rosemary Hennessy. The primary charge against 'ludic' postmodernism is its inability to explain social inequality and transform it. In the third section, therefore, I demonstrate how it is possible to generate a mode of critique from an allegedly 'ludic' position (namely a Foucauldian one) that both explains the emergence of phenomena in the present and opens up space for change. In the final section, I turn my attention to the politics of truth. Since critics often attempt to garner legitimacy for their theories by contending that these theories tell the truth about the world, it is important to consider the politics of truth: the challenge, that is, to the idea that truth is innocent of power.

Ludic Postmodernism and the Failure of Critique

Defining critique, Ebert notes that it is first and foremost a practice oriented towards the development of an historical understanding of how certain social institutions (she suggests motherhood, love, and taxation, by way of examples) come to be and how they change. In other words, critique explains the origination of particular social formations, institutions and practices. In the course of this explication, critique has a second effect; it 'points to what is suppressed by the empirically existing: what *could be* (instead of what actually *is*)'. In other words,

> critique is a mode of knowing that inquires into what is not said, into the silences and the suppressed or missing, in order to uncover the concealed operations of power and underlying socioeconomic relations connecting the myriad details and seemingly disparate events and representations of our lives. (Ebert, 1993: 9)

Critique not only diagnoses the current situation; it also reveals the historicity of that which is and, thus, indicates where change may be possible by revealing what is hidden beneath present arrangements. It is in the execution of these dual functions that ludic postmodernism is deficient. According to Ebert, the basic problems with ludic postmodernism are simple: it 'substitutes validation for critique and affirmation for opposition' (ibid.: 7). It other words, ludic postmodernism fails to

113

explain how social difference comes to be produced (rather it merely affirms such difference) and, in place of an interventionist critique prompting change, it focuses (as previously noted) on pleasure 'in/of textuality, the local, the popular, and, above all, the body (*jouissance*)' (ibid.: 7). Of the two species of postmodernism that concern Ebert (ludic and resistance), only resistance postmodernism is explanatory; its mode of critique alone leads to: 'the production of historical knowledges that mark the transformability of existing social arrangements and the possibility of a different social organization – an organization free from exploitation' (ibid.: 9).

Two sets of questions are raised by Ebert's proclamations. First, how precisely does resistance postmodernism effect the work of critique? What are its methodological presuppositions? To address these questions, in the next section, I examine how resistance postmodernism manages the activity of critique and the operational tools it uses to do so. Second, is it accurate to describe what Ebert calls 'ludic postmodernism'[1] as deficient in explanatory capacity? Leaving to one side the question of the primacy of the economic that underpins resistance postmodernism, does 'ludic postmodernism' necessarily fail to offer an account of – or the tools for the development of – a mode of critique that is not only diagnostic but also transformative? I argue later in this chapter that because Ebert attempts to offer an overview of developments within postmodernism per se, she pays insufficient attention to the significant differences between individual thinkers, not least in respect of the relation between critique and politics.[2] I propose that it is possible to develop a mode of critique from a purportedly 'ludic' position, which is both *explanatory* and *interventionist* and this is through use of the work of Foucault. Moreover, I contend that the kind of historical analysis generated by this approach resonates with the demands of resistance postmodernism, at least of the variety developed by Rosemary Hennessy, to whose work I now turn.

Resistance Postmodernism: Reading between the Lines

Hennessy, like Ebert, endeavours to develop a feminist critical theory that amalgamates aspects of postmodernism and materialism. Drawing on the work of Althusser and Gramsci, in particular, Hennessy seeks to strengthen feminist standpoint theory in such a way that it becomes a more interventionist critical-political strategy, and less a potentially homogenizing and essentializing epistemology based on experientialism. In this section, I explore Hennessy's conception of critical practice. In particular, I examine the mode of reading that she proposes where discourse is read as ideology. Before doing so, a number of preliminary remarks are necessary. Like Ebert, Hennessy offers a version of 'resistance postmodernism' that is resolutely interventionist; that seeks to transform the social world; and that is based upon a social analytic that allows for systemic explanation. In a manner that echoes Foucault (see below), Hennessy argues for an understanding of historical analysis as an 'intervention in the present' (1993: xvii). This means that the kind of vision of democratic political life thereby entailed is always provisional. In addition, like Ebert, Hennessy is severely critical of an overemphasis on linguistic phenomena at the expense of the 'real' material inequalities of patriarchal capitalism. Discourse and language are seen as purely cultural phenomena which, although significant, are secondary to other, more important, economic and political (i.e. emancipatory) concerns. Hennessy reads discourse (of a non-Althusserian kind) as textual not material and as divorced from social practices and power.

The approach that Hennessy favours marries together Althusser's notion of symptomatic reading with Gramsci's concept of hegemony to produce an account of discourse as ideology. Hennessy rejects Althusser's opposition between ideology and science (which accords the latter privileged access to the truth) and instead she substitutes Gramsci's idea of counter-hegemonic discourses as a mechanism to provoke crisis. Ideology is read by Hennessy as the 'array of sense-making practices' that decide what counts in any determinate historical context (1993: 14). It includes, as such, the struggles over meaning that occur as competing discourses become the site of political battle (such as when feminism challenges aspects of patriarchal ideology). Importantly, ideology also produces, and is produced by, the economic and political arrangements of a particular social formation. It is, therefore, never merely textual but always material. It is ideology, for Hennessy, that generates 'what counts as socially made "reality"' (ibid.: 75).[3] This theorization of the materiality of ideology is used by Hennessy to counter the idea of an objective reality outside discourse. Rather, following Althusser, she makes a distinction here between the actual Real – 'the actual world' – and the socially produced real.[4] The actual Real is, she states, unknowable: it is the limit to what can be known historically. The social real, by contrast, is that which makes intelligible the material structures through which ideology works. Significantly, the Real can always disrupt the real. This means that crisis is not *necessarily* the product of the collective critical action of groups, as she contends, but an intrinsic feature of the relation between the actual and the social real/Real. It is here that her turn to Gramsci is significant.

What Gramsci offers is an account of the contestation of discourses within the struggle to assert hegemony that does not rely upon the notion of science as the truth (as opposed to ideology as distortion). Ideological contest is oriented around not a rejection of ideology per se but around attempts to reconfigure the dominant cultural and intellectual framework. It is the mode by which competing discourses are articulated within a coherent matrix of intelligibility that determines the ability of the dominant group to maintain its hegemony. What is implicit in this account of the battle for ideological supremacy is the notion of contradiction, for hegemonic discourses can never fully suture or seal over the incoherence in their narratives (ibid.: 92). 'The dominating ideology never dominates without contradiction. Therefore it cannot exhaust all social experience' (ibid.: 76). From the perspective of critique this means that there are always gaps and cracks within hegemonic discourse, gaps and cracks that are ripe for ideology critique. This Althusserian–Gramsci blend is useful, Hennessy asserts, because it lends itself to a systemic analysis of power relations entailing social transformation. It allows feminism to puncture patriarchal ideology, for instance, in order to challenge its construction of gendered reality.

The aim of symptomatic reading as Hennessy understands it is to concentrate on the aporias within a *text*. This involves a three-fold strategy: first, attending to the self-contradictory moments in the logic of a text; second, reading these contradictions as instances of the ideological displacement of competing historical forces – what she refers to as de-fetishizing; and, finally, producing an alternative narrative that enables social transformation (ibid.: 92). Symptomatic reading makes visible the political unconscious that, in Freudian parlance, is condensed, displaced, and substituted in the articulation of meaning. These symptoms do not disappear, however, rather they indicate the existence of another logic operative in everyday life. The point of critique for Hennessy is to reveal this other (truer?) logic. The resuscitation of the unsaid (the *non dit*) opens a discursive text up to denaturalization (something, she acknowledges, that is shared with the work of Foucault et al.) and, more significantly, both to reconfiguration and to dis-identification.[5] These 'silences' in a text, she suggests, 'may be read as the irruption of counter-hegemonic discourses into the thread of the narrative' (ibid.: 94).

There is a lot that is plausible and persuasive in this account, and as I suggest below, much of the approach resonates with the Foucauldian one I offer. There is, of course, one principal difference. The significant feature of the silences that Hennessy draws attention to is that they represent the text's 'unconscious' – with all this connotes. Just as the psychoanalytic unconscious comes to haunt and disrupt the conscious, so too does the political unconscious haunt and disrupt ideology by revealing what ideology somewhat ineffectually suppresses. So, even though Hennessy wants to disarticulate this mode of reading from Althusserian notions of truth and science, her adherence to the idea of history as the development of exploitative social arrangements means that, while ideology critique offers a form of political criticism, it is one predicated not just upon a necessary logic; it implies that there is something real (or true) hidden beneath the veneer of daily life as currently organized (socially, economically, and politically) that awaits revelation.

Part of Hennessy's critique is that postmodernists fail adequately to differentiate the non-discursive from the discursive or to posit properly the causal, and systematic, relationship that exists between them (ibid.: 25, 41). Frustratingly, however, Hennessy never explains her own conception of these two terms. The best that can be said is that near the start of her book she aligns discourse with feminist critique and the non-discursive with women's lives (ibid.: xvi); between, I surmise, culture and economics, a position that resonates with that of Ebert as discussed in Chapter 4. As I contended then, to argue that all accounts of feminist politics informed by postmodernism emphasize the textual rather than the material is not only to operate with a very narrow conception of materialism but it is to derogate culture and cultural politics. As noted in my earlier discussion, the alignment of materialism with the economic occludes the manner in which discourse itself connotes institutional and social arrangements as well as the ordering of linguistic categories into statements, utterances, and so forth. In addition, it implies that culture is immaterial. Moreover, it instates a mode of neo-Marxist materialism that fails to deal with the multiplicity, or perhaps more accurately with the undecidability, of the political. Hennessy, like Ebert, operates with a very traditional conception of politics as pertaining to collective social transformation or emancipation. Culture – or what is sometimes conceded as cultural politics – is seen thus as tangential to the real concerns of socio-economic exploitation and politics. While it is conceded that cultural politics has value as a mode of denaturalizing taken-for-granted assumptions, it is deemed insufficient because it describes and affirms. It cannot challenge the real bases of exploitation in society nor the manner in which different local manifestations of power are always subservient to the greater logic of patriarchal capitalism. Without repeating too much the earlier arguments, there is thus the problematic assumption once again that labour relation struggles are of greater significance than other struggles.

Is it the case, however, that 'ludic postmodernism' only produces descriptive and affirmative analyses or can it generate a form of critique that is explanatory and interventionist? In the next part of this chapter, I argue that 'permanent critique' of a loosely Foucauldian kind does, in fact, lend itself both to critique understood in Ebert's terms as a species of historical understanding and as an indicator of what might be, and also to political intervention. The one difference is that this mode of critique is not part of a social logic of necessity, though it may be aligned with a global strategy of the kind I outlined in Chapter 4.

Thinking Critically, Thinking Genealogically

In the essay 'What is Enlightenment?' (his famous reflection on Kant's essay of the same name), Foucault (1984d) explores the ways in which subjects are located in an historical present that shapes the ways they have of understanding, and of acting upon, themselves. Through a process of what he elsewhere terms genealogy, Foucault advocates the construction of an historical ontology of the self. He thus proposes the excavation of the chance, contingent and aleatory events that have led to the construction of specific subject positions. By exposing the singularity and historicity of various modes of experience, he contends, it becomes possible to expose the arbitrariness of moral, economic, social and political arrangements. In tracing the localized limits of subjectivity in order to 'eventalize' them, it enables subjects to think differently about the things that they have come to regard as normal and natural. As Lee Quinby formulates it:

> Genealogy attempts to put on display the places where force relations dig in, below the surfaces of the skin, not quite visible yet making themselves felt, governing behaviour, posture, gesture, becoming the truth of one's being. Genealogy exposes how that truth appraises certain behaviours and relationships as sinful or abnormal and designates others as virtuous and proper. (1997: 146–7)

It is, that is, part of a process of making 'facile gestures difficult' (Foucault, 1988d: 155) and of rendering abnormal and unnatural what has come to be normal and natural. Only through the generation of such historical ontologies can the critic create an aperture through which to view contemporary certainties as just so many 'historical coagulations' (Dreyfus and Rabinow, in Foucault 1984b: 350). It is this historicization of the gaps and fullness within discourse, therefore, which is of political significance. (For an alternative, though congruent reading, see Brown, 2001: 91–120.)

The construction of an historical ontology represents, for Foucault, a mode of critique that focuses on 'what we are saying, thinking, and doing' in order to identify the means of 'no longer being, doing, or thinking what we are, do, or think' (1984d: 46) as these things are revealed as historical events rather than natural occurrences or moral certainties. In other words, by examining the limits of the present, it is possible to think and move beyond them. As Foucault observes in *The Use of Pleasure*, the second volume of *The History of Sexuality*, 'the effort to think one's own history can free thought from what it silently thinks, and thus enable it to think differently' (1985: 8-9). Part of this process involves what Foucault terms, in 'Critical theory/intellectual history', a 'diagnosis' of the present (1988e). Such a diagnosis,

> does not consist in a simple characterization of what we are but, instead – by following lines of fragility in the present – in managing to grasp why and how that-which-is might no longer be that-which-is. In this sense, any description must always be made in accordance with these kinds of virtual fracture which open up the space of freedom understood as a space of concrete freedom, i.e. of possible transformation. (Foucault, 1988e: 36)

The work of critique involves, therefore, a double movement. First, there is the unveiling of the historical nature of discourse and its constructions, which involves, among other things, 'pointing out on what kinds of assumptions, what kinds of familiar, unchallenged, unconsidered modes of thought the practices we accept rest' (Foucault, 1988d: 154). Second, there is the putting to 'the test of reality, contemporary reality' that historical inquiry in order to identify the points both where change is possible and desirable and the form that it should take (Foucault, 1984d: 46). It covers both the moment of deconstruction of the historical present and the moment of the creation of something new: transgression of the limit. Genealogy thus focuses on opening up spaces in the present so that non-hegemonic voices may begin to articulate themselves and create a new future.[6] These may be voices silenced in the present or they may be new voices, which have yet to emerge. Either way, genealogy on my reading is concerned, first, to demonstrate how, historically, certain voices, ideas, discourses and truths come to be viewed as natural or legitimate. Second, through a process of problematization,[7] it generates a practical critique capable of engendering change.

The doubled process of critique that Foucault sketches is not one that is limited to questions of subjectivity, although the interdependence between the subject and the social ensures that questions about subjectivity are potentially always implicated in such work. 'Society' is potentially contested by it. Since the social is an historical effect, its contours also may be challenged and changed. The social does not represent reality in an absolute sense nor does it have an inherent character or self-presence; it is only ever constructed. In this regard, as Mouffe points out, 'any social objectivity is ultimately political' (2000: 99; see also Mouffe, 1994). It too is open to denaturalization and, *crucially*,

119

thereby to transformation. For Foucault yokes the two together. In this his sentiments coalesce with those of Ebert:

> For it is through the struggle over theory, the critique of the limits and uses of existing modes of knowing and the effort to construct new frames of intelligibility, that we can produce emancipatory knowledges (rather than merely subversive pleasures) and thus generate the new subjectivities necessary to transform the world as it is. (Ebert, 1993: 32)

There is, after all, no point in a critique that fails to open up the space for change. Critical thinking generates such material effects; potentially at least it spawns new ways of being, becoming, doing and saying, new subjects and new 'realities'.

Discussing the hegemony of discourses of heterosexuality in the construction of gender, Teresa de Lauretis echoes this view of the productivity of the gaps and fissures within discourse: *'the terms of a different construction of gender also exist, in the margins of hegemonic discourses'* (1987: 18; see also Probyn, 1993). These non-heterosexual terms, while less visible or obvious, have a part in the construction of heteronormativity but also suggest the possibility of change. They hint at feminism's work to create 'new spaces of discourse' written from a different perspective to that which dominates – 'a view from "elsewhere"' (de Lauretis, 1987: 25). This view from elsewhere is a view from the 'blind spots, or the space-off' of discourse, from the 'social spaces carved in the interstices of institutions and in the chinks and cracks of the power–knowledge apparati' (ibid.: 25). The term 'space-off', taken from film theory, offers a suggestive image of what is meant by operating interstitially: it is 'the space not visible in the frame but inferable from what the frame makes visible' (ibid.: 26). Put differently, it is virtual rather than actual. Political practice aimed at the interstices of discourse *and practice* works as a form of liminal critique insofar as it moves back and forth across the boundaries that inscribe dominant forms of subjectivity.[8] This is not a movement into the 'real' world outside of discourse nor is it a movement of science against ideology or a movement prompted by the slippage of signifiers (différance). Instead, it is a movement *within* discourse to the implied, to the as-yet-unthought, to what Hennessy and indeed Foucault might term the unsaid (*non dit*). It is this movement that, for de Lauretis, signals the possibility not only of counter-practices but also of new kinds of community; it is transformative. Or, as Biddy Martin observes, Foucauldian deconstruction is 'off-center, out of line ... It is not the point of an imagined absolute otherness', rather it is 'an "alterity" that understands itself as an internal exclusion'. And, she continues, 'it is possible' from such a perspective 'to grasp and restructure the organization of our bodies, psyches, and lives through discourse' (Martin, 1988: 10). Critique, viewed in this way as a particular critical posture towards the present that opens up the virtual spaces within discourse, in particular, and within the field of power relations, in general, not only facilitates but is vital to practical intervention and political action.

Critical thinking as practised by Foucault, Martin, and de Lauretis suggests, I propose, a mode of critique that *is* consonant with the demands of both Ebert and Hennessy for an explanatory and transformative feminist political analysis. Indeed, there is a strong parallel here between Hennessy's form of resistance postmodernism and the mode of critical thinking just sketched. Change is generated for Hennessy because of the ability of symptomatic reading to isolate cracks in ideology, to revive the *non dit* of the text. In the case of genealogy, reference is also made to the presence of fractures, at once present but not actual, that create the conditions for an interrogative relationship with the present which, in turn, produce space for change. This interrogative relationship, by exposing the mechanisms that have been used to naturalize factors in the present, is able to de-naturalize them by revealing them as aleatory effects of chance and contingent phenomena. It historicizes them. By disclosing these virtual fractures, a breach is generated for potential political transformation; what Foucault terms the work of 'concrete freedom'. So resistance postmodernism and the kind of critical thinking I am advocating are closely aligned; both regard the fissures in existing discourse as a necessary precondition for critique and thus for transformative change. The difference is that, for Hennessy, ideology (both hegemonic and counter-hegemonic) is necessarily connected to the organization of productive life, whereas in my Foucauldian account, discourse is not. Moreover, the shape that change takes, for Foucault, is not logically entailed by genealogy nor can it be deduced from any condition in the present (Brown, 2001: 119). Change is, rather, the outcome of specific opportunities and different modes of political creativity, working at the virtual fractures that trace across and through the present.

An important question concerning the truth is raised by approaches that historicize the present: can truth also be historicized and, if so, what does this mean about the relation between critique and truth? Feminists are presently divided in this debate between those who reject the idea of truth as a metaphysical reality and those who hold onto truth as the ground of feminism. The former see truth as implicated in power relations, such that neutral 'authoritative views' actually express the values and ideas of the dominators (Fraser, 1989: 181). The latter, by contrast, see truth as innocent of power, an impartial tool serving the interests of all. In the following section, therefore, I ask: what is at stake in contending that truth is political? In order to begin to answer these questions, I start by sketching briefly feminist approaches to truth. This is not my primary focus, however, for I am more interested in how the idea of the subject-in-process connects with how truth is conceptualized. My aim is to show that the same critical method outlined above can usefully be applied to truth claims.

The Politics of Truth

The nature of feminism's connections to power and truth has varied considerably. Feminists have exposed as partial and perspectival the truth-claims of the dominant traditions within Western social, political and philosophical thought. Feminist authors have written extensively on the 'malestream' nature of that thought; on the hierarchy of gendered dualisms that sustain it; and on the exclusion from it of women's ways of knowing, writing and existing.[9] In these ways, feminism attuned itself to the way power and truth intersect in phallocentric theory. This disposition, however, did not necessarily translate into a general view that all truth is power-invested; indeed, the initial aim of feminist epistemological work was to resolve the problem of partiality and perspectivism by seeking better (less partisan) ways of validating truth. Feminists thus sought a 'successor science' (Harding, 1986, 1991), 'one that better reflects the world around us than the incomplete and distorting accounts provided by traditional social science' (Harding, 1987b: 187).

In the course of this search, two main strands of feminist epistemology have emerged. The first, feminist empiricism, contends that androcentrism is eliminable from academic inquiry through closer adherence to the norms of scientific methodology. 'Good' science needs to replace 'bad'. At the same time feminist standpoint theorists, of radical, socialist and Marxist feminist hue, proposed an alternative process. Echoing the Marxian idea of 'consciousness', standpoint feminists contended, initially at least, that women's experiences like those of the proletariat within Marxism offered them privileged access to the truth.[10] Nancy Hartsock in her now classic formulation of this position, thus argued that 'An analysis which begins from the sexual division of labor ... could form the basis for an analysis of the *real* structures of women's oppression' (1987b: 175, my emphasis). Such an approach would allow the analyst to 'go beneath the surface of appearances to reveal the *real* but concealed social relations' (ibid.: 175, my emphasis). Women's lives create a privileged vantage point from which to see through the oppressive veneer of patriarchy. Like feminist empiricism, standpoint theory concurs with the basic tenets of the scientific approach 'for it still accepts the existence of a "true reality" and the

122

methods of science as the means to establish it' (Stanley, 1990: 27). Both retain, therefore, a commitment to the possibility of access to the Truth per se and both share the belief that objective knowledge is possible. Feminist knowledge is, additionally, privileged by both as being better and more progressive than masculine knowledge. Almost as soon as these views were expressed, however, criticisms were raised.

Standpoint, in its earliest formulations at least, usually presumed that women were a unified and stable category and that difference could thus be ignored or downplayed. It was, as might be expected, sharply criticized for its partiality. Reformulating standpoint from a difference perspective had a number of important implications. The logic of standpoint potentially entails infinite regression: that is, since the most marginalized in any society are those most able to see society's faults, including its structures of oppression, then only knowledge generated from their perspective is true knowledge. This involves, therefore, a quest for those who *are* the most oppressed, a quest that for Donna Haraway involves endeavouring to find what she calls 'a "full" and total position' from which epistemological claims can be made. This entails 'the search for a fetishized perfect subject of oppositional history, sometimes appearing in feminist theory as the essentialized Third World Woman' (Haraway, 1991c: 193). In other words, ontology takes priority over epistemology. It is the ontological validity conferred by marginalization and exclusion that guarantees the validity of the epistemological claims that are made. Given the onslaught in poststructuralist quarters on ontology, it is not surprising that epistemology also came under scrutiny. Here Haraway's idea of 'situated knowledges', her term for her own unique blend of radical constructivism and feminist critical empiricism, is important, not least because in addition to taking difference seriously it engages with these poststructuralist ideas.

Rejecting the opposition that is often appealed to between relativism and totalization, both of which for Haraway 'deny the stakes in location, embodiment, and partial perspective', she champions the potential of radically constructivist feminist science (ibid.: 191). 'Situated knowledges' do not imply a relativist 'way of being nowhere while claiming to be everywhere equally', rather, they refer to 'partial, locatable, critical knowledges sustaining the possibility of webs of connections called solidarity in politics and shared conversations in epistemology' (ibid.: 191). Haraway's rejection of a standpoint feminism grounded in ontological certainty does not translate into a simple endorsement of the idea that if there is no absolute basis for truth, then all truth claims must be equal. Rather, it implies that since all knowledge is partial and motivated, one needs to be critical of all and any knowledge claims. It is for this reason that Haraway contends that feminist situated knowledges are forms of knowledge that centre both responsibility and critical inquiry. As she notes of such knowledge in relation to oppressed groups: 'the standpoints of the subjugated are not "innocent" positions' exactly because such standpoints recognize the 'critical and interpretative core of all knowledge' (ibid.: 191). Or as she puts it earlier in the same piece, 'All knowledge is a condensed node in an agonistic power field' (ibid.: 185); it is all radically and historically contingent (ibid.: 187) and politically invested. Seeing from the stand-point of the oppressed is not a matter of ontology but entails an 'optics of the politics of positioning' (ibid.: 193). Vision is key and 'vision', for Haraway, 'is *always* a question of the power to see – and perhaps of the violence implicit in our visualizing practices' (ibid.: 192; see also 194). In other words, those who make truth claims never do so from a posi-tion of complete objectivity. They are always located in a particular place at a particular time and governed by a determinate set of con-ventions. It is their ability to recognize this that is important for it implies, for Haraway at least, the potential of connection with others and the potential of 'objective knowledge'. The 'split and contradictory self' (entailed by the crisis of the unified subject), as Haraway under-stands her, can only ever see from a mediated position (there is no fal-lacy here of 'immediate vision') and, as such, must rely on the vision of others in order to overcome the idea of one-dimensional knowledge. Unlike some other writers, Haraway holds onto the idea of objective knowledge but it is a radically reformulated notion of objectivity. As she notes: 'a scientific knower seeks the subject position not of iden-tity, but of objectivity; that is, partial connection' (ibid.: 193). She can never merely identify with other subjects – since all vision is partial – but she can engage with them, converse with them, and thus connect with them. Critical optical positioning is the only way to generate objective knowledge, a knowledge that is multidimensional through and through.

Although there is some ambiguity, to my mind, about the extent to which Haraway lets go of the possibility of the truth (which seems now to be a composite of knowledge derived from competing visual posi-tionings),[11] her deconstruction of the link between ontology and knowl-edge points to an important moment of convergence with other forms of poststructuralist work. The challenge to, or rather politicization of, ontology by poststructuralists, also necessarily implies a challenge to epistemology. If subjects are the effects of particular discourses, insti-tutions and practices, then the knowledge that these subjects have, far from being universal (or universalizable) must be particular and local-ized. One way to establish this is to subject such truth claims to criti-cal interrogation. It is to recall Fraser's injunction to historicize: an historical ontology implies historical conditions of possibility for the positing of truth claims. Instead of following the route opened up by Haraway which is to find ways of validating feminist knowledge claims against those of others (an important task in itself), other critics have attended to the consequences for conceptualizations of the truth of accepting that the relation between truth and power is constitutive rather than oppositional. In place of discerning generalizable modes of grounding the truth, they have charted the mechanisms by and through which particular truths are established, maintained, reinforced and, potentially, subverted. They have produced genealogical analyses of the kind outlined in the last section.

Many of the theories examined in this book rely upon a reconfigured understanding of this link between truth and power. Indeed, far from categorizing truth as some kind of transcendent guarantor of particular assertions, facts or claims, truth is understood, by many, as what Foucault calls a 'thing of this world' (1980c: 131), an effect of discourses, language and practices. In this respect, the kinds of structures, statements and conditions that govern what counts as truth at any one juncture are themselves historically and culturally specific. Knowledge, that is, is a matter of power and politics. Truth claims are generated by certain constellations of discourses, practices, and institutions and they secure particular effects in the world. They determine whose voice matters in a specific context; they govern what qualifies as legitimate knowledge and what is bogus; they set the boundaries between 'truth' and 'falsity'. This delimitation of the field of knowledge and who can legitimately acquire and transmit knowledge is predicated on forms of disqualified or subjugated knowledges; that is, forms of knowledge that emerge in ways that are seen to be illegitimate and/or are uttered by those discounted from rightly uttering knowledge (and here, of course, there is an affinity with Haraway's idea of a positional optics). Such an approach shifts inquiry away from epistemology understood as a theory of the *general* grounds, methods or conditions that generate truthful knowledge claims (who knows, what can be known, how is it known) to what Michèle Barrett describes as the 'processes by which the effects of truth are secured' (1991: 143); that is to the production of knowledge claims and their effects in determinate and conditional contexts. This process is equally appropriate for the truth claims of the dominated as for the dominators. The emphasis for practitioners is thus on the historical contingency and aleatory conditions of possibility for the generation of truth effects: on their partiality, localization and temporary foreclosure of alternatives. Acknowledging that truth is 'discourse dependent', as Flax puts it (1993: 138), does not, however, entail consequentially the idea that such truth is relative. Relativism is, as Susan Hekman has argued (and as Haraway also noted), part of the Enlightenment opposition between absolutism and relativism

125

that discourse critics refuse (1990: 152–3). Indeed, what seems to occur in the politics of truth production is an agonistic battle between the two poles, a battle that reveals the politics of truth production.

Where the Enlightenment (or, its dominant tradition at least) held that truth was both uninfected by power and prejudice, and was also empowering,[12] discourse critics posit in varied and often very distinctive ways a conception of knowledge predicated upon a 'highly politicised' relation between truth and power (Barrett, 1991: 139), leading Flax to proclaim the 'end of innocence' (1993: 131–47). The implications for feminism of a mode of conceptualizing truth that involves the additional step of feminism acknowledging its own will to power are profound. First, it means, I suggest, that feminism needs to abandon the dichotomies that structure Enlightenment thinking: power and truth, prejudice and neutrality, domination and emancipation, corrupt knowledge and innocent knowledge and see them for the co-implicated entities that they are. Second, as Flax recognizes, justificatory strategies based on so-called neutral knowledge must be displaced by justifications based on political demands (a position hinted at, if not explicitly developed in Haraway's idea of an optical politics of positioning). In other words, since truth is itself fragile and uncertain, feminist demands for justice or democracy need to be grounded in politics. Next, feminists must take responsibility for their own desire for power rather than abdicate it on the grounds of epistemological certainty (Flax, 1993: 144–7; Haraway, 1991c). If feminism thinks in terms of, what Foucault calls, a '"general politics" of truth', that is, 'the types of discourses which it [society] accepts and makes function as true' (1980c: 131), then the nature of feminist knowledge claims changes. Instead of searching for a method that could establish absolute, final truth, feminist work would self-consciously recognize its own contingency and partiality; it would, as Haraway implies, become ultra-reflexive. In this way it bolsters its responsibility to others. Instead of a firm belief in truth per se, it implies accepting the fact that all truth claims endeavour to secure particular (political) effects in the here and now. Far from feminist truth being more innocent and purer than preceding malestream versions, all truth claims, including feminist ones are contingent.

In *Whose Science? Whose Knowledge?* Sandra Harding proclaims that 'the right to define the categories through which one is to see the world and to be seen by it is a fundamental political right' (1991: 252). Although this process of definition is tied, for Harding, to the possibility of objective truth about the world, the sentiment driving her assertion is nevertheless suggestive. If truth itself is an historical phenomenon, then it means following the logic of the earlier sections, that it is possible to generate a new politics of truth by exposing its historicity, although the contours of this new politics of truth remain provisional and cannot be determined in advance. What genealogical inquiry reveals is the conventionality and artifice of historically specific and contingent truth claims and the part they play politically, economically, and socially in maintaining different forms of hegemony. What it opens up is the space for thinking differently about the truth, for producing an alternative reality of truth. Who, in this context, knows what contingent events might lead to a reconfiguration of the politics of truth? This does not mean that appeals to the truth cannot be made in order to validate particular claims. Much in the way that appeals have been made to the idea of stable subjectivity (to recall my claims from Chapter 3), there may be strategic reasons for so doing. It is, nevertheless, an inescapable fact that certainty about truth has corroded under its intense scrutiny by feminists and others, and in this context one effect of the historicization of truth may be its displacement by other forms of justificatory strategy as the basis of feminist calls for recognition, rights and equity.

Conclusion

I began this chapter by pondering the question of *how* it was possible for feminism to interrogate and resist the operations of power. What mechanisms, in other words, would such feminism have at its disposal for contesting limiting practices and for changing them? Contrary to the claims of Ebert and Hennessy, I contended that critical genealogical thinking could generate space for, and indeed could foment, change, including in respect of truth. Critical genealogy is, as I outlined it, itself a *political* intervention in the present that has the capacity to reshape both our understanding of present 'reality' and the material present. This model of critique does not formulate a politics; it creates an opening for one. In demonstrating that the present is an historical present, a construct of chance and contingent events, critique denaturalizes the present. This denaturalization, in its turn, can prompt not only a disruption of the familiar and everyday but also, and more importantly, a reordering of that reality. The shape that this transformed reality takes, however, is unknowable and unpredictable in advance. While materialist feminism appears to hold onto the idea that transformative change is necessarily progressive change in some sense, that comfort is not possible from this other perspective. As I show in the next chapter, this does not mean that it is not possible to plan and co-ordinate political action but it does mean that the broad effects of this action cannot be fixed ahead of their implementation. In order, therefore, to examine in more detail the politics of denaturalization engaged by the examination of the gaps and fissures that cross-cut contemporary practices, discourses, ideologies and norms, I turn to one of the most influential of such accounts: the politics of parody. My aim: to consider its effectiveness.

Notes

1 I am using the terms 'ludic postmodernism' and 'resistance postmodernism' in this chapter in order to locate my remarks within the context of the debate established by Ebert and Hennessy. As indicated previously, I think the terms are over-general and reductive, particularly in terms of Ebert's use of them.

2 Hennessy is more circumspect in her scope, concentrating on selected post-Marxists (Foucault, Laclau and Mouffe and Kristeva), thus her analysis is more attuned to the specificity of their respective positions.

3 This might include certain presumptions, for instance, about what men and women are like, how they should behave, and so on.

4 The Real for Hennessy is not the same as Lacan's version of the Real, which she sees as posited 'in terms of an individualized metaphysical emptiness or fullness – death or *jouissance*' (1993: 146, n. 7).

5 By dis-identification Hennessy does not mean a simple reversal of position (akin to reverse discourses) but to the 'disruption and re-arrangement of the preconstructed categories [i.e. naturalized assumptions] on which the formation of subjects depends'. In other words, it allows for sweeping transformation of the social order by 'a counterhegemonic collective subject' (1993: 96).

6 It is different from forms of feminist historiography that have attempted to retrieve the voices of those (such as women) hidden from traditional historical narratives. For an account that does interpret genealogy in terms of such retrieval, see Quinby (1997).

7 By problematization, Foucault means the process that makes 'possible the transformations of the difficulties and obstacles of a practice into a general problem for which one proposes diverse practical solutions' (1984a: 389; see also Foucault, 1985: 11; 1991: 76–8; and Rajchman, 1992: 220). In typical Foucauldian fashion, the line of causality is not unilinear (from problematization to practice) but bi-linear (even multiple): just as problematization can prompt alternative practices, so too can practices prompt further problematization.

8 It is significant that de Lauretis (like Foucault) does not see critical work as functioning only at the level of the text as Ebert and Hennessy imply. It is also work in/on institutions and in/on the field of power relations.

9 The classic account of this is clearly Lloyd (1984), but see also Nye (1988); O'Brien (1981); Okin (1980); and Pateman (1988, 1989).

10 On feminist empiricism, see, for instance, Harding (1987b); Millman and Kanter (1975). On feminist standpoint theory, see Collins (2000); Harding (1987b, 2000); Hartsock (1987b, 2000); Hekman (2000b, 2000c); Ramazanoglu with Holland (2002); and Smith (2000).

11 It is unclear to me exactly what the mechanisms would be for adjudicating between or balancing alternative knowledge of the same situation. While it is clear that no one

can be in all positions of subjugation and/or domination at once and as such cannot have knowledge of all those positions at once, it is unclear how 'connection' between split subjects works to generate objective knowledge.

12 That is, that truth is neutral insofar as it does not serve the interests of specific groups nor seek to advance partial and perspectival claims about the world. It is empowering in the sense that armed with the truth we can overcome prejudice, inequity and oppression by showing that it is mistaken; it becomes a source for political struggle. For a similar argument, see Flax (1993).

seven

politics and parody

In the Preface to *Gender Trouble*, Judith Butler declares:

> As a strategy to denaturalize and resignify bodily categories, I describe and *propose* a set of *parodic* practices based in a performative theory of gender acts that disrupt the categories of the body, sex, gender, and sexuality and *occasion their subversive resignification and proliferation beyond the binary frame.* (1990a: xii, my emphasis)

She claims to offer, that is, a parodic strategy capable of disrupting the reigning sex–gender hegemony. That strategy is the focus of this chapter. What precisely does it entail? Does it imply, as some have contended, a politics of dressing-up? Should we take it to mean that we can choose our genders willy-nilly? Or, is what seems to be a permissive politics actually more constrained? In order to answer these questions, I pick up two particular threads of argument from earlier in this book. I return to the account of performativity sketched in Chapter 1 in order to flesh out how it relates to understanding the interconnections between sex and gender. I also link parody to the theory of agency developed in Chapter 5 by demonstrating how parody is predicated upon, or perhaps more accurately prefigures (since, chronologically, *Gender Trouble* precedes *Excitable Speech*), the possibility of political catachresis.[1] The focus of my exploration of catachresis in Chapter 5 was how words that wound could be re-appropriated, even expropriated. In this chapter, I extend that discussion to the question of how to trouble gender. I examine, therefore, the possibilities for transforming and/or transgressing the normative materialization of bodies as male or female, heterosexual or homosexual generated by the confluence of a series of discourses and practices. This is not simply, however, a chapter about Butler. I also consider the work of a number of other writers who have taken parody as their starting point. These writings are of particular interest insofar as they reveal the importance of being very clear about the relationship pertaining between performativity and performance. As I argue, to reduce performativity to performance obfuscates the power relations that constitutively enable and limit performativity. Moreover, treating the two synonymously paradoxically reinstates the very conception of the subject put into question by performativity (that is, the sovereign subject). This discussion in turn raises questions about the political potential of parody. I argue that parody is not commensurate with drag as is often assumed, though drag is *an* instance of parody. There are, rather, multiple possibilities for disruption. The real concern for me is the issue of the efficacy of parody in those contexts where it occurs as a politics. This raises questions not just about outcomes (what can parody do?) but also about its relation to the political and whether parody can be a collective endeavour. I dispute the idea that performativity is either apolitical or that it advocates a hypervoluntarist politics, but as my examination of agency in Chapter 5 suggested, I consider the politics of performativity to be uncertain in its consequences. I start with the performative theory of gender.

Thinking about Gender

'Something's bothering you ...'

'You want to know what it is? It's that Julia, man.'

'Oh.'

'I mean, what is she? She a man or a woman?'

'Well, we keep sayin' "she". We wouldn't do that if we didn't think of her as female.'

'She ain't like no dude I ever met.'

'No.'

'Don't look like none, either. See her on the street, you never 'spect she anything but a woman.'

'You wouldn't.'

'Even up close you wouldn't. Lot of 'em, you can tell right away, but she'd fool you.'

'I agree.'

'Say a dude goes with her, what do that make him?'

'Probably make him happy.'

'Be serious, man. Would it make him gay?'

'I don't know.'

'If you was gay,' he [TJ] said, 'then you be wantin' men, right? So why'd you be lookin' to get down with someone that looks like a woman?'

'You wouldn't.'

'But if you wanted a woman,' he went on, 'why would you pick one's got a dick on her?' (Block, 1993: 191)

TJ's confusion and his search to find a way of categorizing both Julia and any male who desires her exemplify the drive to isolate what is real and determining about identity. Julia confounds TJ because he cannot pin her down: he cannot decide what she really is (or even if she qualifies as a 'she' in the first place). Julia's success in masquerading as a woman (attested to by TJ's claim that one would never suspect her of being anything else) is, of course, exposed as a masquerade by the presence of her penis. The 'reality' of her sexed body belies the illusory nature of her gender identity. She cannot 'be' female because her body is male. Yet without this anatomical knowledge, she appears female to those who see her. Moreover, because TJ cannot determine her gender, he also cannot make sense of the sexuality of any man who might desire her: would he be straight because he desires someone who looks female? Or, would he be gay, because Julia is really male? But, if he were gay, why would he want someone who looked like a woman rather than a man? Julia confounds all the binaries that make TJ comfortable in the world: male and female, straight and gay, and reality and illusion. (Compare TJ's reaction to that of Matt Scudder, his interlocutor, who seems nonplussed both by Julia and the questions about sexuality and desire raised by her.) Julia, to borrow from Judith Butler, puts into crisis 'the *reality* of gender' (Butler, 1999: xxiii). She threatens the naturalized presumption that body morphology, indeed body dimorphism, grounds gendered identity by disorganizing easy connections between anatomy, gender and sexuality. She demonstrates fictionally what Butler's work argues theoretically: the normalizing and prescriptive nature of gender.

One of the defining features of feminist work has been its attention to the issue of sex and gender. Challenging the formulation that 'biology is destiny', feminists proposed the alternative view that sex is natural, grounded in the biological body, whereas gender is cultural. It relates, that is, to the various attitudes, behaviours, styles of dress and social norms that determine whether one is masculine or feminine. Since gender is cultural, it also varies across time and across societies and is cut across by considerations of class, race, age, and so forth. As such, there is thus no direct link back to the sexed body. In *Gender Trouble*, Butler offers a critique of this dominant mode of reasoning about sex and gender. Through detailed readings of a number of leading feminist thinkers (including Kristeva, Witting, and Irigaray), Butler contends that sexual difference feminism is predicated upon a heterosexual presumption that limits the meanings of gender to conventional notions of masculinity and femininity and, in the process, occludes other minority expressions of gender. This heterosexual presumption relies on two claims: the first relates to gender, the second to sex.

Although contesting the idea that sex pre-determines gender identity, sexual difference feminists, Butler argues, nevertheless hold onto the idea of a binary gender system (where masculinity opposes femininity in the way that male opposes female). This incorporates the idea that there is a direct mapping between sex and gender such that femininity is connected to the female body and masculinity to the male. As such, gender operates far more restrictively that a purely cultural conception might allow, where potentially there could be more genders than sexes and where masculinity could easily accrue to female bodies and vice versa. This presumption reveals a second problem: the failure to historicize sex. Sex, that is, is assumed to be natural and immutable, without history. If, however, sex is an historical construction, then it cannot be categorially distinguished from gender for both are cultural (in the senses just noted). This means that it cannot be conceived as the prediscursive surface upon which gender writes. Butler, however, goes further: sex, she contends, is itself a gendered concept. It is the cultural apparatus of gender that produces binary sex and it does so in a way that normalizes certain bodies, genders and sexualities and pathologizes others. This is where the mechanism of *compulsory* heterosexuality fits; it produces a specific relationship between sex, gender and desire in which gender follows from sex, and desire follows from gender. Furthermore, heterosexuality as a regulatory ideal negates those 'gender discontinuities' in which 'gender does not necessarily follow from sex, and desire, or sexuality generally, does not seem to follow from gender' (Butler, 1990a: 135–6). A man who desires a man, a woman who desires a woman, or a man who desires a woman with a penis (to return to my opening example) cannot be accommodated within this matrix, except as abnormal.

A crucial implication of Butler's claim that heterosexuality is a fiction produced through practices and discourses is, of course, to challenge the idea that any individual's sexual identity reveals the 'truth' about them. This returns us to the account of performativity outlined in Chapter 1. As I indicated then, what appears to be the truth of identity is, actually, the effect of repeating over time a series of gestures and acts. They create the *impression* of an essential gendered identity but there is no essential gender identity underpinning them (ibid.: 138). The gendered subject is thus not established through a single constitutive act; any and every impression of gendered identity is achieved through the process of (re)-citation. One never 'is' one's gender, only in a perpetual and uncertain, though inescapable, condition of 'doing' gender, of repeating the acts and gestures that produce and sustain the notion of gender identity. This need for repetition also means that the potential for failing to produce a coherent or convincing gendered identity is ever present. Indeed, what Butler terms the 'temporal and contingent groundlessness of ... [the] "ground"' of gender identity is revealed precisely through an 'occasional *dis*continuity' in performance (ibid.: 141). This is where Butler's account of drag has bearing.

Drag, for Butler, exposes the fallacy of the dominant belief in an original or primary gender identity. In drag, three distinct 'contingent dimensions of significant corporeality' are discernible, and played upon: anatomical sex (contingent maleness), gender performance (the feminine figure displayed in the impersonation), and gender identity (hetero- versus homosexuality). That drag can produce a coherent picture of woman discloses the *'imitative structure of gender itself'* (ibid.: 137). The recitation of 'heterosexual constructs in non-heterosexual frames', such as drag, 'brings into relief the utterly constructed status of the heterosexual original', exposing 'gay to straight *not* as a copy to the original, but, rather, as copy is to copy' (ibid.: 31). Butler's point is not that drag copies authentic femininity (as some would argue) but that it reveals *all* gender as only ever parody or simulacra (including femininity, whoever performs it). In this way, all gender enactment comprises a failure to 'become "real" and to embody "the natural"' (ibid.: 146). Drag is important in this context because it discloses vividly, through its dramatic denaturalization of the links between sex, gender and desire, the culturally fabricated nature of coherent gender in all its forms. There is no heterosexual original that straight men and women embody and that gay, lesbian, or transvestite subjects deviate from; the original is itself a mythical figuration. It is not the 'theatricality of the performative process' as it applies to drag that is key here but the fact that 'theatrical acts of mimesis circle back to the centre, to insist that all gender identification is constituted through the imitative process' (Campbell and Harbord, 1999: 229). What, then, does mimesis and the failure to become real mean for gender politics?

Strategies of Subversion: The Politics of Dressing Up

In the closing pages of *Gender Trouble*, Butler describes the 'critical task of feminism' in relation to the idea that gender is constructed. It is, she points out, 'to locate strategies of subversive repetition enabled by those constructions, to affirm the local possibilities of intervention through participating in precisely those practices of repetition that constitute identity and, therefore, present the immanent possibility of contesting them' (1990a: 147).

The task is thus 'not whether to repeat, but how to repeat or, indeed, to repeat and, through the radical proliferation of gender, *to displace* the very gender norms that enable that repetition itself' (ibid.: 148; see also 138, 146). But what does this mean? What kinds of strategies have the potential to displace hetero-normative gender? In order to address these questions and to contemplate the political efficacy of parody, I turn my attention away from Butler towards a range of writers who, drawing inspiration from her work, articulate what they perceive to be the political potential of drag.[2]

'If "drag" is the verbal shorthand for the performative use of gendered dress codes to subvert the hegemonic twinning of gender and sexuality, then we can speak', writes Gail Hawkes, 'of dress as performance, of women "dragging up as women". Or of men "dragging up as men".' To read such dressing up as a 'performance', Hawkes continues, not only repositions that dressing-up as 'playful' but it makes it harder to know anything authoritative about the subject of drag. The meanings of the chains 'the male/masculine/heterosexual, female/butch/lesbian, male/camp/homosexual, are not reversed but deliberately scrambled' (Hawkes, 1995: 269). Taking her cue from Butler's idea that all gender is imitative, Hawkes discerns in 'dressing up' the potential for queering gender identities so that one is left with a game of 'guess the sexuality(ies)' (ibid.: 269; see also Martin, 1992: 107). Hawkes's account certainly seems to represent the 'sort of feel-good gender discourse' found, as Elspeth Probyn notes, in the work of those drawing on Butler where it is assumed that '*we can have whatever type of gender we want*, and that there are as many genders as there are people, and that we wear our genders as drag' (1995: 79, my emphasis; see also Heinämaa, 1997: 21). If this were the case, then gender identities would surely proliferate, 'opening up', as Jackson comments, the prospect of 'a range of alternatives to hegemonic forms of patriarchal heterosexuality' (1995: 107). As Butler indicates in the preface to *Bodies that Matter*, however, her intention was never to offer a theory of gender that implied, 'one woke up in the morning, perused the closet or some more open space for the gender of choice, donned that gender for the day, and then restored the garment to its place at night' (1993a: x). Gender performativity is, rather, a matter of 'cultural survival' (Butler, 1990a: 139). Yet this permissive, celebratory reading of it circulated; the question is, why? My argument is that the main reason is because of the confusion that occurred concerning the relation between performativity and performance. By taking out of context Butler's remarks on drag, in particular, scholars turned a non-voluntarist account of agency and subjectivity into a voluntarist, even hyper-voluntarist, account.

Performativity and Performance: What's in a Word?

In *Gender Trouble*, Butler asks a particularly pertinent question: 'what kind of gender *performance* will enact and reveal the *performativity* of gender itself in a way that destabilizes the naturalized categories of

136

identity and desire?' (1990a: 139, my emphasis). It is here, in my view, that drag should be located – as a performance that exposes gender performativity.[3] Drag disjoins and re-assembles the connections between sex, gender identity and gender performance. But what does it mean to talk about drag in terms of performances and performativity as Butler does? Does it mean that subjects can instrumentally perform gender in ways of their own choosing or that they can act out some kind of gender 'masquerade'? Can they bring about a specific identity by their deliberate actions? Certainly, this is how some have read Butler, and I will examine a specific example of this shortly when I consider the case of Bell et al. Suffice to say, that this is not, in my view what is implied by a performative theory of subjectivity; at least, not of the kind offered by Butler.

Butler's account of performativity is, as already noted, indebted to the speech-act theory of J.L. Austin. One way of differentiating between performativity and performance might be to follow Austin in distinguishing between pure speech acts and parasitic speech acts. Pure speech acts refer to utterances issued in 'ordinary circumstances' while parasitic speech acts refer to theatrical or poetic uses of the same words, which are 'in a peculiar way hollow or void' (Austin, 1962: 22). It might, pursuing this interpretation, be possible, though with some difficulty I suspect, to distinguish gender performativity in 'ordinary circumstances' from parasitic performances: say, when someone who is ordinarily male drags up as a woman. Butler, however, follows Derrida rather than Austin in refusing such a distinction. She argues that ordinary speech-acts and their parasitic performances are underpinned by the same linguistic conventions that 'have traditionally worked to bind or engage certain kind of effects' (Butler, 1995b: 134–5). She uses, that is, Derrida's notion that performativity is intrinsically connected to citation and repetition. For a performative utterance to succeed, it has to conform to an iterable model. It is this model that underpins or 'codes' the performative. This applies to theatre just as much as to 'real life'. (The same linguistic conventions are cited, for instance, in a 'real' wedding as in a stage wedding.) Applied to gender, therefore, real life and theatrical performances are indistinguishable in terms of citationality. The 'real' woman and the man performing femininity are *both* reciting the same conventions.[4] Crucially, the biggest difference between Austin and Butler relates to how they conceptualize the subject. Austin regards agents as responsible for their utterances (which is why he seeks to exclude parasitic speech acts from consideration because they reduce or abrogate 'the agent's responsibility' [1962: 22]). He sees them, thus, as autonomous authors of their speech and actions. Butler does not.

In 'Critically queer' (1993b), Butler observes that a performance is a 'bounded "act"' that can be differentiated from performativity on the grounds that performativity: *'consists in a reiteration of norms which pre-cede, constrain, and exceed the performer and in that sense cannot be taken as the fabrication of the performer's "will" or "choice"'* (ibid.: 24). Butler clearly rejects the idea, therefore, that subjects are the authors of their actions. Performatively, there is no subject that precedes or enacts the repetition of norms rather the subject is the effect of their compulsory repetition. 'There is no "one" who takes on a gender norm'; the 'one' is produced by reiterating gender norms (ibid.: 23). Butler rejects the idea of gender as performance where this assumes the existence of a prior subject (see Butler, in Osborne and Segal, 1994: 33). Performing – doing – gender is neither an expression of a subject's will or the revelation of some gendered truth about them.[5] Even though performativity may acquire 'act-like status', this is an effect – of the dissimulated repetition of discursive conventions. The idea that a performer controls when and where they perform their gender – that they 'act' in a bounded way – is simply unsustainable. Doing gender is culturally compulsory; it is a form of reiteration vital to viable subjectivity.

Despite a wealth of confusion surrounding these two terms (per-formance and performativity), brought on in part by the way that the two terms are elided in Butler's own various uses of them and in part because of the complexity (and, some would suggest, counter-intuitive-ness) of the ideas involved, it should be clear by now that Butler refuses the idea of performance where this presupposes an autonomous subject. Just because she argues against the notion of gen-der as performance (or theatre), does not mean, however, that she repu-diates the possibility of theatricalizing gender. When theatricality is linked to attempts to oppose normalizing gender interpellations by tak-ing up and citing the terms that are used to denigrate or abject partic-ular groups, it is an example of the kinds of catachresis discussed in Chapter 5. It is *'theatrical* to the extent that it *mimes and renders hyper-bolic* the discursive convention that it also *reverses'* (Butler, 1993a: 232; see also Butler, in Osborne and Segal, 1994: 38). Hyperbolic gender performances occur because of the (performative) compulsion to do gender. Because the subject neither precedes its constructions, nor is fully determined by them, the potential always exists for reworking the terms of subjectification so as to expose its underlying heteronormative imperative. As Fuss puts it, 'to be excessively excessive, to flaunt one's performance as performance, is to unmask all identity as drag' (1995: 81n.). Fuss's remark brings us almost full circle back to drag and its potential (or otherwise) to expose homophobia. Since drag in Butler's writing is closely connected to parody (indeed, it is often written of in the same sentence), before attempting to assess the political potential of parody it is necessary to explore in more detail what is meant by parody.

The Ambivalence of Drag

When Butler talks of parody, she uses it to refer to the performative constitutivity of all gender identity, including especially that which is deemed most natural – heterosexuality. Parody, for Butler, is linked to the idea of mocking 'the very notion of an original' gender identity (1990a: 138). All gender is parodic in the sense that it is all imitative, but some forms are more parodic than others because that imitativeness is exposed. As the discussion of Butler's conception of agency in Chapter 5 demonstrated, the practices that produce gendered subjects are also the sites where critical agency is possible. In the gaps between the impossibility of identical recitation and the need for reiteration, there is the possibility of a 'failure to repeat, a deformity, or a parodic repetition' (ibid.: 141), a possibility that Butler declares may lead to 'gender transformation'. This is linked, in *Gender Trouble*, to the possibility of a 'new configuration of politics' where 'cultural configurations of sex and gender might then proliferate' and where the 'present proliferation' could be properly articulated in culturally intelligible discourses (ibid.: 149). This reconfiguration of the political appears to be predicated upon exposing the unnaturalness of binary sex, and thus denaturalizing gender. That is, in *Gender Trouble* at least, gender proliferation alone appears potent enough to produce a fundamental restructuring of sex and gender norms.

This optimism about the diversification of gender identity is visible in the article 'All hyped up and no place to go' (1994), by cultural geographers David Bell, Jon Binnie, Julia Cream and Gill Valentine. Citing Butler's work, they aim to explore what happens to the gendering, or rather the heterosexualization, of space when bodies that parody masculinity and femininity occupy that space. Their account focuses on the two such instances: the lipstick lesbian and the gay skinhead. I want to discuss the latter, the gay skinhead, since it reveals most clearly the problems in assuming that parody is *ipso facto* transgressive. According to the authors, during the 1990s the skinhead look became 'fashionable in gay London' turning into a popular 'form of gay "uniform"' (Bell et al., 1994: 34). More than this it represented a politically affirmative 'way of life': 'the gay skinhead', they claim, 'can be seen as a progressive identity' (ibid.: 35) because it 'consciously inhabits a publicly acceptable one which is, in fact, its enemy' (Bristow cited in Bell et al., 1994: 36).[6] In 'passing for straight', that is, the gay skinhead both challenges the idea that masculinity accrues only to 'straight' men and subverts heterosexual space; through it 'gay skinheads create a queer space in a heterosexual world, which is in itself empowering' (Bell et al., 1994: 37). But in what sense is passing subversive, or empowering? To whom is this queer space open or visible?

139

Bell et al. build their case by asserting, simplistically in my view, that the appropriation by gay men of a 'straight' image not only makes that image transgressive but also politically *progressive*. The evidence for this is unclear, however. In the example of drag that Butler offers, the performance denaturalizes gender by calling attention to its fabrication. It presents a theatricalization of gender through hyperbole. The gay skinhead subverts heterosexual space, however, precisely by not rendering visible the fabricated nature of his identity. This makes it harder to demonstrate that this instance of parody does anything to destabilize heterosexual norms since paradoxically its efficacy derives (in part, at least) from its invisibility, conjured through the believability of the 'straight' performance. Instead of de-naturalizing or de-idealizing the dominant norms of masculinity, I argue, it re-idealizes them. To many who encounter him, the gay skinhead may in fact *only* be legible as heterosexual.

There is an additional difficulty in assuming that the gay skinhead represents a progressive identity, which relates to the idea that his progressiveness resides in parodying another 'publicly acceptable' identity. On what grounds, and to whom is this identity acceptable? In the historical present, the skinhead is frequently associated in popular consciousness with neo-Nazism, racism and violence.[7] Given this, it is entirely possible that the gay skinhead may be interpellated by another subject not just as straight but, more specifically, as a straight racist; that is, as embodying a particularly aggressive form of masculinity. Citing the marches through London in response to the Spanner trial, in support of consensual gay sado-masochism, Bell et al. declare emphatically that the 'queer march is not a march of fake fascists taking place in a straight space' (1994: 38). Presumably the specific context of the march, in relation to the well-publicized trial, helps locate it on the terrain of gay rights but what happens outside of this collective encounter when a gay black man, for instance, sees the hypermasculine gay skinhead heading his way? As Lisa Walker notes, this image 'excludes black men from the [white male] ga(y)ze, the queer space created on the street amongst those "in the know", by not acknowledging that it could be dangerous for a black gay man to initiate construction of that space' (1995: 73; see also Kirkby, 1995). The gay black male, in other words, will not automatically know that the gay skinhead he sees is masquerading as a hypermasculine straight male in neo-Nazi garb. He may simply assume that he is a hypermasculine neo-Nazi with a violent racist agenda in mind. To simply propose that the skinhead's identity is progressive because he intends it that way will not suffice (Bell et al., 1994: 34).

Without dwelling too much on the analysis that Bell et al. offer here,[8] their conclusions concerning the subversiveness of the parodic gay skinhead reveal a number of issues relating to parody. To be sure, the gay skinhead is reciting a particular set of conventions not naturalistically associated with gay men; he is, of course, disrupting the often perceived association between homosexuality and effeminacy. His performance, thus, does support the idea of imitation central to Butler's theory. Within particular gay communities, it may even be recognized as hyperbolic, though for the reasons attested to above, not necessarily to those 'outside'. This example also indicates a point that was understated in *Gender Trouble*, which is that it is not only the denaturalization of heterosexuality that is secured through parody but also its perpetual *re-naturalization*. Indeed, it is this fact that undermines, just as it enables, the potential of parody to destabilize gender norms. Butler makes this link more forcefully in *Bodies that Matter* when she comments:

> The critical promise of drag does not have to do with the proliferation of genders, as if a sheer increase in numbers would do the job, but rather with the exposure or the failure of heterosexual regimes ever fully to legislate or contain their own ideals. Hence it is not that drag *opposes* heterosexuality, or that the proliferation of drag will bring down heterosexuality; on the contrary, drag tends to be the allegorization of heterosexuality. (1993a: 237)

It is no longer the upsurge in the number of genders that counts; it is what this upsurge discloses: the impossibility or 'inefficacy' of normative heterosexuality containing its own ideals. Subversion is now a consequence of 'working the weakness in the norms' generating heteronormativity (ibid.: 237). This is important.

The idea, common to readings of *Gender Trouble*, that dressing-up *tout court* would lead to a proliferation of genders and, therefore, to gender transformation is explicitly refuted in *Bodies that Matter*. The norms which form the matter of recitation 'taken not as commands to be obeyed, but as imperatives to be "cited", twisted, queered, brought into relief as heterosexual imperatives' may not be 'subverted in the process' (ibid.: 237; see also Butler, 2000b: 158). They may simply be re-idealized. This is what Bell et al. miss with the case of the gay skinhead: that his performance of hypermasculinity may not denaturalize heterosexuality. Instead by 'working in the context of these traditional categories [masculinity and femininity]', as Andrew Kirkby points out, 'gay or lesbian pastiches' of the kind prescribed by Bell et al. may only 'stretch the category of heterosexual normality rather than undermine it' (1995: 93). Since it is not possible to stand outside of gender, politically parody may actually reproduce what it seeks to displace, not least because 'the gender meanings taken up in these parodic styles are

141

clearly part of hegemonic, misogynist culture' (Butler, 1990a: 138). At best, drag is a, therefore, 'site of a certain ambivalence' (Butler, 1993a: 125), occasioned by the fact that it is a product of the same regime of power that it endeavours to oppose and to denaturalize. The price of this ambivalence is illustrated touchingly in Jennie Livingston's film, *Paris is Burning*.

In the film, director Livingston documents the annual balls held in Harlem, New York. Here black and Latino gays and transvestites compete to win prizes in categories such as 'Best Dressed Butch Queen', 'Executive Realness' and 'Miss Cheesecake'. According to the advertising blurb on the video, '*Paris is Burning* is a remarkable and moving portrait of disenfranchised individuals chasing the American Dream.' For the 'men' who participate, the balls offer an opportunity to be what they are prevented, for reasons of poverty, lack of education, homophobia and racism, from being in the outside world. As Dorian Corey (one of the participants) poignantly observes, dressing up is 'not a take-off or a satire. No, it's actually being able to be this.' The balls thus offer a world of phantasmatic promise. The performances in *Paris is Burning* aim not at the explicit denaturalization of gender norms but rather at as convincing an imitation of those norms as possible (though, of course, this imitation is nevertheless a denaturalization). They provide a comparative safe haven within which to expropriate heteronormative gender. As the plight of Venus Xtravaganza demonstrates all too starkly, however, when her ability to pass as a light-skinned woman in the outside world fails, she doesn't merely fail to win a prize; she is strangled to death. Although the film does not speculate upon the precise reasons for her death,[9] that death nevertheless points to the potential costs for those (knowingly or not) transgressing gender norms and thus threatening heteronormativity. As Butler herself makes clear in her commentary on the film, Venus Xtravaganza's death is the result of a social order 'that would eradicate those phenomena that require an opening up of the possibilities for the resignification of sex' (1993a: 131); that cannot, that is, countenance non-normative forms of sexuality. If, as Butler surmises, heterosexuality is not just an imitation of an unattainable, phantasmatic ideal, but also a '*panicked* imitation of its own naturalized idealization' (1991: 23), then how much more panicked and panic-inducing are those imitations that serve to denaturalize and de-idealize it? When those who advocate drag proclaim it as an unambiguously positive and productive form of politics, they disregard or, at least, underemphasize 'when, where and to whom gendered performances are either "passable" for straight or readable as queer' (Walker, 1995: 71) and the consequences that might attach to failed performances and failed readings.

If there is no necessary connection between drag and subversion, does this mean that politically the dominant sex/gender system is unassailable? How, if at all, can heteronormativity be breached? As I have already stipulated in this chapter, one of the reasons for the overly optimistic gloss that some critics have put on Butler's notion of parody derives from a sense that actors can manipulate their gender identities at will and that this manipulation is enough to diversify gender in ways that denaturalize the dominant binary system. I have argued that this view is at variance with both the account of performativity that Butler posits and with her explanation of agency; with, that is, the idea that actors do not choose their gender, but that rather gender produces him or her through its performance. Given the ambivalence of parody (and drag), the fact that it may or may not challenge heteronormativity, is there anything that can be said definitively about the kinds of political activity that are subversive?

Political Performativity and its Incalculable Effects

In *Bodies that Matter*, Butler considers the ways in which the theatricalization of death in the practice of 'die-ins' helped to publicize an otherwise 'privatized' issue – AIDS (1993a: 233). By prompting the public to ask questions about the events symbolized in these performances (who was dying in them), Act-Up both raised public consciousness of AIDS and highlighted governmental failure to fund its research. The die-ins performed on the streets of New York by Act-Up are described by Butler, in a later interview, as not only 'extremely dramatic' and displaying 'shocking symbolization', but also as a 'renovation' of the conventions of other protest movements. They involve, she notes, a 'new adumbration of a certain kind of civil disobedience' (Butler, in Osborne and Segal, 1994: 38). A pre-existing mode of protest is here successfully resignified. This is important, for Butler further observes that:

> I think that we need to pursue the moments of degrounding, when we're standing in two different places at once; or we don't know exactly where we're standing; or when we've produced an aesthetic practice that shakes the ground. That's where resistance to recuperation happens. It's like breaking through to a new set of paradigms. (In Osborne and Segal, 1994: 38)

A practice that problematizes most graphically what we take for granted appears, from this quotation at least, to be that best able to resist instant re-incorporation to the dominant norms it opposes. By forcing a rethinking of those norms, it is able to destabilize them. Such

143

'transgressive reinscriptions', as Osborne and Segal call them, seem powerful indeed (1994: 38). But are they unequivocally so?

In 'Critically queer', Butler insists that what renders a performance subversive is that it 'is the kind of effect that *resists calculation*'. The reason for this is that the effects of discourse, as we saw in Chapter 5, are not bounded by particular acts of legislation, the utterance of specific statements, or by specific events. Those who generate these effects (whether through speech or writing) cannot control the 'reach of their signifiability', precisely because these productions are not 'owned' by them (1993b: 29). Unintended consequences will occur. Performatives will circulate in unexpected ways. The earlier gay skinhead example is a case in point. The deployment of certain signs by gay (white) men may be read by others, particularly black gay others, in way different to that intended and may, additionally, provoke all kinds of inadvertent and deeply troubling effects. Because discourse is not 'fully controlled by intention', the aims that *are* intended, can easily 'become subverted by other operations of power to effect consequences that we do not endorse' (Butler, 2000b: 158)[10] as well, presumably, as ones 'we' do (although questions remain about who 'we' are; see Chapter 8). Even 'transgressive reinscriptions' may, that is, be turned to other, non-transgressive ends. Indeed, it may only be in retrospect and with the aid of genealogical analysis of the kind outlined in the last chapter that it is possible to gauge how effective an intervention or an expropriative reinscription has been. Given the iterability of language, one crucial factor of course is, as noted earlier in this book, the extent to which a reinscription is able to break with its 'prior context' (Butler, 1997b: 147; see Chapter 5), for as Butler demonstrates in *Excitable Speech* context conditions though it does not foreclose the operation of any performative.[11] Decontextualization opens performatives up to other and to new signifying contexts.

Extrapolated to questions of political action in general, this reasoning implies that delimiting a context may also be important in conditioning and/or evaluating which goals and which actions might be most apposite at certain times and in certain places (for instance, appealing to a 'truth' of the self in order to claim legitimacy for one's sexual orientation as demonstrated in Chapter 2) though the inherent potential for a decontextualizing rupture impedes anything other than a provisional delimitation. My point is not, however, that Butler must furnish an account of these contextualized goals and actions or of more general aims and strategies (as a number of normative theorists aver). Quite the contrary: this would be to recuperate the ideal of the 'universal intellectual', to borrow from Foucault and Deleuze, the 'representing or representative consciousness' of the masses speaking 'the silent truth of all' (1973: 103, 104); the intellectual, that is, who prophesies, legislates and guides the actions and practical political endeavours of others. Rather, it is to see the process of planning and strategizing as an inherent part of the work of what might be better described as the 'specific intellectual' (to borrow once more from Foucault and Deleuze), the person who 'uses his [sic] knowledge, his competence and his relation to truth in the field of political struggle' (Foucault, 1980c: 128). In other words, the work of those who operate within the sphere of 'real, material everyday struggles' (ibid.: 126). It is here that political action is planned, and its subversive potential sketched even as it cannot be guaranteed; it is here that contexts are delimited, meanings provisionally halted, and breaks with past conventions plotted. This takes us back, I suggest, to the need for the kinds of critique considered in the last chapter, since intellectual work of the democratic kind envisioned for the specific intellectual is of necessity critical work. Critical reflection upon present practice provides the focus for future activity. Through identifying gaps and points of weakness in the hegemonic discourses and norms conditioning our lives, it is possible to identify where change may be possible (see Foucault, 1988c: 124). Exploiting these potential spaces *may* (or, may not) produce some form of alteration in power relations. Crucially, a critical attitude of this kind engenders a form of reflexivity that encourages constant interrogation of the effects and effectiveness, actual and possible, of particular goals, aims, tactics and strategies. This can be seen in Butler's discussion of gay marriage rights.

In 'Competing universalities', Butler debates the efforts of gay and lesbian movements to gain rights of marriage (2000b: 175–7). The rationale behind the campaign is simple: it is seen as an egalitarian move that extends citizenship rights to those currently denied them and it de-heterosexualizes marriage in the process. In other words, if such rights were granted, marriage could no longer be conceived in its current restrictive terms; that is, in terms of the union of male and female. Butler, however, is uncomfortable with the goal of marriage rights for gays and lesbians because the political campaign fails to problematize the institution of marriage itself. It reinforces, rather, the fact that particular legal benefits ought to accrue only to those with marital status (for instance, adoption rights, inheritance rights, and rights of hospital access). It also intensifies the distinction between those in state-approved relationships and those who are not, between legitimate subjects and illegitimate abjects. Operating in a similar manner to the reverse discourses discussed in Chapter 5, it presumes it is necessary to occupy the dominant norm in order to undermine or subvert it. Butler suggests, however, that political performativity need not operate in this way.[12] For the alternative to petitioning for the same rights (and duties) as heterosexual married subjects is to challenge the necessity of marriage as the basis of those rights in the first place. The only 'possible route for a radical democratization of legitimating effects would be to relieve marriage of its place as the precondition of legal entitlements of various kinds' (ibid.: 177). Instead of seeing the extension of marriage to non-heterosexual couples as a positive instance of the continuing universalization of rights, forcing the universal to resignify catachrestically as it were, Butler proposes dismantling the norm altogether.[13] This is 'performativity proper to refusal' in which what is reiterated is not marriage but sexuality 'beyond the dominant terms' (ibid.: 177), beyond marriage as the main form of human sexual organization.

To parodic or theatrical politics, Butler here adds a politics of refusal. It would be a mistake, however, to see either or both as exhausting the potential politics generated by performativity. Although the process of repetition grounding citationality underpins parodic politics and the politics of refusal (and surely other not-yet described forms), the point is, that for Butler (as for Foucault) 'politics has a character of contingency and context to it that *cannot be predicted at the level of theory*' (in Bell, 1999: 166, my emphasis). There is no single site 'from which to struggle effectively' (Butler, in Osborne and Segal, 1994: 38), nor a single mode of struggle. Political decisions are made 'in that lived moment and they can't be predicted from the level of theory' (Butler, in Bell, 1999: 167). Theory can help to sketch them, schematize them and even prepare for them by troubling received wisdom and casting doubt on naturalized assumptions but it cannot forecast what will happen and when. This is why the theory of gender performativity is not programmatic. It exposes the mechanisms through which change becomes possible but it does not legislate what those changes ought to be. It does not advocate as the only legitimate political strategy a politics of drag or, indeed, of anything else (refusal, appropriation, etc.). Context determines the mode(s) of political attachment and action. What the theory of gender performativity does highlight, however, is the potential ambivalence of all forms of political intervention. To this end, all politics contains an element of the unexpected as it aims to secure particular outcomes in a context of contestation. It is this that generates the possibility of moments of radical rupture within the present. It is this also that might scupper the best-laid plans of a political group. Far better, however, to try to act in concert to change things, even with the vagaries of politics and the uncertainty of its outcomes, than to hope that things will somehow improve of their own accord.

Conclusion

In her article, 'The professor of parody', Martha Nussbaum accuses Butler, and those influenced by her, of 'hip quietism' (1999). Butler's politics, for Nussbaum, are no politics at all. They fail to address 'mass movements of resistance or campaigns for political reform' and focus wrongly on 'only personal acts carried out by a small number of knowing actors' (Nussbaum, 1999). Butler's contention that the outcomes of political acts are incalculable, and may also be recuperable, is read by Nussbaum as a form of passive acceptance of the status quo. But what sense does it make to call quietist a theory that endeavours to interrogate the very ways in which gender norms are hegemonized and stabilized? What is the purpose of challenging those norms if not to demonstrate ways in which they might be contested? Can any theory actually guarantee that the strategies it proposes (the calls for legal reform that Nussbaum appears to favour) will succeed in producing the outcomes it desires, and only those, and only in ways that benefit those they were intended for? The answer is, surely not. What Butler demonstrates is the paradox that the conditions that actually generate heteronormativity are precisely those that create the possibility of change (of catachresis and resignification, of appropriation, expropriation and misappropriation) and that might jeopardize it. Nor, as I have shown earlier in this chapter, should the account of agency implicated in this paradox be misread as a form of hyper-voluntarism (as Nussbaum's remark that Butler's is a politics comprising 'only personal acts carried out by a small number of knowing actors' implies) where actors can, with volition (knowingly), change their gender to their own ends. The appearance of volition is itself an effect of the changes that occur rather than its cause.

What, then, of the charge of individualism? Certainly Butler does cite plenty of instances of individual insubordination – Rosa Parks and Antigone to take examples from Chapter 5 – but she also draws attention to collective acts: the activities of Act-Up, drag balls, and so on. The point is that just as performativity explains how individual gender identity is comprehended on a day-to-day basis as the reiterative effect of an historically specific ensemble of practices, gestures, and ideas, so too are collective identities explained: the lesbian 'we', the heterosexual 'we', and so on, themselves produced in and through a process of compulsory and in-identical recitation. There can, moreover, be no absolute universalization of the claims or political activities of any group – women, or gays and lesbians – of the kind that Nussbaum appears to desire, for the reason that 'the universal cannot be finally identified with any particular content' if the 'open-endedness that is essential to democratization' is to be secured (Butler, 2000b: 161).

Future democratic contestation, as Butler reads it, requires the constant deferral of the universal. This is what Nussbaum misses. To define the universal – by legislating particular political strategies as the only ones capable of securing a particular group's interest – goes against the grain of Butler's project. This is also what other writers overlook when they deduce a politics of drag or dressing-up from Butler's work as the only politics capable of shattering binary sex/gender. There is neither a single nor a guaranteed way of contesting heteronormativity. There is no common cause that unites all women or all gays or all lesbians or any other group, not even such notions as universal rights or citizenship, except in a very abstract sense. For what is meant by a right or by citizenship is as much a matter of political debate, division and contestation as anything else. Rather political positions, values, imaginations and judgements are all contingent; a 'matter of opportunity ... [and] limits' (Brown, 2001: 116).

As I stated at the outset of this chapter, my aim was to examine the relation between politics and parody. That relation is far more complex than often assumed by readers drawn to Butler's work. Parody is not synonymous with drag, though it is often taken to be; rather, all gender is, in some sense, parodic. This implies that all gender performances are just as capable of denaturalizing acts and gestures that are coded as 'natural' to one sex or the other as those identified as drag (where some form of cross-dressing is implied). This does not, however, imply that performances can be manipulated at will since this assumes a subject prior to the performance, which as I have demonstrated above, is at variance with an understanding of the performative subject. Subjects are effects of their performances, not the origins of them. What it does suggest, however, is the importance of activities that challenge how one reads and understands them, that force one to think. No acts, on this count, are inherently subversive. It is the degree to which they compel new possibilities of interpretation that indexes them as such. They are, furthermore, subversive only in certain determinate contexts, and these contexts change. This indeterminacy is not disabling; conversely it reveals the contradictory but productive nature of politics and democracy. Democracy does not entail achieving a specific set of goals once and for all; rather, it opens up the future, it does not foreclose it. Democratic subjects thus need to be vigilant to the ways in which subversive acts and norms may become domesticated, installing a new regime of power that operates its own exclusions and abjections. In the next chapter, therefore, I consider the politics of radical democracy. In particular, I explore the idea of inessential coalitions as a response to the radical insufficiency of conventional identity categories and their relation to the open-endedness of democratic struggle.

Notes

1 As in Chapter 1, my discussion of Butler makes selective use of her work. For a more extended and systematic treatment, see my forthcoming book *Judith Butler: From Norms to Politics*.

2 Drag in these accounts is usually construed not as *an* exemplar of parody but as *the* exemplar.

3 In *Bodies that Matter*, confusingly and unhelpfully, Butler refers to drag as 'an example of performativity' not performance (1993a: 230).

4 What separates the two are, of course, differently 'sexed' bodies. To use the body as the touchstone that determines real from fake performances, however, goes against the logic of Butler's thesis. Moreover, it would fail as a test for cases where male bodies are performing different sorts of masculinity or females performing different sorts of femininity.

5 This is not to deny the unconscious a role in the performative enactment of gender identities, though I do not have the space here to discuss what that role is. See Butler (1993a, 1993b, 1997a, 2000a), and Lloyd (1998–99).

6 The idea that sexuality is reducible to progressive lifestyle choice needs to be treated with caution. It ignores the material structures, and institutions that inaugurate and police gender and sexuality (Jackson, 1995).

7 The history of the skinhead look extends, of course, beyond its neo-Nazi incarnation. During the late 1960s and early 1970s one of the characteristics of the skinhead was his imitation of 'black' subcultures around ska and later reggae. A 'gay' appropriation of the skinhead style could be subversive if, to recall the discussion of catachresis from Chapter 5, it could render 'innocent' its current 'sullied' history.

8 I outline what I perceive to be additional problems with this analysis in Lloyd (1999).

9 The film leaves unclear whether the attack is racist or homophobic, prompted, that is, by the discovery that she is Hispanic not white, a biological male not a female, or because of some combination of the two. Given the importance of race in the film (what is emulated in the balls is affluent *white* America), Butler pays it too little attention. For an alternative reading discussing race, see hooks (1992b).

10 Interestingly, this quotation seems also to imply that aims that are intended may also be successful.

11 Although Butler in 'Critically queer' (1993b) contested the idea of demarcating contexts for effects on the grounds that it constitutes an attempt to prefigure the result of an action, this view is quickly (and, in my view, rightly) dropped. In fact, in *Excitable Speech*, she argues that one should endeavour to 'delineate a context' but that 'any such delineation is subject to a potentially infinite revision' (Butler, 1997b: 148). In the article on which part of this chapter is based, I examined changes in Butler's arguments from *Gender Trouble*, to 'Critically queer' and the later *Bodies that Matter* relating to parody/drag and, briefly, to context (Lloyd, 1999). The analysis I developed there did not extend to either *Excitable Speech* or *The Psychic Life of Power* and should not be taken to do so. Unfortunately, in a critical engagement with this article, Catherine Mills wrongly imputes to me certain views about *Excitable Speech* and *The Psychic Life of Power* that I

have never expressed or held (2000: 275).

12 The point is not that reverse discourses are not political – they clearly are – but that political performativity cannot be reduced to them.

13 It might plausibly be argued that extending marriage rights to gays and to lesbians might itself bring about a fundamental change in the nature of marriage, though while marriage is state-sanctioned, it would not necessarily reduce the state's role in its regulation.

eight

radical democracy and inessential coalitions

If, as I have argued throughout this book, identarian logic cannot provide the basis for collective politics, and if we cannot *assume* pre-given common cause or shared interests in the articulation of democratic demands, then what kinds of collective democratic politics are possible? I proposed in Chapter 3, that the fact that I, and other theorists, have cast doubt on the validity of pre-given identities as the basis of politics, does not evacuate identity of all conceptual or political value. There will be times when feminism can do no other than make demands in the name of women's needs or interests *but* these interests and needs should be seen as political constructions not entities existing prior to politics. In this chapter, therefore, I examine a number of accounts centring on the production of collectives and their goals. More specifically, I focus on coalitions as inessential political groupings, what Elam describes as 'the ungrounded politics of women's solidarity' (1994: 42). The meaning of coalition is crucial here. It is not sufficient to simply replace identity politics (in its unitary sense) with coalitions, if this just assumes assembling otherwise discrete groups whose identities are left unaffected by the process of coalescence. Nor is it sufficient to presume that beneath miscellaneous struggles there is some kind of underlying unity that grounds coalition work, such as a common history of oppression or the promise of liberation in the future (Elam, 1994: 69). So, after some introductory remarks about coalitions, I begin by exploring the idea of cyborg politics articulated by Donna Haraway. Starting from the idea that cyborg subjects are multiple, open, and impure, Haraway considers the kind of collective politics that cyborgs might generate. Taking 'women of colour' as an incidence of cyborg politics, I reflect on Haraway's account of its production as an inessential coalition. Relating this discussion back to my argument in Chapter 3, I show how a certain vagueness in Haraway's discussion of affinity (the basis of coalitions) is indicative, once again, of the agonism between constation and performativity. I then explore the ideas of Shane Phelan who, drawing on Haraway, raises questions about the tendency towards nationalism within identity groups. Examining Phelan's use of 'queer' as her example, I consider the tension exhibited within this collective politics between naturalizing identity and deconstructing it. I also explore Phelan's contention that a local politics is the most apt for inessential coalitions. One of the features of both of these accounts is the assumption that the 'we' of the coalition is not a given but an effect. In my final section, I consider another similar argument, that offered by Chantal Mouffe. Here I explore the role of articulation. This theory is important, first, because articulation foregrounds the mechanism whereby new political identities are forged, and second, because more explicitly than Haraway or Phelan, Mouffe ties her discussion to democracy. I end, therefore, with a brief discussion of radical democracy.

Coalitions

Katherine Adam, discussing the potential in the work of Hannah Arendt for a so-called 'self-interested practice of coalition discourse', observes that:

> Coalition work brings us face to face with the absence of universal truths, the danger of safe assumptions, the falsity of common sense – or the lack of any supposed common basis in reason or rationality that promises to simultaneously transcend and unite difference. Rather today's diverse political communities require approaches to discourse that will promote negotiation among divergent identities, histories and desires ... coalitions also seek to address differences without reifying them or falling into binary logics. (2002: 2)

The contention that coalitions offer feminism a mechanism for dealing with identity's complexity has a relatively long history within second-wave feminism. Here there are, at least, two divergent understandings of what coalition work means for identity.

When, the Combahee River Collective published 'A Black Feminist Statement' in 1978, one of its central messages was the need for coalition work with 'other progressive organizations and movements' as a way of dealing with interlocking systems of oppression (in Hull et al., 1982: 13). Likewise, Bernice Johnson Reagon in her 1983 article 'Coalition politics: turning the century' confronts the 'fear' and discomfort of coalition work, contending that it is nonetheless a vital 'survival' strategy when the exclusionary 'home' of separatism (hiding behind the 'red door' of sameness) turns into a barred room (1998: 242–53). Reagon is clearly attuned here to the shortcomings of a 'nationalist' conception of identity, arguing instead, as Mohanty notes, for 'survival, rather than shared oppression as the ground for coalition' (Mohanty, 1998: 264). The Combahee River Collective, by contrast, contend that the most radical form of political work is that 'embodied in the concept of identity politics', issuing 'directly out of our own identity, as opposed to working to end somebody else's oppression' (in Hull et al., 1982: 16). Where Reagon's conception of coalitions acknowledges the 'differences and potential divisions *within* political subjects as well as collectives' and accords coalition work a transformative capacity of some kind in respect of identity (Mohanty, 1998: 266), the Combahee River Collective emphasize the affirmation of identity. Coalitions are merely mechanisms for bringing people together, in their difference, in some kind of 'strategic alignment' over a particular issue (Phelan, 1994: 139).

Reagon's work, I suggest, prefigures in various ways some of the concerns motivating advocates of the subject-in-process: the anxious scepticism about the exclusionary nature of identity politics, the possibility of coalitions as a mechanism to move beyond the confines of identity politics, and the apprehension of those coalitions not in terms of 'deep similarity', as Anne Phillips observes, but of 'political process' (1998: 14). It hints at coalitions as practices capable of generating 'new identities, new agendas, new alliances, and new political forms' (Adams, 2002: 2).

Before I turn to Haraway's cyborg politics, I want to make one final prefatory remark. Interest group pluralism has formed one of the dominant paradigms for thinking about coalitions within democratic theory. Related to feminism, this translates to a concern with women's interests. Indeed, the identification between women (as identity) and interests is so strong that one often seems to be synonymous with the other; interests come to appear as 'compulsions – reflexes of desire' (Adams, 2002: 8). My argument in this book questions not only the assumption that political demands issue from pre-given group identities but also the characterization of democracy as the satisfaction of group interests, for if nothing can be taken for granted about groups, then neither can anything be taken for granted about interests. Both are forged in the crucible of politics. Interests thus, I propose, require reconceptualization in the light of identity critique.[1] They too are constructions, negotiable and open to reformulation and, like identity, they too may become reified to the degree that they appear to be natural.

Cyborg Politics

In 'A cyborg manifesto',[2] Donna Haraway asks: 'What kinds of politics could embrace partial, contradictory, permanently unclosed constructions of personal and collective selves and still be faithful, effective – and, ironically, socialist-feminist?' (1991b: 157). Without pursuing the needs explicitly of a socialist feminist agenda here,[3] Haraway's question is important. It reminds the reader that with the loss of ontological certainty entailed when the subject is conceived as in-process, the structure and grounding of feminist politics must necessarily change. This is a change, paradoxically, that must be able to accommodate the need for political unity in the face of the multiple 'dominations of "race", "gender", "sexuality" and "class"' in a context where '[n]one of "us" have any longer the symbolic or material capability of dictating the shape of reality to any of "them"' (ibid.: 157). If, as Haraway claims, 'the cyborg is our ontology; it gives us our politics' (ibid.: 150) then what precisely do 'cyborg politics' look like?

The cyborg, it should be recalled from Chapter 1, is a hybrid produced across a range of discourses, practices, and materials; it may be, among other things, simultaneously animal and human, machine and animal, human, machine and animal, even male and female (Alaimo, 1994: 140). It stands, therefore, as a metaphor for subjective existence as fragmented and in process. As an image, the cyborg, like that of the nomad, trickster or coyote, encapsulates the instability and hybridity of subjectivity. Since cyborgs negate the unity and/or singularity underpinning conventional identity politics, it is safe to say that cyborg politics will not be grounded in pre-discursive essentials (shared identity, natural features, and so on). Nevertheless, according to Haraway, '[c]yborgs have a natural feel for united front politics' (1991b: 151).[4] So, why does cyborg politics imply a collective politics? Moreover, what, if anything, unifies that politics?

In 'Situated knowledges', Haraway remarks, it is the partiality and openness of the self that allow for the possibility of connection. Because 'it is always constructed and stitched together imperfectly' this self is '*therefore* able to join with another, to see together without claiming to be another' (1991c: 193). It is the lack of closure endemic to cyborgs that allows their connection to and unity (in some form) with others. Cyborg subjectivity is thus, to borrow from Adam in a slightly different context, constituted '*through* rather than in advance of its association with others' (2002: 3). Like the *mestiza*, discussed in Chapter 2, the cyborg's intersubjective connections are multiple and shifting, not bound by a pre-existing shared identity. In coalitional terms, for Haraway, the cyborg is open to a variety of 'monstrous and illegitimate' alliances (1991b: 154), grounded not in identity, but in affinity. Or, as she notes later, cyborgs are 'not related by blood but by choice' (ibid.: 155).[5] Cyborg politics has no inevitable grounding, then, in natural(ized) identities nor in singularity, rather, it emerges out of the affinity of one group for another; it is a form of 'political kinship' (ibid.: 156). To support her somewhat abstract discussion of cyborgs, Haraway offers a concrete example of a cyborg affinity group: 'the new political voice called "women of colour"' (ibid.: 155).[6] Importantly, this is an example of cyborg politics that is historically grounded. I suggest this historical specificity and retrospective analysis must be kept in mind when contemplating inessential coalitions. I will come back to this point later.

According to Haraway's reading, the term 'women of colour' signi-fies the construction of a 'postmodern identity' out of 'otherness, speci-ficity and difference' (ibid.: 155); a 'potent subjectivity synthesized from fusions of outsider identities' (ibid.: 174). It is a fully political identity wrought out of deep contestation. First, many of the women who would later identify with it initially disputed the name, fearing it would homogenize them (Sandoval, 1990: 60). Second, 'women of colour' implies a form of consciousness fashioned in opposition to a declining, though once, hegemonic power (Man, as a universal signifier – in the West, at least). Through exclusion from existent categories (women, black, etc.) and the 'conscious appropriation of [that] nega-tion', 'women of colour' evolved as a political grouping (Haraway, 1991b: 156).[7] Women of colour, thus, denotes a 'self-consciously con-structed space' developing out of inassimilable differences. Unlike con-ventional modes of identity, 'women of colour' does not signify completeness, wholeness, or closure. As Sandoval writes, 'What US third world feminists are calling for is a new subjectivity, a political revision that denies any one perspective as the only answer, but instead posits a shifting tactical and strategic subjectivity that has the capacity to re-center depending upon the forms of oppression to be confronted' (1990: 67). Cyborg politics, as exemplified by women of colour, is incomplete and shifting – and this is the source of its strength. As Haraway proclaims in the introduction to Simians, Cyborgs and Women, cyborg politics is 'perhaps more able [than Euro-American feminism] to remain attuned to specific historical and political positionings and per-manent partialities without abandoning the search for potent connec-tions' (Haraway, 1991a: 1).

Like a number of other feminist thinkers, Haraway sees inessential coalitions as a necessary corollary of the subject-in-process. As just indicated, one reason for this is that such coalitions are acutely sensi-tive to historical specificity and to difference. This raises the issue of their conditions of possibility. In Haraway's case coalitions are made possible by affinity.[8] So, what are the conditions of possibility for affin-ity? The idea of affinity as the basis of coalition rests on the assump-tion that certain aspects of existing groups lead them (or enable them) to discern in others something that is appealing, and it is this that gen-erates the affinity forming the basis for coalitions. What, though, forms the basis of this appeal? To attempt to answer this, it is necessary to work out what precisely Haraway herself takes affinity to mean.

Haraway derives the term 'affinity' from chemistry (unsurprisingly, given her background in the natural sciences), where it is defined as 'the appeal of one chemical nuclear group for another' (1991b: 155). Assuming that chemical nuclear groups share essential qualities that define them, it might be assumed that affinity, in coalitional terms, is essentialist, grounded in a pre-existing identity. Indeed, as Stacy Alaimo notes, discussing feminist environmentalism, 'affinity (... often slides into essentialist definitions of "woman")' (1994: 150). In terms of the (chemical) process of affinity, it may, however, be objected that identity is less important than appeal: the 'tendency of certain substances to combine with others' (as the *OED* puts it). Such a clarification seems only to muddy the conceptual waters further, for the question then becomes, what constitutes the 'tendency' that produces 'combination'? We saw with regard to Haraway's non-scientific example, women of colour, that it was their shared experience of negation (the tendency) that brought them together (in combination). Affinity, in this case, then was not based on positivity (the assumption of a set of substantive ontological characteristics joining women of colour) but rather on negativity (what they were not). Moreover, Haraway's idea of 'monstrous' affinities further suggests, in my view, an attempt to avoid overt essentialism. Take her observation of a potential ironic affinity between 'corporate executives reading *Playboy* and anti-porn radical feminists' (1991b: 162). This affinity is not predicated upon a shared nature or set of experiences, but instead loosely on a set of beliefs and values; as Crosby frames it, both groups 'find it irrational that sex is natural or necessarily linked to reproduction' (1989: 208). In this regard, cyborg politics appears to be very much an improvisational politics drawing on what is around at the time (see Scott, 1989: 217). This poses a problem: as one critic notes, it is unclear whether the cyborg 'knows how to say no' to potential points of connection; knows, that is, the 'proper (although not natural, not necessary, not essential) limits and boundaries of coalitions' (Crosby, 1989: 208), though one might of course wonder what 'proper' means in this context.

If affinity is an inessential phenomenon (as Haraway's examples seem to indicate), the contours, parameters and points of connection of which cannot be determined in advance, then what needs to happen in order to generate it? Fuss and Alaimo are, I think, right in this regard to raise questions about the priority of the relation between affinity and politics. 'Politics marks the site', as Fuss observes, 'where Haraway's project begins' rather than ends (1989: 36; see also Alaimo, 1994: 150); it is what happens once the coalition is formed. Affinity, that is, often appears to be pre-political. Another of Haraway's claims, however, counters this for she reads the emergence of 'women of colour' specifically as the generation of a political identity. In other words, politics does not simply follow from affinity; it occasions the affinity that pulls cyborgs together. The ambiguity present in Haraway's work is, I propose, another version of the agonistic relation I charted in Chapter 3 between constation and performativity. It testifies to the problems of opposing essentialism to anti-essentialism in stark terms, when what exists is simply the essentialism within inessentialism and, of course, the inessentialism within essentialism. Predicated as it is on an anti-essentialist conception of subjectivity, cyborg politics still ends up embroiled in a potential essentialism when it shifts to considering the grounds of coalition politics. By attempting to posit affinity as the cement that holds together the elements of a coalition (even while disclaiming any real content to that cement), Haraway turns affinity into a term with the potential to become essentialized. This is the case even though affinities are themselves political constructions, crafted through negotiation and interaction.

The focus of Haraway's account is, as discussed, the potential of cyborgs for intersubjective political connection with others. This is revealed through the example of women of colour as a form of in-process political kinship. In the next section, I turn to another thinker, Shane Phelan, who, drawing on Haraway, explores further the idea of inessential coalitions. Significantly Phelan, unlike Haraway, directly addresses the propensity for inessential coalitions to develop essentialist agendas.

'Alliances and Coalitions: Nonidentity Politics'

In her book, *Identity Politics: Lesbian Feminism and the Limits of Community* (1989), Shane Phelan criticizes the tendency of some lesbian feminists to deploy an essentialist account of identity that ignores the differentiated ways of being-lesbian. Not only does such a style of thinking and doing politics treat identity as homogenous, but it is also, Phelan claims, 'nondemocratic' in the sense that it silences voices that do not fit the unitary schema it establishes (1994: x). Concrete differences between lesbians disappear as the need to generate a unified identity wins out. At the end of *Identity Politics*, Phelan suggests, as a solution to the incipient separatism of essentialist lesbianism, with its demand for 'purity in our allies', the need for 'workable coalitions and porous but meaningful communities' (1989: 166). In an effort to think through this problem of, what she terms, 'nonnegotiable identities' (ibid.: 170), Phelan turns her attention in her next book, *Getting Specific: Postmodern Lesbian Politics* (1994), to the question of what kind

157

of democratic lesbian politics could best encompass specificity and difference. Her answer, in short, is one based on postmodern coalition
politics. Contending for a recuperation of the broad political vision
advocated by the earliest exponents of identity politics (that is, the idea
of working with other marginalized groupings), though not for the
identarian logic that often accompanied it, Phelan argues in *Getting
Specific* for an anti-essentialist account of identity. She construes identities, that is, as 'fluid and negotiable locations' rather than 'reified into
solid chunks' that ontologically define people as x or y (ibid.: x). Taking
difference as a resource that can contribute to the generation of political solidarity, and not as a hindrance that stymies it, Phelan contemplates the vitality of coalitions and alliances as the way out of
essentialism and as a counterweight to the kinds of interest group politics that, in her opinion, dominate society in the USA.[9]

'Lesbian' for Phelan, as discussed in Chapter 2, does not connote an
unchanging or timeless identity. Lesbians are simply 'people occupying
provisional subject positions in heterosexual society' (ibid.: 140).
Lesbians, thus, actively construct selves out of the resources (discursive and practical) that currently constitute sexuality. They articulate a
subject position from them at the same time as they are themselves
subjected by these discourses and resources. As she comments, 'To
paraphrase Foucault, "we must insist on *becoming* [lesbian], rather than
persist in defining ourselves as such"' (ibid.: 140). Lesbian identity is
not fixed; rather, it operates as a landscape for potential political
change. As already indicated, the purpose of Phelan's theory is to
develop a form of lesbian politics that is not narrowly sectarian but can
embrace difference and specificity. This is a politics orchestrated
through coalitions, coalitions predicated upon the idea that lesbian
identity is malleable and potentially transformable. As with Haraway,
since the basis of such coalitions is not what individuals already share,
the crucial question becomes 'What *might* we share as we develop our
identities through the process of coalition?' (Phelan, 1994: 140; see also
Butler, 1990a: 14). An affinity between groups and individuals might
facilitate the development of an alliance but it is politics – the work of
negotiation, give-and-take and a willingness to change – that will determine whether a coalition gels and whether it can generate shared goals.

To exemplify the politics of coalition formation, Phelan examines the
emergence of 'queer' politics. The parallels here with Haraway's consideration of women of colour are striking, not least because both queer and
women of colour emerge from very specific historical conditions making
possible their formation. As a mode of political kinship, to borrow
Haraway's term, queer politics (and theory), are products of the 1980s
and, more pertinently, as Phelan notes, of the accidental convergence of
four factors: (1) the tiredness and disillusionment of some lesbians with

the sex wars of the 1980s; (2) the effect of AIDS on male–female relationships and as the grounds for political alliances; (3) the significance of
poststructuralist theory within the academy (in the USA at least); and (4)
the problematization of the heterosexual–homosexual binary and of the
relation between politics and sexuality engendered by bisexuals seeking
inclusion within an extended (and modified) gay and lesbian movement
(for fuller details, see Phelan, 1994: 151–3 and 2001). Queer has, furthermore, been expressly identified as constituting 'a coalitional identity'
(1994: 153) – what Lisa Duggan calls 'a "new community"' moving
beyond the confines of the earlier gay and lesbian movements to encompass previously excluded sexual minorities.

This 'new community', for Duggan, is unified not by a shared identity but by 'a shared dissent from the dominant organization of sex and
gender' (Duggan, cited in Phelan, 1994: 153). In other words, just as
'women of colour' emerged *against* other forms of identity (in negation,
that is), so too 'queer' is also defined *against* that which it rejects. While
acknowledging some of the benefits that have accrued to the emergence of queer politics (including humour attached to some of its
demonstrations), Phelan cautions wisely that queer does not *ipso facto*
'guarantee a better alliance politics than "gay" or "lesbian" have' (1994:
154) for the simple reason that the term operates in a variety of ways.
'To many,' Phelan notes, '"queer" is simply a new label for "lesbian"
and "gay".' For at least some of these people, queer thus 'implies a
nationalist politics', one in which 'queerness' operates as a 'cross-cul-
tural and transhistorical "natural" identity or position' (ibid.: 153, 154).
Once again, the agonism I outlined in Chapter 3 between essentialism
and anti-essentialism emerges. In this case, it emerges from a tension
between nationalist and deconstructionist uses of the sign 'queer';
between, that is, queer apprehended as a natural identity and queer
theorized as a provisional identity category generated at the nexus of
gender and sexuality. To simply assume that a coalitional identity, even
that of an inessential identity such as queer or women of colour, is
somehow naturally immune to the dangers of identity-naturalization
(or essentialism) is naïve. For it to remain inessential – or open to new
articulatory possibilities (and I explore what this means below) – it has
to work at that openness. It cannot simply be presumed. For that way
lies nationalism.

As my earlier argument makes clear, and as Phelan also contends,
although the twin polarities (nationalism–deconstruction, or constation–performativity, as I put it) help configure the field of politics, the
answer is not to opt for one side or the other as a means of resolving
the tension between them. Instead, these two sides should be seen as
the site of political contestation, a scene of agonism. In endeavouring
to keep the category of 'queer' open to future resignification, Phelan

thus argues for a problematization of the 'nation' at the heart of nation-alism; that is, for a problematization of essentialist definitions of queer. Or, as she puts it, 'The only fruitful nationalism is one that has at its heart the idea of the nonnation – the nation of nonidentity' (1994: 154). In other words, postmodern coalitional politics is not an identity poli-tics but a non-identity politics, predicated not on the presence of iden-tity but on its absence or undoing. With regard to queer, this means that as a non-identity politics, 'queer' must not become inscribed as *'the* sexual minority', for this is to nationalize it, thereby alienating and excluding those sexual minorities that do not fit in. Far better that it aspire to what Spivak terms 'the practical politics of the open end' (Spivak, 1990; Phelan, 1994: 154), where conflicts within and among those involved in, in this case, coalitional work are recognized as 'inevitable', an inevitability that is regarded as the 'grounds for con-tinued rearticulation, new narratives of political structures and change' (Phelan, 1994: 149) and not as an obstacle to the production of politi-cal goals. Accommodating difference and specificity and accepting the non-unitary nature of subjectivity, means producing a political agenda that is expressly *not* predicated on shared identities and that does not, as far as possible (and this will always be a site of conflict), naturalize alliances so as to render them exclusionary. For Phelan, this portends a local politics.

In her own words, 'local' invokes 'two senses': a first '"postmodern" sense' relating to 'a politics that eschews universal narratives of oppression' and a second political sense, which is a 'return to the orig-inal formulation of identity politics' (ibid.: 145) where political agendas were generated by the groups directly suffering the injustice or oppres-sion. Local politics for Phelan, therefore, makes no claims about a sin-gular mechanism generating oppression identically for all. It seeks instead to highlight the ways in which power works in and through 'social minutiae'. It is anti-statist, based on a plethora of micro-resist-ances, and conceptualizes revolution only as a 'post-factum label' used to describe the multiple resistances reconfiguring power and not as an a priori description of a form of political struggle (ibid.: 146). This is, thus, a highly participatory and on-going form of politics. Translated to lesbian activism, it requires 'the patient simultaneous entry into and subversion of a social field that denies lesbian existence while present-ing hypostatised images of "the lesbian"' (ibid.: 147). This painstaking work is allied (to recall the second sense of local noted above) to a revivified – though de-essentialized – identity politics that takes self-knowledge, the humble and incomplete knowledge of the fractured, in-process postmodern self, as the basis both for generating political analyses and political agendas. Instead of a mass movement mobilizing to seize power, democratic lesbian politics as conceived by Phelan (in

Foucauldian vein) would involve resistance to the effects of power at the social periphery, capillary resistance to suit capillary power.

Without doubt, the accounts of coalition politics that Haraway and Phelan produce are consonant with the need to foster a collective democratic politics consistent with the subject-in-process. To this end, coalitions operate, I suggest, as political spaces where different persons, through various inter-subjective and dialogical encounters, are able to forge an inessential collective identity of some kind. The important point, though, is that the shape and character of such inessential collectives – coalitions – cannot be predicted in advance. They are determined by the dynamics (interpersonal, ideological, etc.) of those involved in its formation. It is their interactions that generate the coalition's scope, form and degree of unity (or otherwise). Both 'woman of colour' and 'queer' demonstrate this; they both reveal, in different ways, the political work involved in producing and maintaining them as inessential coalitions when they are cross-cut with contradictions. It is these contradictions – often very sharp and divisive ones – that give them energy and life, just as they threaten to deaden and deactivate them. Given this, democracy is better conceived, in my view, less as the arrival at (or production of) a consensus than as an unceasing journey towards equality, understood in an incomplete and permanently open sense, which is marked along the way by factionalization, pain and rupture; or conflict. In order to pursue further this theme, of the relation between conflict and democracy, I turn to Chantal Mouffe's neo-Schmittian account of friends, enemies and adversaries and its utility for feminism.

Friends, Enemies, Adversaries and the Creation of Political Frontiers

In a piece entitled 'For a politics of nomadic identity' (1994), Mouffe examines the relations between collective identities and political frontiers occasioned by the collapse of communism. What interests me about her paper here is not Mouffe's discussion of post-Cold War European politics, intriguing as it is, but her contention that conflict is endemic to, indeed constitutive of, politics and that, consequently, all political relations between groups are necessarily conflictual relations.[10] In order to understand this relationship, I want briefly to reprise her ideas on identity and subjectivity.

As sketched in the opening chapter, in her work with Laclau in particular, Mouffe combines the idea of the Subject constituted in lack with the notion of historically specific subject positions.[11] Since, as I noted then, it is impossible for such subjects to 'realise their identity'

(Howarth, 1998: 134), what happens is that subjects identify, albeit precariously, with phantasmatic representations. They identify, that is, with ideological subject positions produced in determinate historical contexts. These subject positions are 'the ensemble of beliefs through which an individual interprets and responds to her structural positions within a social formation' (Smith, 1998: 58). Every social agent (individual or collective) identifies with a number of social positions, 'corresponding to the multiplicity of social relations in which it is inscribed' (Mouffe, 1992a: 376; see also 82). Identity, for Mouffe, is thus a process of 'permanent hybridization and nomadization' (1994: 110). Further, by assuming that all subject positions are defined relationally, positing an identity (an 'us') involves also positing a difference (a 'them'). The subject position, 'mother' thus requires 'son', 'daughter', 'father' and 'aunt', etc. to constitute her. The (imagined) presence of an Other is, thus, a necessary condition – 'the constitutive outside' – for the formation of any identity. What precisely does this mean? As Mouffe writes in *The Democratic Paradox*, the constitutive outside does not refer to an outside understood as a dialectical negation (or concrete opposite) of the inside (the identity that is posited). Rather, it is what is excluded in order to make the inside (the identity) possible (Mouffe, 2000: 13).[12]

It is not simply the relation between identities, defined in terms of the constitutive outside, which renders them political, however. An identity, for Mouffe, only becomes political when:

> the 'other', who up until now has been considered simply as different, starts to be perceived as someone who is rejecting 'my' identity and is threatening 'my' existence. From that moment on, any form of us/them relationship – whether it be religious, ethnic, economic or other – becomes political. (Mouffe, 1994: 108)

The production of a *political* identity is grounded in antagonism, the translation of the other into an 'enemy' as opposed to a 'friend' (to echo the Schmittian lexicon underwriting Mouffe's account). Politics, that is, creates frontiers between subject positions (Laclau and Mouffe, 1985). In this way without enemies, there can be no politics. Politics is, thus, defined by the presence of antagonism. What is crucial here is that it is not just that conflict cannot be separated from politics, for Mouffe, but that the human condition is itself 'permanently conflictual'. Politics is, as such, 'a dimension inherent in all human society which stems from our very ontological condition' (1994: 108). On this reading, any us/them division has the potential to become politicized, when one identity blocks (or appears to block) another (Mouffe, 1993: 2–3), a process most likely to happen when some form of social dislocation occurs and social relations are thrown into disarray. At such times, the potential is created for the generation of new forms of political identity (see Howarth and Stavrakakis, 2000). These political identities are neither homogeneous nor fixed; rather, they construct various categories ('nodal points') with which subjects can identify and around which political campaigns can be crafted (Mouffe, 1992a: 381). It is here that Mouffe's concept of radical or, more recently, agonistic democracy becomes pertinent.

Central to the relation between democracy and political identities is the concept of articulation. As noted earlier, articulation is 'any practice establishing a relation among elements such that their identity is modified as a result of articulatory practice' (Laclau and Mouffe, 1985: 105). New political groupings or movements are, thus, produced through articulatory practices that bring together different subject positions, reconfiguring them in the process through a series of complex negotiations.[13] This works by constructing a 'relation of equivalence' between these subject positions, where different ones are 'substitutible for each other' (Mouffe, 1992a: 379), but in which these differences are not erased by their articulation, even though they are modified.[14] It is worth noting that articulation is not an infinitely open process, however. As Stacy Alaimo notes in a reference to Stuart Hall, 'everything cannot be articulated with everything else' (1994: 134); instead historical factors (the tenacity of certain ideologies, for instance, or the particular landscape of political formations) configure likely articulatory possibilities. So, how does this work in practice? In order to show how articulation operates, I propose, briefly, to re-read the emergence of women of colour from a Mouffean perspective.

Women of colour emerged, as noted earlier, as a new, historically contingent, political identity. Construed in Mouffe's terms, it did so by articulating (bringing together) the subject positions of, *inter alia*, black feminists, Latina feminists, Asian feminists, and lesbian feminists of colour, all of whose identities were partially modified thereby, but whose differences from one another were not erased. (It was still possible to differentiate the forms of oppression visited on Latina women from those subjecting lesbians of colour.) In addition, the identity 'women of colour' also articulated various beliefs – anti-racism, anti-sexism and a commitment to democracy – generating, as a consequence, an 'oppositional consciousness'. The process of articulation was, again as previously indicated, the product of complex, often painful, negotiations. Crucially, and a key reason why women of colour is understood by Haraway as a cyborg identity, and why it might be read in Mouffean terms, is that it was produced in negation. The 'we' of women of colour was constructed against a 'them' (which included white women, black men, not to mention racists and sexists of all hues) that denied its existence. (Whether negation and antagonism are the same is, of course, a moot point.[15])

As this example illustrates, articulation is, as Phelan notes, 'a profoundly political act' (1994: 21). It not only creates new political identities but also generates discourses that both make sense of the specific situation of a particular group and identify 'particular political actions and strategies' for it (Phelan, 1994: 21–2). Citing the example of the Radicalesbians of the 1970s, Phelan comments how their generation of the idea of lesbianism as 'woman-identification' (against the prevailing idea that lesbianism was a sexual orientation defined by object choice) occasioned the development of a different political strategy to that operating in the existing gay and lesbian movement of the time, namely, one creating an 'alignment with feminist women, lesbian and (sometimes) heterosexual' (ibid.: 21). And, of course, constructing the category 'women of colour' enabled the production of alternative, ethnically-nuanced, feminist discourses, such as Anzaldúa's account of the *mestiza* discussed in Chapter 2, which themselves suggest alternative political tactics and strategies.

Mouffe is, however, less interested in the potential of articulation for specific feminist struggles than in its relation to democracy, or rather, to what she terms radical or agonistic democracy. This is democracy conceived as a permanently open-ended process (not in terms of institutional arrangements or deliberative procedures). Feminism, according to Mouffe, 'is the struggle for the equality of women' conceived in terms of a struggle against the many ways in which '"woman" is produced as inferior' (1992a: 382). Feminism is not, thus, a quest for the equality of women understood as an empirical group with a shared essence; indeed, Mouffe does not see feminism as a separate mode of politics oriented around the interests of women qua women. For this reason, she opposes calls for sexually differentiated citizenship on the grounds that this would merely reify sexual difference, rendering citizenship unidimensional. Democratic citizenship, instead, should be the mechanism through which struggles against oppression in all their forms (including, but going beyond, feminism) are articulated. Feminism, in her view, is, as such, merely part of the project of radical, plural democracy. Mouffe's work converges at this point with that of other feminist political theorists such as Iris Young who also see democracy as a battle against multiple forms of oppression (see Young, 1990, 1995, 2000). Where they differ, according to Mouffe is that she does not aim, as Young does, to secure representation for pre-existing groups ('women' or African Americans, say). Mouffe proposes, instead, as the way forward the construction of a new form of democratic citizenship, 'a common political identity'. It is this *new* political identity, 'articulated through the principle of democratic *equivalence'* (1992a: 379), that would 'create the conditions for the establishment of a new hegemony articulated through new egalitarian social relations, practices and institutions' (ibid.: 380). Moreover, this new identity, bringing together all kinds of democratic groupings, is established in antagonism to its anti-democratic enemies. Radical democratic practice, thus, embraces both the construction of friends *and* enemies. The concept of 'friend' in this democratic/anti-democratic binary is especially interesting.

Because the establishment of a 'we' constitutively requires the establishment of a 'them', the kinds of democratic consensus espoused by certain liberals and Habermassians are, Mouffe charges, simply unachievable, for every consensus is necessarily founded upon acts of exclusion. As such, democratically, 'the question cannot be any more the creation of a fully inclusive community where antagonism, division, and conflict will have disappeared' (Mouffe, 1992a: 379; see also Mouffe, 1992b, 2000), what is required is 'the constitution of collective identities around clearly differentiated positions' (Mouffe, 1994: 109). The aim of politics, therefore, is to create a particular order and to arrange the co-existence of humans in a situation of inevitable discord. It is thus tasked with what Mouffe terms, 'domesticating hostility'. In other words, politics (as public activity) should be oriented to 'defus[ing] the potential antagonism inherent in human relations' (ibid.: 108), turning antagonism into agonism. Humans cannot escape the differential relations that mark out subject positions; this is the ontological ground of existence. They can, however, try to create the conditions in which the Other is no longer viewed as an enemy that must be eradicated (or excluded) but is transformed into an adversary or a counterpart. Agonistic democracy requires adversaries not enemies. As such, it involves accepting that the Other has a legitimate place in the polity, tolerating their ideas (assuming those ideas are democratic), and allowing space for disagreement over values and goals, thus keeping alive potential contention against their views. In a pluralist, democratic order the category of the enemy would thus be 'displaced'. (It would not be eradicated, however, since it would pertain to those opposed to democracy.) Radical pluralist democracy would, on this count, be messy, 'combative ... partial and erratic' (Nash, 1998: 53), intensely political, (ideally) agonistic rather than antagonistic.[16]

It is for these reasons that Mouffe regards feminism as entailing more than an attempt to attain the equality of women as an empirical group. If feminist struggles are also democratic struggles, then feminists have, for her, to engage in the construction of political friendships that cut across gender lines. This is not to deny the possibility that, occasionally, feminist democratic struggles will appear which are partially fixed just around the category 'women'; quite the contrary, such

struggles are critical. However, to reduce feminist politics to one identity – a feminism grounded in a singular conception of women – is to
miss both the diversity and multiplicity of feminist struggles and the
manifold ways in which relations of power and oppression/subordina-
tion are constituted. Concentrating only on women's interests or issues
(as if these exist in unified form prior to political engagement) is to
ignore the productive democratic possibilities emerging out of the articulation of a plurality of democratic demands – an articulation that must
combine and, crucially reconfigure the relative values of those
demands. And, although (to recall Hall) there is a potential question
mark over the degree to which some articulatory possibilities are open
to reconfiguration, this does not detract from the basic thrust of
Mouffe's argument, which is that through articulation, the political
field can be altered and new subject positions generated. What aids in
this is the fact that politics derives from the antagonisms that underpin
human life. Turning antagonism into agonism is, as such, one of the
processes that can bring about a changed political terrain (even though,
in my opinion, such a turning can only ever be provisional and insecure, since the terrain of politics is always haunted by the potential
threat of a resurgence of discord).

Conclusion

The aim of this chapter was to think through what inessential coalitions or non-identity politics might look like. The thinkers I examined
share certain affinities in their representations of collective political
endeavour. All begin from anti-essentialist conceptions of subjectivity;
all see coalitions as based on something other than identarian logic,
indeed, all are 'suspicious', as Elam puts it, 'of identity as the essential
grounding for meaningful political action' (1994: 69); all note the work
– the politics – that goes into generating coalitions across specificity
and difference. Each is also sensitive, to a greater or lesser degree, to
the historical conditions of possibility for the production of new forms
of collective political (non-)identities. Though there are affinities in particular between the three in respect of how they think about the generation of new identities, there are also differences, the greatest of
which concerns the role of antagonism in the process of coalition formation. Haraway's treatment of women of colour and Phelan's account
of queer resonate with the notion of articulation evinced by Mouffe in
so far as something akin to a chain of equivalence is seen to be constructed between the groups that together produce the new political
identities they discuss (women of colour and queer). The process
alluded to by Haraway concentrates, for instance, on the joining

together of different groups of women in a way that might be taken to imply a smooth creative process; she talks simply of a 'fusion' of various outsider identities (1991b: 174). Sandoval, whom Haraway cites, reveals, however, the cost involved in this process. It is this sometimes forceful, even violent, aspect of articulation that is brought to the fore in Mouffe's consideration of the place of antagonism and agonism in democratic struggle (a view partially echoed by Phelan). Forging a new political identity on this latter reading is not just a case of benignly assembling the elements in the chain of equivalence; it is also (and here the historical conditions of production of determinate modes of political identity need to be recognized for the way they inflect the nature of those antagonisms) a matter of reshaping or bending them in such a way that antagonism becomes agonism (something that may not always be possible). Articulation may appear in retrospect to be non-violent but, for (Laclau and) Mouffe, this is the result of the discourses generated during this process, masking the pain of conjoining (as, for instance, it presents the connections between groups as natural or inevitable or historically determined, etc.) and not the nature of the process itself.

More than anything, though, what these debates bring to the fore expressly are questions concerning the nature of politics and the political. Poststructuralist-inflected (feminist) political theory has often been accused of being either apolitical or, worse, anti-political. Throughout this book my aim has been to argue that neither reading is accurate. It is not the case that the writers I have examined are uninterested in political concerns or in questions of political strategizing; it is rather that they deal with these issues in ways that differ from earlier feminist theories. They thus reconfigure how politics and the political are understood. This is just as true for writers such as Haraway and Phelan who engage with questions of politics and political constitutivity without tendering a comprehensive conceptualization of what they mean by these terms, as it is for someone like Mouffe who offers in her writings a definition of the differences between politics and the political. It is to questions about how these conceptions of politics (implicit or explicit) differ from mainstream feminist approaches that I now turn in the concluding chapter of this book.

Notes

1 Here the work of Anna Jónasdóttir (1988) is important. See also Phelan (1994) and Adams (2002).

2 This essay was originally published as 'Manifesto for cyborgs: science, technology, and socialist feminism in the 1980s', in *Socialist Review* in 1985. My references are to the

revised version included in Haraway's 1991 collection of essays, *Simians, Cyborgs, and Women: The Reinvention of Nature*.

3 For a critical engagement with Haraway's vision of socialist politics, see Scott (1989).

4 Of course, the connections for Haraway's cyborgs need not only be with humans but may be with animals, machines and other cyborg entities. It is not entirely clear what political possibilities this may entail.

5 Although Haraway rejects the liberal idea of choice, which assumes an individual prior to the text, the idea that choice is the basis of affinity opens up a range of questions for discussion, not least relating to Haraway's implied opposition between choice and nature and the extent to which this echoes that between free will and determinism. See Doane (1989), and Scott (1989).

6 Haraway here cites Sandoval, as well as the work of Audre Lorde and her conception of 'Sister Outsider' (Lorde, 1984b) and Cherríe Moraga's treatment of the narrative of Malinche (the mother of the *mestizo*) in *Loving in the War Years* (1983).

7 A series of negations captured in the title of the edited collection *All the Women are White, All the Men are Black, but Some of Us are Brave* (Hull et al., 1982).

8 See also Shane Phelan (1994) and Iris Marion Young (1990) for two different accounts that prioritize 'affinity' as the basis of politics in one way or another.

9 Phelan tends for the most part to use these terms synonymously until the final chapter of her book, *Getting Specific*, when she treats alliances and coalitions as different in terms of motive and purpose (1994: 154–9). Although I do not have the space here to explore why she makes this differentiation, suffice to say, alliances appear better able than coalitions to avoid foundering on the rocks of identity, where shared oppression is privileged and where more attention is paid to discerning the ground of coalition than to constructing that ground communally. In terms of this chapter, alliances appear closer to the sorts of inessential coalitions that I am discussing.

10 According to her own argument, Mouffe's form of radical democratic pluralism should be differentiated from liberal pluralism on the grounds that the latter defines group relations in terms of a competition over scarce resources and, thus, in terms of interest satisfaction. By assuming that conflicting interests can be satisfied by the appropriate allocation of resources, 'Relations of power and antagonism are erased.' In other words, liberal pluralism is 'pluralism without antagonism' (2000: 20).

11 There is a question concerning the compatibility of the theories Mouffe deploys: between the historically sedimented subject positions of Foucault, the Lacanian idea that any totality is illusory, the deconstruction of Derrida and Schmitt's friend/enemy distinction. I do not, however, have space here to do more than note it.

12 It also makes that identity impossible – by threatening to disrupt any attempt to define it in a comprehensive and all-encompassing way.

13 Here Anzaldúa's categorization of alternative strategies of coalition building is suggestive of the kinds of negotiation that might be pertinent. She offers four different forms of connection between groups and individuals that are particularly appropriate for the relation between people of colour and dominant white groups: to 'bridge', or to mediate; to 'drawbridge', where there is an option of engaging or disengaging; to 'island', that is to separate without connection, to work only within one's community; and to 'sandbar', a link that is sometimes visible, sometimes not depending on the 'tide'

of politics (Anzaldúa, 1990b: 223–4). Obviously, other additional or alternative negotiating positions may also be possible. For an account of the ethics of coalitions, see Elam (1994: 105–20).

14 Mouffe offers an account, I suggest, that bridges the polarity between the two modes of coalition I sketched in the introduction to this chapter.

15 In *Hegemony and Socialist Strategy*, Laclau and Mouffe contend 'in the case of antagonism … the presence of the "Other" prevents me from being totally myself … it is because the peasant *cannot* be a peasant that an antagonism exists with the landowner expelling him from his land' (1985: 125). The same might be said about women of colour, prevented from being themselves not only by racists but also within their own communities by the men who perceived feminist struggles as less meaningful than anti-racist struggles and within the feminist movement by those who ignored or de-prioritized race.

16 In defining democracy as related to principles of freedom and equality, Mouffe subscribes to a form of universalism, however, the actual contents of these principles – what they mean in certain contexts and for certain groups – are the focus of the agonism characterizing democracy.

conclusion
interrogating the political

If there is one feature that has defined contemporary feminist discussions on subjectivity, identity and politics over the past two decades, it has been contention. For every advocate of the idea that women share a common identity, there has been one who has argued for the radical insufficiency of identity categories; for every critic of the idea that identity is constructed, there has been one claiming that it is not constructed, or if it is, then not in the ways suggested. In a way, the intensity of the debate should surprise no one with a background in political theory. For what it demonstrates is akin, in some ways, to what W.B. Gallie referred to 50 years ago as the essential contestability of political concepts (1955–56), the fact that certain evaluative concepts are so complex and open that several plausible interpretations of them are possible at any one time. When political theorists took up the mantle thrown down by Gallie, they turned their attention to ideas such as power, authority, liberty, justice, and democracy, the staple components of political discourse. More recently, feminist theorists have not only contested the meanings attaching within mainstream political theory to these staple terms; they have also scrutinized notions such as public and private, and the body (Hirschmann and Di Stefano, 1996; Shanley and Narayan, 1997). Like the essentially contested concepts noted by Gallie, these later ones also are capable of sustaining both a potentially interminable dispute over their 'proper uses', and a range of 'perfectly respectable arguments and evidence' (1955–56: 169). While Gallie talked in terms of essential contestability, I prefer, however, to construe the disputes surrounding, for instance, power, subjectivity or politics as evidence of their *political* contestability.

Essential contestability assumes a conceptual essence that necessarily becomes the subject of disputation. Political contestability not only queries the idea that any concept has an essential meaning, seeing both meaning and the exclusions that constitute it, instead, as determinate, historically specific effects, however, but it also sees conceptual contestation as contingent (not necessary). By this I mean that different concepts will become politicized – and thus subject to dispute – in specific contexts at particular times. It is this that has occurred with such categories as 'woman', 'man', 'heterosexual' or 'homosexual', terms once ascribed a naturalness or normalcy that seemed to put them beyond dispute. They have become politically significant, as battles ensue over how they are defined, how they operate, what they exclude and include. Indeed, so far have things developed that even the notion of an essence has, as demonstrated in Chapter 3, itself become subject to political contestation. Far from regarding this contestability as a hindrance to theory, and to feminist political theory in particular, I view it as a resource, opening up new avenues. The open-textured nature of concepts, discourses and practices, is precisely what invigorates political theorizing as they are scrutinized, critiqued and resignified in ways that attempt to displace their hegemonic meanings. It is this that helps to reconfigure the terrain of politics. This is not to assume too permissive a reading of this openness, since critiquing certain hegemonic practices, ideas or theories is no guarantee of their displacement. Nor does this imply, however, that one need be too pessimistic. Understanding political theory as a form of critique, focused on eventalizing specific phenomena, compels forensic attention to how the present configuration of politics emerged and took hold, what it makes possible and what it forecloses, and how it might be reshaped.

Throughout this book, I have addressed myself specifically to the ways in which the subject–politics relation has become a site of discord within feminism. Obviously my treatment of these topics has been selective. There are a number of themes that I could have considered that I chose not to; questions, for instance, relating to the politics of undecidability or to the decisionism found in some of the theories encountered here; the relation between the body and subjectivity; or the debate within feminism between discourse ethicists and poststructuralists about the normative dimensions of feminist theory. Some of these I will return to in later work, some I leave for others to explore. I want to end this book by thinking in general about some of the issues this debate about the subject and politics raises for politics. Specifically, two issues are pertinent: first, the problem of what is meant by politics; and, second, what this indicates about the role and nature of feminist political theory.

As I noted in the Introduction, 'what is politics?' has been a topic of debate within and outside of feminism for many years. Throughout this book, evidence of this questioning of politics in the thinkers under review has been plentiful. One of the most common characteristics of this work – though not shared by all authors considered here – has been a distinction of sorts between politics apprehended as a daily activity and politics (or the political) understood in a generative sense. Sometimes this is explicitly formulated, as in Mouffe's contention that the political (understood as the site of contestation, or *polemos*) is an intrinsic dimension of human ontology, which can be demarcated from politics (conceived as the ordering of human existence through a domestication of hostilities, the *polis*) (1994: 108 and 2000). Sometimes it is not. Butler thus, for instance, repeatedly remarks that the activity of politics is contingent and contextual and that it cannot be predicted or prescribed but rather is dependent upon decisions taken at opportune political moments. She also talks of what might be termed political constitutivity – what the political institutes: thus, as my discussion in Chapter 1 indicated, defining the 'domain of the political' (Butler, 1992: 4), for Butler, is political in a productive sense, as is the argument that politics logically requires a subject as its guarantor. This kind of reasoning relates to my contention, in Chapter 3, that the relation between the subject and politics in the debate on essentialism may be thought of as circular: that is, the generation of political subjects relies upon their prior political subjection. It is, furthermore, evidence of the complexity, perhaps even the undecidability, of politics as it circulates simultaneously as activity, process, policy *and* productive force.

Where mainstream political science often conceives of 'political reality' in terms of institutions (such as, for instance, elections and modes of representation), or activities (competition between ideologically differentiated parties or, say, citizenship [Stavrakakis, 1999: 71–2]), advocates of the subject-in-process – and here I include myself – tend to construe it differently. For me, politics it is a dense web of variable power relations: a circulating dynamic. Political reality is thus neither limited to a particular group of activities nor to a separate system – a discrete sphere with its own distinguishing characteristics (the political system as opposed to the economic system, juridical system or the realm of culture) – though it includes them. Politics, instead, exceeds this delimited realm and set of practices. This excess cannot, however, be dealt with just by extending existing definitions of politics to incorporate activities (say, the sexual division of labour), institutions (say, the family or marriage), or spheres (civil society) that a more restricted political science conception excludes, though it is important to do so. Political reality is never, however, simply commensurate with politics per se. What passes for political reality is always the effect of historically sedimented practices and discourses; these circumscribe what politics is and what it disavows. There are, thus, only ever specific political realities, operative in particular places at particular times. Determining what counts as politics (and disqualifying what doesn't) is, as I have argued throughout, an inherently *political* process. This

173

applies just as much to the political discourses avowed by feminists as to the political practices formally recognized by national, sub-national and supranational bodies. Recognizing this is one of the defining features of the relation between subject and politics articulated in this book. This is why it is a mistake to construe accounts of the subject-in-process, as their detractors often do, as either anti-political or apolitical; they are engaged intensely with political questions. The difference between them and more traditional accounts (including feminist ones) is that they appreciate that an *exclusively* topographical or spatial account of politics occludes not only the constituted nature of the political realm, as such, but also hides the constitutive work the political does, in, for instance, generating society, conditioning the parameters of debate, and effecting forms of subjectivity. If politics is reformulated in this way, what does it portend about feminist political theory?

Anyone who reads this book looking for a set of political prescriptions about what feminists ought to do will be disappointed. By and large, though there are exceptions, the theories covered here are not prescriptive. This is not to say, however, that the theories discussed here are not driven by particular normative political values, by a commitment to enhancing democracy and extending equality, for example, for they are. This is what makes them feminist. Pursuing these values, I propose, does not necessitate furnishing a detailed programmatic account of what needs to be done to achieve them, however, though it may sometimes generate certain pointers (as in Mouffe's contention that a new form of radical democratic citizenship is needed). Rather, it means giving up on the kind of fundamentalist fantasy of completion or resolution associated with some political theories (Brown, 2003) – the contention that democracy can be attained once and for all or that equality can be firmly and finally secured – in recognition of the fact that neither can ever be realized permanently. In fact, it is precisely the openness of democracy and equality to reformulation that generates their very capacity for perpetual political renewal. Moreover, and here I concur with Butler, it is the role of politics to keep the 'universal' (democracy or equality, in my examples) indeterminate (2000b), for it is precisely unsettling it – subjecting it to critique – that keeps it alive.

Unlike earlier generations of feminists who followed the trajectory of, for instance, Marxism in believing that such theories not only offered radical political critique, but could also furnish guidance on the *correct* political action to bring about progressive social and political change and could identify the political agent of such change, the contemporary writers under discussion in this book eschew this mode of political reasoning. Accounts of history that assume a particular linear logic are read as totalizing; all-encompassing global and universal explanations of patriarchy are regarded as examples of meta-narrative authoritarianism, and so on. There is no feminist subject of history, no single direction for political action and no unitary set of political values that can be read off, or deduced from, any analysis of women's lives no matter how comprehensive it may claim to be. There is, consequently, a rejection of the types of political normativity that are present within other strands of feminist political theory, say, feminist discourse ethics.[1]

Rethinking political theory as a form of critique, I suggest, means actively embracing the fact that political outcomes will not *necessarily* follow from a particular theory – though they may be made possible by it. It thus means yielding the idea that political theory ought necessarily to advise on political strategy or to command what needs to be done. Critique is important to politics in terms of revealing what is disavowed in a discourse, not in terms of furnishing blueprints for political action. If, as Nikolas Rose observes, many forms of political 'engagement' are minor, lacking 'the arrogance of programmatic politics', this does not make them apolitical (1999: 279–80; Lawler, 2002: 110).[2] Quite the reverse, the absence of a programme to validate them does not depoliticize or delegitimize them; it serves as a reminder that one should be cautious about any account that endeavours to theorize appropriate forms of political activity, since that authorization is always at the expense of the proscription of other forms of activity. Political theory as critique asks what interests are served by this distinction between activities and what privileges they establish for those who act in certain ways.

Since political activity, on my reading, is not governed (though it may be enabled) by theoretical practices such as deconstructive analysis or genealogical inquiry, what interests me is the way in which the thinkers I treat challenge the notion that politics is 'about acquiring certainty ... and acting on it' (Elam, 1994: 67). What most of them share, in some measure, is a disposition towards questioning and a critical suspicion of attempts to foreclose what counts as political. Eve Sedgwick's remarks, contemplating her own project in *Epistemology of the Closet*, are apposite here: the point of such an approach is '*not to know* how far ... insights and projects are generalizable, not to be able to say in advance where the semantic specificity of these issues gives over to (or: itself structures?) the syntax of the "broader" or more abstractable critical project'. It is to operate against such 'deadening pretended knowingness' (1990: 12). The same could be said of many of the positions debated in this book; that the issue is to query and to interrogate instances of 'pretended knowingness' in order to challenge their authority and their capacity to normalize and pathologize those subject(ed) to them. This pertains equally to feminism, with its own discourses that claim to 'know' women in their commonality or universality, as to other discourses and practices (such as democracy, medicine, psychoanalysis or the law) that structure and condition women's lives. Political theory as critique, on this count, is not concerned with positing alternatives to the present and charting how to arrive at these new utopias, though, as indicated earlier, it is driven by a desire to see political changes that bring about a more egalitarian or democratic society. It concentrates instead on the critical examination and denaturalization of current norms, practices and political subjectivities. In other words, feminist work is political not because of the recommendations it makes for the future, but because it is animated by specific concrete problems in the present, problems pertaining to women in their variety and multiplicity.

Treating the enterprise of political theory as a mode of critique thus permits a distinction to be drawn between the question of what to do with the disruptions produced by, for instance, genealogical intervention and the interrogatory impulse that initially prompted that intervention, an impulse firmly located within the history of the present. The process of denaturalization immanent to genealogy and deconstruction, what Foucault termed the 'desacrilization' of the social and what Butler calls 'decontextualization', is politically effective and valuable *in itself* not for what it prescribes. Its effectiveness and value, in part at least, as noted in Chapter 6, are that it opens up the space for *potential* political transformation. What results from this critique politically is, of course, contingent and unpredictable, and sometimes even wholly unexpected. Critique, in this sense, has no predetermined shape or necessary outcome. It entails neither logical political consequences nor particular normative solutions; it is neither predictive nor prescriptive. Or, as Gayatri Spivak puts it in relation to deconstruction: 'there is no absolute justification for *any* position', 'no politically correct deconstructive politics', only a critical questioning and exploring of limits (1990: 104).

Political theory *in these modalities* is non-programmatic but, crucially, it is not non-political. As Wendy Brown eloquently observes:

> Once the radical contingency of political views and judgments is avowed, it is possible to partially and productively depoliticize the theoretical enterprise without thereby rendering it apolitical. It becomes thinkable to distinguish between the political possibilities that a certain body of theory affords, the political uses to which it can be put, the political positions of the theorist, and a particular political deployment of the theory. *Political truth* then ceases to be sought *within* a particular theory but is, rather, that which makes an explicit bid for hegemony in the political realm. And theory may be allowed a return to its most fertile, creative, and useful place as, *inter alia*, an interlocutor of that domain. (2001: 120)

The theories explored in this book are political, I contend, in some of the senses elucidated by Brown: not in terms of fostering a particular cause through the generation of a set of political protocols or platforms, or because they issue from the pen of someone with a particular political bent but in terms of the questions they ask. It is for how they contest received wisdom and the opportunities this contestation creates for concrete (though indeterminate) acts of political intervention, acts that contingently articulate together such factors as political desire and imagination, political connections, not to mention political judgement and values. Whether they succeed in convincing others or bringing about significant change is a matter of the struggle for political hegemony.

The issue for feminist theory operating in this register is not primarily to oppose existing theories (feminist or otherwise) in terms of their political or moral assumptions, as when radical feminism criticizes Marxist feminism because the latter emphasizes class-based politics at the expense of sex-based politics. The purpose is to open up spaces – political, discursive – through which to probe the constituent elements of these (and other) theories (including, for example, the essentialist idea of a unitary subject or the possibility of a uniform account of patriarchy) and to denaturalize, and potentially delegitimize, our most cherished and unquestioned assumptions. In particular, in this book, I have traced manifold accounts of how the relation between the subject and politics has been problematized in just such ways: from the idea of cyborg subjectivity, through non-identity politics to 'becoming out', from the *mestiza* through agency as catachresis, to the interconnectivity of essentialism and inessentialism. Each of these moments of questioning and scrutiny is *political* because it exposes the generation and emergence of these varied phenomena and events as aleatory, arbitrary and haphazard and thus as contestable. Moreover, it helps to divulge, among other things, the radically contingent mechanisms through which norms are configured, sexual life organized, and bodies materialized. It reveals the historical conditions that make possible the performative invocation of specific political rationalities, centring determinate regimes of power and securing particular truth effects. In short, the political is revisioned as a field that is perpetually open to reconfiguration, amenable to unending revitalization and *never* immune from scrutiny and critical excavation. This is the site of political theory.

Notes

1 This is not to repudiate the motivations behind or the practice of such work. It has been a persistent characteristic of work from Aristotle onwards for political theory to posit a positivity; that is, to delineate shared goals, interests and ideal institutions. The effect of this is to impose meaning on politics and the political by fixing its boundaries

and by attempting to arrest the flow and flux that mark them. My point is that much of the writing under consideration in this book has a different aim: to problematize and to denaturalize that which is supposedly beyond question. It is still, however, *political* theory even if it does not guarantee a politics. (For a recent discussion of questions of politics and negativity, see Coole, 2000.)

2 In other words, these actions happen in specific contexts and it is in these contexts that particular judgements are made, specific values appealed to, political imaginations given rein, and so on (see Brown, 2001). Obviously this opens up questions about the relations between norms, judgement and context that I do not have space to pursue here. Suffice to say that, unlike political theories that have an investment in specifying what Nancy Fraser calls 'a comprehensive moral-political vision' (1995b: 163) that assists in determining where feminists ought to be heading and whether what they are doing will get them there, the alternative forms of political theory considered here do not make such a vision central to their concerns. Instead, they raise questions about what is foreclosed or disallowed by such attempts to generate universal, indeed, universalizable, criteria of judgement.

bibliography

Adam, Katherine (2002) 'At the table with Arendt: toward a self-interested practice of coalition discourse', *Hypatia*, 17 (1): 1–33.

Ahmed, Sara (1998) *Differences that Matter: Feminist Theory and Postmodernism*. Cambridge: Cambridge University Press.

Alaimo, Stacy (1994) 'Cyborg and ecofeminist interventions: challenges for an environmental feminism', *Feminist Studies*, 20 (1): 133–52.

Alcoff, Linda (1988) 'Cultural feminism versus post-structuralism: the identity crisis in feminist theory', *Signs: Journal of Women in Culture and Society*, 13 (3): 405–36.

Anzaldúa, Gloria (1987) *Borderlands: The New Mestiza/La Frontera*. San Francisco, CA: Aunt Lute.

Anzaldúa, Gloria (ed.) (1990a) *Making Face, Making Soul: Haciendo Caras – Creative and Critical Perspectives by Women of Color*. San Francisco, CA: Aunt Lute Foundation.

Anzaldúa, Gloria (1990b) 'Bridge, drawbridge, sandbar or island: lesbians-of-color Haciendas Alianzas', in Lisa Albrecht and Rose M. Brewer (eds), *Bridges of Power: Women's Multicultural Alliances*. Philadelphia, PA: New Society Publishers, pp. 216–31.

Appiah, Kwame Anthony (1995) 'African identities', in Linda Nicholson and Steven Seidman (eds), *Social Postmodernism: Beyond Identity Politics*. Cambridge: Cambridge University Press, pp. 103–15.

Austin, J.L. (1962) *How to Do Things with Words*, 2nd edn. Oxford: Oxford University Press.

Aziz, Razia (1997) 'Feminism and the challenge of racism: deviance or difference?', in Heidi Safia Mirza (ed.), *Black British Feminism: A Reader*. London: Routledge, pp. 70–7.

Balsamo, Anne (1996) *Technologies of the Gendered Body: Reading Cyborg Women*. Durham, NC: Duke University Press.

Barrett, Michèle (1991) *The Politics of Truth: From Marx to Foucault*. Cambridge: Polity.

Bartky, Sandra Lee (1988) 'Foucault, femininity and the modernization of patriarchal power', in Irene Diamond and Lee Quinby (eds), *Feminism and Foucault: Reflections on Resistance*. Boston, MA: Northeastern University Press, pp. 61–86.

Begum, Nasa (1992) 'Disabled women and the feminist agenda', in Hilary Hinds, Ann Phoenix and Jackie Stacey (eds), *Working Out: New Directions for Women's Studies*. London: Falmer Press, pp. 61–73.

Bell, David, Binnie, Jon, Cream, Julia and Valentine, Gill (1994) 'All hyped up and no place to go', *Gender, Place and Culture: A Journal of Feminist Geography*, 1 (1): 31–47.

Bell, Diane and Klein, Renate Duelli (eds) (1996) *Radically Speaking: Feminism Reclaimed*. London: Zed Books.

Bell, Vikki (1993) 'Governing childhood', *Economy and Society*, 22 (3): 390–405.

Bell, Vikki (1999) 'On speech, race and melancholia: an interview with Judith Butler', *Theory, Culture and Society*, 16 (2): 163–74.

Benhabib, Seyla (1992) *Situating the Self: Gender, Community and Postmodernism in Contemporary Ethics*. Cambridge: Polity Press.

Benhabib, Seyla (1995) 'Feminism and postmodernism: an uneasy alliance', in Seyla Benhabib, Judith Butler, Drucilla Cornell and Nancy Fraser, *Feminist Contentions: A Philosophical Exchange*. New York: Routledge, pp. 17–34.

Benhabib, Seyla, Butler, Judith, Cornell, Drucilla and Fraser, Nancy (1995) *Feminist Contentions: A Philosophical Exchange*, with an introduction by Linda Nicholson. New York: Routledge.

Bland, Lucy (1995) *Banishing the Beast: English Feminism and Sexual Morality 1885–1914*. Harmondsworth: Penguin Books.

Bland, Lucy and Doan, Laura (eds) (1998) *Sexology Uncensored: The Documents of Sexual Science*. Cambridge: Polity.

Block, Lawrence (1993) *The Devil Knows You're Dead*. London: Phoenix.

Bordo, Susan (1990) 'Feminism, postmodernism and gender-scepticism', in Linda Nicholson (ed.), *Feminism and Postmodernism*. London: Routledge, pp. 133–56.

Braidotti, Rosi (1991) *Patterns of Dissonance: A Study of Women in Philosophy*. Cambridge: Polity.

Braidotti, Rosi (1994) *Nomadic Subjects: Embodiment and Sexual Difference in Contemporary Feminist Theory*. New York: Columbia University Press.

Brown, Wendy (1987) 'Where is the sex in political theory?', *Women and Politics*, 7 (1): 3–23.

Brown, Wendy (1991) 'Feminist hesitations, postmodern exposures', *Differences: A Journal of Feminist Cultural Studies*, 3 (1): 63–83.

Brown, Wendy (1995) *States of Injury: Power and Freedom in Late Modernity*. Princeton, NJ: Princeton University Press.

Brown, Wendy (2001) *Politics out of History*. Princeton, NJ: Princeton University Press.

Brown, Wendy (2003) 'Women's studies unbound: revolution, mourning, politics', *Parallax*, 9 (2): 3–16.

Butler, Judith (1990a) *Gender Trouble: Feminism and the Subversion of Identity*. London: Routledge.

Butler, Judith (1990b) 'Gender trouble, feminist theory and psychoanalytic discourse', in Linda Nicholson (ed.), *Feminism and Postmodernism*. London: Routledge, pp. 324–40.

Butler, Judith (1991) 'Imitation and gender insubordination', in Diana Fuss (ed.), *Inside/Out: Lesbian Theories, Gay Theories*. London: Routledge, pp. 13–31.

Butler, Judith (1992) 'Contingent foundations: feminism and the question of "post-modernism"', in Judith Butler and Joan W. Scott (eds), *Feminists Theorize the Political*. London: Routledge, pp. 3–21.

Butler, Judith (1993a) *Bodies that Matter: On the Discursive Limits of 'Sex'*. London: Routledge.

Butler, Judith (1993b) 'Critically queer', *GLQ: A Journal of Lesbian and Gay Studies*, 1: 17–32.

Butler, Judith (1995a) 'Contingent foundations: feminism and the question of "postmodernism"', in Seyla Benhabib, Judith Butler, Drucilla Cornell and Nancy Fraser, *Feminist Contentions: A Philosophical Exchange*. New York: Routledge, pp. 35–57.

Butler, Judith (1995b) 'For a careful reading', in Seyla Benhabib, Judith Butler, Drucilla Cornell and Nancy Fraser, *Feminist Contentions: A Philosophical Exchange*. New York: Routledge, pp. 127–43.

Butler, Judith (1997a) *The Psychic Life of Power: Theories in Subjection*. Stanford, CA: Stanford University Press.

Butler, Judith (1997b) *Excitable Speech: A Politics of the Performative*. New York: Routledge.

Butler, Judith (1998) 'Merely cultural', *New Left Review*, 227: 33–44.

Butler, Judith (1999) *Gender Trouble: Feminism and the Subversion of Identity*, 10th anniversary edn. New York: Routledge.

Butler, Judith (2000a) *Antigone's Claim: Kinship between Life and Death*. New York: Columbia University Press.

Butler, Judith (2000b) 'Competing universalities', in Judith Butler, Ernesto Laclau and Slavoj i ek (eds), *Contingency, Hegemony, Universality: Contemporary Dialogues on the Left*. London: Verso, pp. 136–81.

Butler, Judith (2000c) 'Dynamic conclusions', in Judith Butler, Ernesto Laclau and Slavoj i ek (eds), *Contingency, Hegemony, Universality: Contemporary Dialogues on the Left*. London: Verso, pp. 263–80.

Butler, Judith, Laclau, Ernesto and i ek, Slavoj (eds) (2000) *Contingency, Hegemony, Universality: Contemporary Dialogues on the Left*. London: Verso.

Butler, Judith and Scott, Joan W. (eds) (1992) *Feminists Theorize the Political*. New York: Routledge.

Campbell, Jan and Harbord, Janet (1999) 'Playing it again: citation, reiteration or circularity?', *Theory, Culture and Society*, 16 (2): 229–39.

Caputo, John D. (1997) 'Dreaming of the innumerable: Derrida, Drucilla Cornell, and the dance of gender', in Ellen K. Feder, Mary C. Rawlinson and Emily Zakin (eds), *Derrida and Feminism: Recasting the Question of Woman*. New York: Routledge, pp. 141–60.

Carter, Bob (1997) 'Rejecting truthful identities: Foucault, "race" and politics', in Moya Lloyd and Andrew Thacker (eds), *The Impact of Michel Foucault on the Social Sciences and Humanities*. Basingstoke: Macmillan, pp. 128–46.

Childers, Mary and hooks, bell (1990) 'A conversation about race and class', in Marianne Hirsch and Evelyn Fox Keller (eds), *Conflicts in Feminism*. London: Routledge, pp. 60–81.

Christian, Barbara (1988) 'The race for theory', *Feminist Studies*, 14 (1): 67–79.

Cixous, Hélène and Clément, Catherine ([1975] 1986) *The Newly Born Woman*, trans. Betsy Wing. Minneapolis: Minnesota University Press.

Cixous, Hélène and Clément, Catherine (1994) 'The newly born woman', in Susan Sellers (ed.), *The Hélène Cixous Reader*. London: Routledge, pp. 37–46.

Clough, Patricia Ticineto (1994) *Feminist Thought: Desire, Power and Academic Discourse*.

Cambridge, MA: Blackwell.

Collins, Patricia Hill (1989) 'The social construction of black feminist thought', *Signs: Journal of Women in Culture and Society*, 14 (4): 745–73.

Collins, Patricia Hill (1990) *Black Feminist Thought: Knowledge, Consciousness, and the Politics of Empowerment*. London: HarperCollins.

Collins, Patricia Hill (2000) 'Comment on Hekman's "Truth and method: feminist standpoint theory revisited": where's the power?', in Carolyn Allen and Judith A. Howard (eds), *Provoking Feminisms*. Chicago, IL: University of Chicago Press, pp. 43–9.

Coole, Diana (1993) *Women in Political Theory: From Ancient Misogyny to Contemporary Feminism*, 2nd edn. London: Harvester Wheatsheaf.

Coole, Diana (2000) *Negativity and Politics: Dionysus and Dialectics from Kant to Poststructuralism*. London: Routledge.

Cornell, Drucilla (1991) *Beyond Accommodation: Ethical Feminism, Deconstruction and the Law*. New York: Routledge.

Cornell, Drucilla (1992) *The Philosophy of the Limit*. New York: Routledge.

Cornell, Drucilla (1995) 'Rethinking the time of feminism', in Seyla Benhabib, Judith Butler, Drucilla Cornell and Nancy Fraser, *Feminist Contentions: A Philosophical Exchange*. New York: Routledge, pp. 145–56.

Crosby, Christina (1989) 'Commentary: allies and enemies', in Elizabeth Weed (ed.), *Coming to Terms: Feminism, Theory, Politics*. New York: Routledge, pp. 205–8.

Dean, Mitchell (1991) *The Constitution of Poverty*. London: Routledge.

Defert, Daniel (1991) '"Popular Life" and insurance technology', in Graham Burchell, Colin Gordon and Peter Miller (eds), *The Foucault Effect: Studies in Governmentality*. Hemel Hempstead: Harvester Wheatsheaf, pp. 211–34.

De Lauretis, Teresa (1987) *Technologies of Gender: Essays on Theory, Film and Fiction*. Basingstoke: Macmillan.

De Lauretis, Teresa (1990) 'Eccentric subjects: feminist theory and historical consciousness', *Feminist Studies*, 16 (1): 115–50.

Deleuze, Gilles (1992) 'What is a dispositif?', in Timothy J. Armstrong (ed.), *Michel Foucault, Philosopher*. London: Harvester Wheatsheaf, pp. 159–66.

Deleuze, Gilles and Guattari, Félix (1987) *A Thousand Plateaus: Capitalism and Schizophrenia*, trans. and with an introduction by Brian Massumi. London: Athlone Press.

Derrida, Jacques (1991) 'Signature event context', in Peggy Kamuf (ed.), *Between the Blinds: A Derrida Reader*. Hemel Hempstead: Harvester Wheatsheaf, pp. 82–111.

Diamond, Irene and Hartsock, Nancy (1998) 'Beyond interests in politics: a comment of Virginia Sapiro's "When are interests interesting? The problem of the political representation of women"', in Anne Phillips (ed.), *Feminism and Politics*. Oxford: Oxford University Press, pp. 193–202.

Diamond, Irene and Quinby, Lee (eds) (1988) *Feminism and Foucault: Reflections on Resistance*. Boston, MA: Northeastern University Press.

Disch, Lisa (1999) 'Judith Butler and the politics of the performative', *Political Theory*, 27 (4): 545–59.

Di Stefano, Christine (1990) 'Dilemmas of difference: feminism, modernity, and postmodernism', in Linda Nicholson (ed.), *Feminism and Postmodernism*. London: Routledge, pp. 63–82.

Doane, Mary Ann (1989) 'Commentary: cyborgs, origins, and subjectivity', in Elizabeth Weed (ed.), *Coming to Terms: Feminism, Theory, Politics*. New York: Routledge, pp. 209–14.

Donzelot, Jacques (1979) *The Policing of Families: Welfare versus the State*. London: Hutchinson.

Douglas, Susan (1994) *Where the Girls Are: Growing up Female with the Mass Media*. Harmondsworth: Penguin.

Ebert, Teresa L. (1993) 'Ludic feminism, the body, performance, and labor: bringing materialism back into feminist cultural studies', *Cultural Critique*, Winter: 5–50.

Eisenstein, Zillah (1988) *The Female Body and the Law*. Berkeley, CA: University of California Press.

Elam, Diane (1994) *Feminism and Deconstruction: Ms. en Abyme*. London: Routledge.

Elshtain, Jean Bethke (1998) 'Antigone's daughters', in Anne Phillips (ed.), *Feminism and Politics*. Oxford: Oxford University Press, pp. 363–77.

Faith, Karlene (1994) 'Resistance: lessons from Foucault and feminism', in H. Lorraine Radtke and Henderikus J. Stam (eds), *Power/Gender: Social Relations in Theory and Practice*. London: Sage, pp. 36–66.

Feder, Ellen K., Rawlinson, Mary C. and Zakin, Emily (eds) (1997) *Derrida and Feminism: Recasting the Question of Feminism*. London: Routledge.

Feder, Ellen K. and Zakin, Emily (1997) 'Flirting with the truth: Derrida's discourse with "woman" and wenches', in Ellen K. Feder, Mary C. Rawlinson and Emily Zakin (eds), *Derrida and Feminism: Recasting the Question of Feminism*. London: Routledge, pp. 21–51.

Ferguson, Ann (1990) 'Is there a lesbian culture?', in Jeffner Allen (ed.), *Lesbian Philosophies and Cultures*. Albany, NY: State University of New York Press.

Ferguson, Kathy E. (1993) *The Man Question: Visions of Subjectivity in Feminist Theory*. Berkeley, CA: University of California Press.

Ferguson, Margaret and Wicke, Jennifer (eds) (1994) *Feminism and Postmodernism*. Durham, NC: Duke University Press.

Firestone, Shulamith (1970) *The Dialectic of Sex: The Case for Feminist Revolution*. New York: Morrow.

Flax, Jane (1987) 'Postmodernism and gender relations in feminist theory', *Signs: Journal of Women in Culture and Society*, 12 (4): 621–43.

Flax, Jane (1990) *Thinking Fragments: Psychoanalysis, Feminism and Postmodernism in the Contemporary West*. Berkeley, CA: University of California Press.

Flax, Jane (1992) 'The end of innocence', in Judith Butler and Joan W. Scott (eds), *Feminists Theorize the Political*. London: Routledge, pp. 445–63.

Flax, Jane (1993) *Disputed Subjects: Essays on Psychoanalysis, Politics and Philosophy*. New York: Routledge.

Fortier, Anne-Marie (1999) 'Re-membering places and the performance of belonging', *Theory, Culture and Society*, 16 (2): 41–64.

Foucault, Michel (1977) *Discipline and Punish: The Birth of the Prison*, trans. A. Sheridan. Harmondsworth: Penguin.

Foucault, Michel (1978) *The History of Sexuality*, Vol. 1: An Introduction, trans. R. Hurley. Harmondsworth: Penguin.

Foucault, Michel (1980a) 'Two lectures', in Colin Gordon (ed.), *Michel Foucault: Power/Knowledge – Selected Interviews and Other Writings 1972–77*. London: Harvester Wheatsheaf, pp. 78–108.

Foucault, Michel (1980b) 'The confession of the flesh', in Colin Gordon (ed.), *Michel Foucault: Power/Knowledge – Selected Interviews and Other Writings 1972–77*. London: Harvester Wheatsheaf, pp. 194–228.

Foucault, Michel (1980c) 'Truth and power', in Colin Gordon (ed.), *Michel Foucault: Power/Knowledge – Selected Interviews and Other Writings 1972–77*. London: Harvester Wheatsheaf, pp. 109–33.

Foucault, Michel (1984a) 'Polemics, politics, and problematizations: an interview', in Paul Rabinow (ed.), *The Foucault Reader*. Harmondsworth: Penguin, pp. 381–90.

Foucault, Michel (1984b) 'On the genealogy of ethics: an overview of work in progress', in Paul Rabinow (ed.), *The Foucault Reader*. Harmondsworth: Penguin, pp. 340–72.

Foucault, Michel (1984c) 'Politics and ethics: an interview', in Paul Rabinow (ed.), *The Foucault Reader*. Harmondsworth: Penguin, pp. 373–80.

Foucault, Michel (1984d) 'What is enlightenment?', in Paul Rabinow (ed.), *The Foucault Reader*. Harmondsworth: Penguin, pp. 32–50.

Foucault, Michel (1985) *The History of Sexuality*, Vol. 2: The Use of Pleasure. Harmondsworth: Penguin.

Foucault, Michel (1986) *The History of Sexuality*, Vol. 3: The Care of the Self. Harmondsworth: Penguin.

Foucault, Michel (1988a) 'Technologies of the self', in Luther H. Martin, Huck Gutman and Patrick H. Hutton (eds), *Technologies of the Self: A Seminar with Michel Foucault*. London: Tavistock, pp. 16–49.

Foucault, Michel (1988b) 'The ethic of care as a practice of freedom: an interview', in James Bernauer and David Rasmussen (eds), *The Final Foucault*. Cambridge, MA: MIT Press, pp. 1–20.

Foucault, Michel (1988c) 'Power and sex', in Lawrence D. Kritzman (ed.), *Michel Foucault: Politics, Philosophy, Culture – Interviews and Other Writings 1977–1984*. New York: Routledge, pp. 110–24.

Foucault, Michel (1988d) 'Practising criticism', in Lawrence D. Kritzman (ed.), *Michel Foucault: Politics, Philosophy, Culture – Interviews and Other Writings 1977–1984*. New York: Routledge, pp. 152–6.

Foucault, Michel (1988e) 'Critical theory/intellectual history', in Lawrence D. Kritzman (ed.), *Michel Foucault: Politics, Philosophy, Culture – Interviews and Other Writings 1977–1984*. New York: Routledge, pp. 17–46.

Foucault, Michel (1991) 'Questions of method', in Graham Burchell, Colin Gordon and Peter Miller (eds), *The Foucault Effect: Studies in Governmentality*. Hemel Hempstead: Harvester Wheatsheaf, pp. 73–86.

Foucault, Michel and Deleuze, Gilles (1973) 'The intellectuals and power', *Telos*, 16: 103–9.

Fowlkes, Diane L. (1997) 'Moving from feminist identity politics to coalition politics through a feminist materialist standpoint of intersubjectivity in Gloria Anzaldúa's Borderlands/La Frontera: The New Mestiza', *Hypatia*, 12 (2): 105–24.

Fraser, Mariam (1999) 'Classing queer: politics in competition', *Theory, Culture and Society*, 16 (2): 107–31.

Fraser, Nancy (1989) *Unruly Practices: Power, Discourse and Gender in Contemporary Social Theory*. Cambridge: Polity.

Fraser, Nancy (1995a) 'False antitheses', in Seyla Benhabib, Judith Butler, Drucilla Cornell and Nancy Fraser, *Feminist Contentions: A Philosophical Exchange*. New York: Routledge, pp. 59–74.

Fraser, Nancy (1995b) 'Pragmatism, feminism and the linguistic turn', in Seyla Benhabib, Judith Butler, Drucilla Cornell and Nancy Fraser, *Feminist Contentions: A Philosophical Exchange*. New York: Routledge, pp. 157–71.

Fraser, Nancy (1997) *Justice Interruptus: Critical Reflections on the 'Postsocialist' Condition*. London: Routledge.

Fraser, Nancy (1998) 'Heterosexism, misrecognition and capitalism: a response to Judith Butler', *New Left Review*, 228: 140–50.

Fraser, Nancy and Nicholson, Linda (1990) 'Social criticism without philosophy: an encounter between feminism and postmodernism', in Linda Nicholson (ed.), *Feminism and Postmodernism*. London: Routledge, pp. 19–38.

Friedman, Susan Stanford (1995) 'Beyond White and Other: relationality and narratives of race in feminist discourse', *Signs: Journal of Women in Culture and Society*, 21 (1): 1–49.

Fuss, Diana (1989) *Essentially Speaking: Feminism, Nature and Difference*. London: Routledge.

Fuss, Diana (1991) 'Inside/out', in Diana Fuss (ed.), *Inside/Out: Lesbian Theories, Gay Theories*. London: Routledge, pp. 1–10.

Fuss, Diana (1994) 'Reading like a feminist', in Naomi Schor and Elizabeth Weed (eds), *The Essential Difference*. Bloomington, IN: Indiana University Press, pp. 98–115.

Fuss, Diana (1995) *Identification Papers*. London: Routledge.

Gallie, W.B. (1955–56) 'Essentially contested concepts', *Proceedings of the Aristotelian Society*, 56: 167–98.

Gilligan, Carol (1982) *In a Different Voice*. Cambridge, MA: Harvard University Press.

Grant, Jaime (1996) 'Building community-based coalitions from Academe: the Union Institute and the kitchen table – women of color press transition coalition', *Signs: Journal of Women in Culture and Society*, 21 (4): 1024–33.

Grant, Judith (1993) *Fundamental Feminism: Contesting the Core Concepts of Feminist Theory*. London: Routledge.

Grewal, Inderpal (1994) 'Autobiographic subjects and diasporic locations: meatless days and borderlands', in Inderpal Grewal and Caren Kaplan (eds), *Scattered Hegemonies: Postmodernity and Transnational Feminist Practices*. Minneapolis, MN: University of Minnesota Press, pp. 231–54.

Grosz, Elizabeth (1989) *Sexual Subversions: Three French Feminists*. St Leonards, NSW: Allen and Unwin.

Grosz, Elizabeth (1990) *Jacques Lacan: A Feminist Introduction*. London: Routledge.

Hall, Stuart (1987) 'Minimal selves', *ICA Documents*, 6: 44–6.

Haraway, Donna (1985) 'Manifesto for cyborgs: science, technology, and socialist feminism in the 1980s', *Socialist Review*, 80: 65–108.

Haraway, Donna (1991a) *Simians, Cyborgs, and Women: The Reinvention of Nature.* London: Free Association Books.

Haraway, Donna (1991b) 'A cyborg manifesto: science, technology, and socialist-feminism in the late twentieth century', in Donna Haraway, *Simians, Cyborgs, and Women: The Reinvention of Nature.* London: Free Association Books, pp. 149–81.

Haraway, Donna (1991c) 'Situated knowledges: the science question in feminism and the privilege of partial perspective', in Donna Haraway, *Simians, Cyborgs, and Women: The Reinvention of Nature.* London: Free Association Books, pp. 183–201.

Harding, Sandra (1986) *The Science Question in Feminism.* Milton Keynes: Open University Press.

Harding, Sandra (ed.) (1987a) *Feminism and Methodology.* Milton Keynes: Open University Press.

Harding, Sandra (1987b) 'Conclusion: epistemological questions', in Sandra Harding (ed.), *Feminism and Methodology.* Milton Keynes: Open University Press, pp. 181–90.

Harding, Sandra (1991) *Whose Science? Whose Knowledge?* Milton Keynes: Open University Press.

Harding, Sandra (2000) 'Comment on Hekman's "Truth and method: feminist standpoint theory revisited": whose standpoint needs the regimes of truth and reality?', in Carolyn Allen and Judith A. Howard (eds), *Provoking Feminisms.* Chicago, IL: University of Chicago Press, pp. 50–9.

Harris, Laura Alexandra (1996) 'Queer black feminism: the pleasure principle', *Feminist Review*, 54 (4): 3–30.

Hartmann, Heidi, Bravo, Ellen, Bunch, Charlotte, Hartsock, Nancy, Spalter-Roth, Roberta, Williams, Linda and Blanco, Maria (1996) 'Bringing together feminist theory and practice: a collective interview', *Signs: Journal of Women in Culture and Society*, 21 (4): 917–51.

Hartsock, Nancy (1985) *Money, Sex and Power: Toward a Feminist Historical Materialism.* Boston, MA: Northeastern University Press.

Hartsock, Nancy (1987a) 'Rethinking modernism: minority vs. majority theories', *Cultural Critique*, 7: 187–206.

Hartsock, Nancy (1987b) 'The feminist standpoint: developing the ground for a specifically feminist materialism', in Sandra Harding (ed.), *Feminism and Methodology.* Milton Keynes: Open University Press, pp. 157–80.

Hartsock, Nancy (1990) 'Foucault on power: a theory for women?', in Linda Nicholson (ed.), *Feminism and Postmodernism.* London: Routledge, pp.157–74.

Hartsock, Nancy (1996) 'Community/sexuality/gender: rethinking power', in Nancy J. Hirschmann and Christine Di Stefano (eds), *Revisioning the Political: Feminist Reconstructions of Traditional Concepts in Western Political Theory.* Boulder, CO: Westview Press, pp. 27–49.

Hartsock, Nancy (2000) 'Comment on Hekman's "Truth and method: feminist standpoint theory revisited": truth or justice?', in Carolyn Allen and Judith A. Howard (eds), *Provoking Feminisms.* Chicago, IL: University of Chicago Press, pp. 35–43.

Hawkes, Gail (1995) 'Dressing-up: cross-dressing and sexual dissonance', *Journal of Gender Studies*, 4 (3): 261–70.

Heinämaa, Sara (1997) 'What is a woman? Butler and Beauvoir on the foundations of the sexual difference', *Hypatia*, 12 (1): 20–39.

Hekman, Susan (1990) *Gender and Knowledge: Elements of a Postmodern Feminism.* Cambridge: Polity Press.

Hekman, Susan (ed.) (1996) *Feminist Interpretations of Michel Foucault.* University Park, PA: Pennsylvania State University Press.

Hekman, Susan (2000a) 'Beyond identity: feminism, identity and identity politics', *Feminist Theory*, 1 (3): 289–308.

Hekman, Susan (2000b) 'Truth and method: feminist standpoint theory revisited', in Carolyn Allen and Judith A. Howard (eds), *Provoking Feminisms.* Chicago, IL: University of Chicago Press, pp. 9–34.

Hekman, Susan (2000c) 'Reply to Hartsock, Collins, Harding and Smith', in Carolyn Allen and Judith A. Howard (eds), *Provoking Feminisms.* Chicago, IL: University of Chicago Press, pp. 66–9.

Hennessy, Rosemary (1993) *Materialist Feminism and the Politics of Discourse.* New York: Routledge.

Hennessy, Rosemary (1995) 'Queer visibility in commodity culture', in Linda Nicholson and Steven Seidman (eds), *Social Postmodernism: Beyond Identity Politics.* Cambridge: Cambridge University Press, pp. 142–83.

Hertz, Noreena (2001) *The Silent Takeover: Global Capitalism and the Death of Democracy.* London: Heinemann.

Hirschmann, Nancy J. and Di Stefano, Christine (eds) (1996) *Revisioning the Political: Feminist Reconstructions of Traditional Concepts in Western Political Theory.* Boulder, CO: Westview Press.

Hobbes, Thomas ([1651] 1991) *Leviathan*, ed. Richard Tuck. Cambridge: Cambridge University Press.

Honig, Bonnie (1992) 'Toward an agonistic feminism: Hannah Arendt and the politics of identity', in Judith Butler and Joan W. Scott (eds), *Feminists Theorize the Political.* New York: Routledge, pp. 215–35.

Honig, Bonnie (1996) 'Difference, dilemmas, and the politics of home', in Seyla Benhabib (ed.), *Democracy and Difference: Contesting the Boundaries of the Political.* Princeton, NJ: Princeton University Press, pp. 257–77.

hooks, bell (1982) *Ain't I a Woman: Black Women and Feminism.* Boston, MA: South End Press.

hooks, bell (1984) *Feminist Theory: From Margin to Center.* Boston, MA: South End Press.

hooks, bell (1989) *Talking Back: Thinking Feminist – Thinking Black.* London: Sheba.

hooks, bell (1990a) *Yearning: Race, Gender, and Cultural Politics.* Toronto: Between the Lines.

hooks, bell (1990b) 'Postmodern blackness', in bell hooks, *Yearning: Race, Gender, and Cultural Politics.* Toronto: Between the Lines, pp. 23–31.

hooks, bell (1990c) 'The politics of radical black subjectivity', in bell hooks, *Yearning: Race, Gender, and Cultural Politics.* Toronto: Between the Lines, pp. 15–22.

hooks, bell (1992a) *Black Looks: Race and Representation.* Boston, MA: South End Press.

hooks, bell (1992b) 'Is Paris burning?', in bell hooks, *Black Looks: Race and Representation*. Boston, MA: South End Press, pp. 145–56.

hooks, bell (1994a) *Teaching to Transgress: Education as the Practice of Freedom*. New York: Routledge.

hooks, bell (1994b) *Outlaw Cultures: Resisting Representations*. New York: Routledge.

hooks, bell (1995) *Killing Rage: Ending Racism*. Harmondsworth: Penguin.

Howarth, David (1998) 'Post-Marxism', in Adam Lent (ed.), *New Political Thought: An Introduction*. London: Lawrence and Wishart, pp. 126–42.

Howarth, David and Stavrakakis, Yannis (2000) 'Introducing discourse theory and political analysis', in David Howarth, Aletta J. Norval and Yannis Stavrakakis (eds), *Discourse Theory and Political Analysis: Identities, Hegemonies and Social Change*. Manchester: Manchester University Press, pp. 1–23.

Hull, Gloria T., Scott, Patricia Bell and Smith, Barbara (eds) (1982) *All the Women are White, All the Blacks are Men, but Some of Us are Brave: Black Women's Studies*. New York: Feminist Press.

Hunter, Ian (1988) *Culture and Government: The Emergence of Literary Education*. London: Macmillan.

Hunter, Ian (1994) *Rethinking the School*. St Leonards, NSW: Allen and Unwin.

Hurtado, Aída (1989) 'Relating to privilege: seduction and rejection in the subordination of white women and women of color', *Signs: Journal of Women in Culture and Society*, 14 (4).

Irigaray, Luce (1985) *Speculum of the Other Woman*, trans. Gillian C. Gill. Ithaca, NY: Cornell University Press.

Irigaray, Luce (1993) *Sexes and Genealogies*, trans. Gillian C. Gill. New York: Colombia University Press.

Jackson, Peter (1995) 'Gender trouble – or just shopping?', *Gender, Place and Culture: A Journal of Feminist Geography*, 2 (1): 107–8.

James, Stanlie M. (1993) 'Mothering: a possible black feminist link to social transformation?', in Stanlie M. James and Abena P.A. Busia (eds), *Theorizing Black Feminisms: The Visionary Pragmatism of Black Women*. London: Routledge, pp. 44–54.

James, Stanlie M. and Busia, Abena P.A. (eds) (1993) *Theorizing Black Feminisms: The Visionary Pragmatism of Black Women*. London: Routledge.

Jardine, Alice (1985) *Gynesis: Configurations of Woman and Modernity*. Ithaca, NY: Cornell University Press.

Jónasdóttir, Anna (1988) 'On the concept of interests, women's interests, and the limitations of interest theory', in Kathleen B. Jones and Anna G. Jónasdóttir (eds), *The Political Interests of Gender: Developing Theory and Research with a Feminist Face*. London: Sage, pp. 33–65.

King, Deborah K. (1988) 'Multiple jeopardy, multiple consciousness: the context of black feminist ideology', *Signs: Journal of Women in Culture and Society*, 14 (1).

Kirkby, Andrew (1995) 'Straight talk on the PomoHomo question', *Gender, Place and Culture: A Journal of Feminist Geography*, 2 (1): 89–95.

Kristeva, Julia (1980a) *Desire in Language*. Oxford: Basil Blackwell.

Kristeva, Julia (1980b) 'Women can never be defined', in Elaine Marks and Isabelle de

Courtivron (eds), *New French Feminisms*. Amherst, MA: University of Massachusetts Press, pp. 137–41.

Kristeva, Julia (1984) *The Revolution in Poetic Language*. New York: Columbia University Press.

Lacan, Jacques (1977) *Écrits: A Selection*. London: Tavistock/Routledge.

Lacan, Jacques (1982) 'God and the Jouissance of The Woman', in Juliet Mitchell and Jacqueline Rose (eds), *Feminine Sexuality: Jacques Lacan and the École Freudienne*. Basingstoke: Macmillan, pp. 137–49.

Laclau, Ernesto and Mouffe, Chantal (1985) *Hegemony and Socialist Strategy: Towards a Radical Democratic Politics*. London: Verso.

Landry, Donna and MacLean, Gerald (1993) *Materialist Feminisms*. Oxford: Blackwell.

Lawler, Steph (2002) 'Mobs and monsters: independent man meets Paulsgrove woman', *Feminist Theory*, 3 (1): 103–13.

Lee, Theresa Man Ling (2001) 'Feminism, postmodernism and the politics of representation', *Women and Politics*, 22 (3): 35–57.

Leland, Dorothy (1992) 'Lacanian psychoanalysis and French feminism: toward an adequate political psychology', in Nancy Fraser and Sandra Lee Bartky (eds), *Revaluing French Feminism: Critical Essays on Difference, Agency, and Culture*. Bloomington, IN: Indiana University Press, pp. 113–35.

Lloyd, Genevieve (1984) *The Man of Reason: 'Male' and 'Female' in Western Philosophy*. London: Methuen.

Lloyd, Moya (1993) 'The (f)utility of the feminist turn to Foucault', *Economy and Society*, 22 (4): 437–60.

Lloyd, Moya (1996) 'A feminist mapping of Foucauldian politics', in Susan Hekman (ed.), *Feminist Interpretations of Michel Foucault*. University Park, PA: Pennsylvania State University Press, pp. 241–64.

Lloyd, Moya (1998–99) 'Politics and melancholia', *Women's Philosophy Review*, 20: 25–43.

Lloyd, Moya (1999) 'Performativity, parody, politics', *Theory, Culture and Society*, 16 (2): 195–213.

Lloyd, Moya (forthcoming a) 'Butler, Antigone and the state', *Contemporary Political Theory*.

Lloyd, Moya (forthcoming b) *Judith Butler: From Norms to Politics*. Cambridge: Polity.

Lorde, Audre (1984a) 'An open letter to Mary Daly', in Audre Lorde, *Sister Outsider: Essays and Speeches by Audre Lorde*. Freedom, CA: Crossing Press, pp. 66–71.

Lorde, Audre (1984b) *Sister Outsider: Essays and Speeches by Audre Lorde*. Freedom, CA: Crossing Press.

Lovell, Terri (2003) 'Resisting with authority: historical specificity, agency and the performative self', *Theory, Culture and Society*, 20 (1): 1–17.

MacKinnon, Catharine A. (1987) *Feminism Unmodified: Discourses on Life and Law*. Cambridge, MA: Harvard University Press.

MacKinnon, Catharine A. (1989) *Toward a Feminist Theory of the State*. Cambridge, MA: Harvard University Press.

Macpherson, C.B. (1962) *The Political Theory of Possessive Individualism: Hobbes to Locke*. Oxford: Oxford University Press.

189

Martin, Biddy (1988) 'Feminism, criticism, and Foucault', in Irene Diamond and Lee Quinby (eds), *Feminism and Foucault: Reflections on Resistance*. Boston, MA: Northeastern University Press, pp. 3–19.

Martin, Biddy (1992) 'Sexual practice and changing lesbian identities', in Michèle Barrett and Anne Phillips (eds), *Destabilising Theory: Contemporary Feminist Debates*. Cambridge: Polity, pp. 93–119.

Martin, Biddy and Mohanty, Chandra (1986) 'Feminist politics: what's home got to do with it?', in Teresa de Lauretis (ed.), *Feminist Studies/Critical Studies*. Basingstoke: Macmillan, pp. 191–212.

Matsuda, Mari J., Lawrence, Charles R., III, Delgado, Richard and Crenshaw, Kimberlè Williams (1993) *Words that Wound: Critical Race Theory, Assaultive Speech, and the First Amendment*. Boulder, CO: Westview Press.

McNay, Lois (1992) *Foucault and Feminism: Power, Gender and the Self*. Cambridge: Polity Press.

McNay, Lois (1994) *Foucault: A Critical Introduction*. Cambridge: Polity Press.

McNay, Lois (1999) 'Subject, psyche and agency: the work of Judith Butler', *Theory, Culture and Society*, 16 (2): 175–93.

McNay, Lois (2000) *Gender and Agency: Reconfiguring the Subject in Feminist and Social Theory*. Cambridge: Polity.

Meyers, Diana T. (1992) 'The subversion of women's agency in psychoanalytic feminism: Chodorow, Flax and Kristeva', in Nancy Fraser and Sandra Lee Bartky (eds), *Revaluing French Feminism: Critical Essays on Difference, Agency and Culture*. Bloomington, IN: Indiana University Press, pp. 136–61.

Millett, Kate (1977) *Sexual Politics*. London: Virago.

Millman, Marcia and Kanter, Rosabeth Moss (eds) (1975) *Another Voice: Feminist Perspectives on Social Life and Social Science*. New York: Anchor Books.

Mills, Catherine (2000) 'Efficacy and vulnerability: Judith Butler on reiteration and resistance', *Australian Feminist Studies*, 15 (32): 265–79.

Mitchell, Juliet (1982) 'Introduction – I', in Juliet Mitchell and Jacqueline Rose (eds), *Feminine Sexuality: Jacques Lacan and the École Freudienne*. Basingstoke: Macmillan, pp. 1–26.

Mohanty, Chandra Talpade (1998) 'Feminist encounters: locating the politics of experience', in Anne Phillips (ed.), *Feminism and Politics*. Oxford: Oxford University Press, pp. 254–72.

Moi, Toril (1985) *Sexual/Textual Politics: Feminist Literary Theory*. London: Routledge.

Molina, Papusa (1990) 'Recognizing, accepting and celebrating our differences', in Gloria Anzaldúa (ed.), *Making Face, Making Soul: Haciendo Caras – Creative and Critical Perspectives by Women of Color*. San Francisco, CA: Aunt Lute Foundation, pp. 326–33.

Moraga, Cherríe (1983) *Loving in the War Years: lo que nunca pasó por sus labios*. Boston, MA: South End Press.

Mouffe, Chantal (1992a) 'Feminism, citizenship, and radical democratic politics', in Judith Butler and Joan W. Scott (eds), *Feminists Theorize the Political*. London: Routledge, pp. 369–84.

Mouffe, Chantal (ed.) (1992b) *Dimensions of Radical Democracy: Pluralism, Citizenship and Community*. London: Verso.

Mouffe, Chantal (1993) *The Return of the Political*. London: Verso.

Mouffe, Chantal (1994) 'For a politics of nomadic identity', in George Robertson, Melinda Mash, Lisa Tickner, Jon Bird, Barry Curtis and Tim Putnam (eds), *Travellers Tales: Narratives of Home and Displacement*. London: Routledge, pp. 105–13.

Mouffe, Chantal (2000) *The Democratic Paradox*. London: Verso.

Nash, Kate (1998) 'Beyond liberalism? Feminist theories of democracy', in Vicky Randall and Georgina Waylen (eds), *Gender, Politics and the State*. London: Routledge, pp. 45–57.

Nicholson, Linda (1990) 'Introduction', in Linda Nicholson, *Feminism and Postmodernism*. London: Routledge, pp. 1–16.

Nussbaum, Martha (1999) 'The professor of parody', www.tnr.com/archive/0299/022299/nussbaum022299.html

Nye, Andrea (1988) *Feminist Theory and the Philosophies of Man*. New York: Routledge.

O'Brien, Mary (1981) *The Politics of Reproduction*. London: Routledge and Kegan Paul.

Okin, Susan Moller (1980) *Women in Western Political Thought*. London: Virago.

Oliver, Kelly (1998) 'Woman as truth in Nietzsche's writing', in Kelly Oliver and Marilyn Pearsall (eds), *Feminist Interpretations of Friedrich Nietzsche*. University Park, PA: Pennsylvania State University Press, pp. 66–80.

Ortega, Mariana (2001) '"New Mestizas", "'World'-Travelers", and "Dasein": phenomenology and the multi-voiced, multi-cultural self', *Hypatia*, 16 (3): 1–29.

Osborne, Peter and Segal, Lynne (1994) 'Gender as performance: an interview with Judith Butler', *Radical Philosophy*, 67: 32–9.

Owen, David (1998) 'Nietzsche's squandered seductions: feminism, the body, and the politics of genealogy', in Kelly Oliver and Marilyn Pearsall (eds), *Feminist Interpretations of Friedrich Nietzsche*. University Park, PA: Pennsylvania State University Press, pp. 306–25.

Parmar, Pratibha (1990) 'Black feminism: the politics of articulation', in Jonathan Rutherford (ed.), *Identity: Community, Culture, and Difference*. London: Lawrence and Wishart.

Pateman, Carole (1988) *The Sexual Contract*. Cambridge: Polity.

Pateman, Carole (1989) *The Disorder of Women*. Cambridge: Polity.

Phelan, Shane (1989) *Identity Politics: Lesbian Feminism and the Limits of Community*. Philadelphia, PA: Temple University Press.

Phelan, Shane (1993) '(Be)coming out: lesbian identity and politics', *Signs: Journal of Women in Culture and Society*, 18 (4): 765–90.

Phelan, Shane (1994) *Getting Specific: Postmodern Lesbian Politics*. Minneapolis, MN: University of Minnesota Press.

Phelan, Shane (1995) 'Coyote politics: trickster tales and feminist futures', *Hypatia: A Journal of Feminist Philosophy*, 11 (3): 1–23, 130–49.

Phelan, Shane (2001) *Sexual Strangers: Gays, Lesbians, and Dilemmas of Citizenship*. Philadelphia, PA: Temple University Press.

Phillips, Anne (ed.) (1987) *Feminism and Equality*. Oxford: Basil Blackwell.

Phillips, Anne (ed.) (1998) *Feminism and Politics*. Oxford: Oxford University Press.

Poovey, Mary (1992) 'The abortion question and the death of man', in Judith Butler and Joan W. Scott (eds), *Feminists Theorize the Political*. London: Routledge, pp. 239–56.

Pringle, Rosemary and Watson, Sophie (1998) '"Women's interests" and the poststructuralist state', in Anne Phillips (ed.), *Feminism and Politics*. Oxford: Oxford University Press, pp. 203–23.

Probyn, Elspeth (1993) *Sexing the Self: Gendered Positions in Cultural Studies*. London: Routledge.

Probyn, Elspeth (1995) 'Lesbians in space: gender, sex and the structure of missing', *Gender, Place and Culture: A Journal of Feminist Geography*, 2 (1): 77–84.

Quinby, Lee (1997) 'Genealogical feminism: a politic way of looking', in Jodi Dean (ed.), *Feminism and the New Democracy: Resiting the Political*. London: Sage, pp. 146–67.

Rajchman, John (1992) 'Foucault: the ethic and the work', in Timothy J. Armstrong (ed.), *Michel Foucault: Philosopher*. Hemel Hempstead: Harvester Wheatsheaf, pp. 215–24.

Rajchman, John (ed.) (1995) *The Identity in Question*. New York: Routledge.

Ramazanoglu, Caroline (1993) *Up against Foucault: Explorations of Some Tensions between Foucault and Feminism*. London: Routledge.

Ramazanoglu, Caroline, with Holland, Janet (2002) *Feminist Methodology: Challenges and Choices*. London: Sage.

Randall, Vicky (1987) *Women and Politics: An International Perspective*, 2nd edn. Basingstoke: Macmillan.

Raymond, Janice (1986) *A Passion for Friends: Towards a Philosophy of Female Affection*. Boston, MA: Beacon Press.

Reagon, Bernice Johnson (1998) 'Coalition politics: turning the century', in Anne Phillips (ed.), *Feminism and Politics*. Oxford: Oxford University Press, pp. 242–53.

Rose, Jacqueline (1982) 'Introduction – II', in Juliet Mitchell and Jacqueline Rose (eds), *Feminine Sexuality: Jacques Lacan and the École Freudienne*. Basingstoke: Macmillan, pp. 27–57.

Rose, Jacqueline (1986) *Sexuality in the Field of Vision*. London: Verso.

Rose, Nikolas (1999) *Powers of Freedom: Reframing Political Thought*. Cambridge: Cambridge University Press.

Roseneil, Sasha (1999) 'Postmodern feminist politics: the art of the (im)possible', *European Journal of Women's Studies*, 6: 161–82.

Ruddick, Sara (1990) *Maternal Thinking: Towards a Politics of Peace*. London: Women's Press.

Said, Edward (1978) 'The problem of textuality: two exemplary positions', *Critical Inquiry*, (4): 673–714.

Sandoval, Chela (1990) 'Feminism and racism: a report on the 1981 National Women's Studies Association Conference', in Gloria Anzaldúa (ed.), *Making Face, Making Soul: Haciendo Caras – Creative and Critical Perspectives by Women of Color*. San Francisco, MA: Aunt Lute Foundation, pp. 55–71.

Sandoval, Chela (1995) 'Feminist forms of agency and oppositional consciousness: US third world feminist criticism', in Judith Kegan Gardiner (ed.), *Provoking Agents: Gender and Agency in Theory and Practice*. Urbana, IL: University of Illinois Press.

Sapiro, Virginia (1998) 'When are interests interesting? The problem of the political representation of women', in Anne Phillips (ed.), *Feminism and Politics*. Oxford: Oxford University Press, pp. 161–92.

Sawicki, Jana (1988) 'Identity politics and sexual freedom: Foucault and feminism', in Irene Diamond and Lee Quinby (eds), *Feminism and Foucault: Reflections on Resistance*. Boston, MA: Northeastern University Press, pp. 177–91.

Sawicki, Jana (1991) *Disciplining Foucault*. New York: Routledge.

Schneir, Miriam (ed.) (1995) *The Vintage Book of Feminism*. London: Vintage Press.

Schneir, Miriam (ed.) (1996) *The Vintage Book of Historical Feminism*. London: Vintage Press.

Schor, Naomi and Weed, Elizabeth (eds) (1994) *The Essential Difference*. Bloomington, IN: Indiana University Press.

Scott, Joan W. (1989) 'Commentary: cyborgian socialists?', in Elizabeth Weed (ed.), *Coming to Terms: Feminism, Theory, Politics*. New York: Routledge, pp. 215–17.

Sedgwick, Eve Kosofsky (1990) *Epistemology of the Closet*. Harmondsworth: Penguin.

Segal, Lynne (1990) *Slow Motion: Changing Masculinities, Changing Men*. London: Virago.

Sellers, Susan (ed.) (1994) *The Hélène Cixous Reader*. London: Routledge.

Shanley, Mary Lyndon and Narayan, Uma (1997) *Reconstructing Political Theory: Feminist Perspectives*. Cambridge: Polity.

Sheridan, Susan (2002) 'Words and things: some feminist debate on culture and materialism', *Australian Feminist Studies*, 17 (37): 23–30.

Showalter, Elaine (1987) *The Female Malady: Women, Madness and English Culture, 1830–1980*. London: Virago Press.

Smart, Carol (ed.) (1992) *Regulating Womanhood: Historical Essays on Marriage, Motherhood and Sexuality*. London: Routledge.

Smith, Anna Marie (1998) *Laclau and Mouffe: The Radical Democratic Imaginary*. London: Routledge.

Smith, Dorothy E. (2000) 'Comment on Hekman's "Truth and method: feminist standpoint theory revisited"', in Carolyn Allen and Judith A. Howard (eds), *Provoking Feminisms*. Chicago, IL: University of Chicago Press, pp. 59–65.

Spelman, Elizabeth V. (1990) *Inessential Woman: Problems of Exclusion in Feminist Thought*. London: Women's Press.

Spivak, Gayatri Chakravorty (1988) 'Subaltern studies: deconstructing historiography', in Gayatri Chakravorty Spivak, *In Other Worlds: Essays in Cultural Politics*. New York: Routledge, pp. 197–221.

Spivak, Gayatri Chakravorty (1990) 'Practical politics of the open end', in Sarah Harasym (ed.), *The Post-Colonial Critic: Interviews, Strategies, Dialogues*. New York: Routledge, pp. 95–112.

Spivak, Gayatri Chakravorty (1992) 'French feminism revisited: ethics and politics', in Judith Butler and Joan W. Scott (eds), *Feminists Theorize the Political*. New York: Routledge, pp. 54–85.

Spivak, Gayatri Chakravorty, with Rooney, Ellen (1994) 'In a word: interview', in Naomi Schor and Elizabeth Weed (eds), *The Essential Difference*. Bloomington, IN: Indiana University Press, pp. 151–84.

Stanley, Liz (ed.) (1990) *Feminist Praxis: Research, Theory and Epistemology in Feminist Sociology*. London: Routledge.

Stavrakakis, Yannis (1999) *Lacan and the Political*. London: Routledge.

Thompson, Denise (1996) 'The self-contradiction of post-modernist feminism', in Denise Bell and Renate Duelli Klein (eds), *Radically Speaking: Feminism Reclaimed*. London: Zed Books, pp. 325–38.

Thompson, Denise (2001) *Radical Feminism Today*. London: Sage.

Tress, Darryl McGowan (1988) 'Comments on Flax's "Postmodernism and gender relations in feminist theory"', *Signs: Journal of Women in Culture and Society*, 14 (1): 196–200.

Trinh, T. Minh-ha (1989) *Woman, Native, Other: Postcoloniality and Feminism*. Bloomington, IN: Indiana University Press.

Trinh, T. Minh-ha (1990) 'Not you/like you: post-colonial women and the interlocking questions of identity and difference', in Gloria Anzaldúa (ed.), *Making Face, Making Soul: Haciendo Caras – Creative and Critical Perspectives by Women of Color*. San Francisco, CA: Aunt Lute Foundation, pp. 371–5.

Trinh, T. Minh-ha (1992) *Framer Framed*. New York: Routledge.

Truth, Sojourner (1996) 'Ain't I a woman?', in Miriam Schneir (ed.), *The Vintage Book of Historical Feminism*. London: Vintage Press, pp. 94–5.

Walker, Alice (1984) *In Search of Our Mothers' Gardens: Womanist Prose*. London: Women's Press.

Walker, Lisa (1995) 'More than just skin-deep: fem(me)ininity and the subversion of identity', *Gender, Place and Culture: A Journal of Feminist Geography*, 2 (1): 71–6.

Waters, Kristin (1996) '(Re)turning to the modern: radical feminism and the postmodern turn', in Denise Bell and Renate Duelli Klein (eds), *Radically Speaking: Feminism Reclaimed*. London: Zed Books, pp. 280–96.

Webster, Fiona (2000) 'The politics of sex and gender: Butler and Benhabib debate subjectivity', *Hypatia*, 15 (1): 1–22.

Weedon, Chris (1987) *Feminist Practice and Poststructuralist Theory*. Oxford: Basil Blackwell.

Weir, Allison (1996) *Sacrificial Logics: Feminist Theory and the Critique of Identity*. London: Routledge.

Whitford, Margaret (1991) *Luce Irigaray: Philosophy in the Feminine*. London: Routledge.

Williams, Patricia J. (1993) *The Alchemy of Race and Rights*. London: Virago Press.

Yeatman, Anna (1994) *Postmodern Revisionings of the Political*. New York: Routledge.

Young, Iris Marion (1990) *Justice and the Politics of Difference*. Princeton, NJ: Princeton University Press.

Young, Iris Marion (1995) 'Gender as seriality: thinking about women as a social collective', in Linda Nicholson and Steven Seidman (eds), *Social Postmodernism: Beyond Identity Politics*. Cambridge: Cambridge University Press, pp. 187–215.

Young, Iris Marion (2000) *Inclusion and Democracy*. Oxford: Oxford University Press.

Žižek, Slavoj (2000) 'Class struggle or postmodernism? Yes, please!', in Judith Butler, Ernesto Laclau and Slavoj Žižek (eds), *Contingency, Hegemony, Universality: Contemporary Dialogues on the Left*. London: Verso, pp. 90–135.

index